NetWorld!

What People Are **Really** Doing on the **Internet**, and What It Means to **You**

David H. Rothman

PRIMA PUBLISHING

With 88s to Carly,
my dearest company
in life and on the 'Bahn.

Library of Congress Cataloging-in-Publication Data

Rothman, David H.
    Networld!: what people are really doing on the Internet, and what it
means to you / David H. Rothman.
        p. cm.
    Includes index.
    ISBN 0-7615-0013-8
    1. Internet (Computer network)   I. Title.
TK5105.875.I57R69 1995
004.6'7–dc20   95-5287
                                                                CIP

95 96 97 98 99 AA 10 9 8 7 6 5 4 3 2 1
Printed in the United States of America

How to Order:
Single copies may be ordered from Prima Publishing, P.O. Box 1260BK, Rocklin, CA 95677; telephone (916) 632-4400. Quantity discounts are also available. On your letterhead, include information concerning the intended use of the books and the number of books you wish to purchase.

Contents

A Note to Visitors (and Natives)

Everyone in *NetWorld!* is real, even me. Chapter 1 tells how to reach some good people who let their electronic addresses go on the Web site for this book.

In a few cases—most notably "Sue" and "Greg" in Chapter 7—I've guarded my subjects' privacy with aliases and changes of identifying details. Asterisks show up after the first occurrences of their revised names.

Please note, too, that I've smoothed out people's informal online prose to accommodate the printed page. A "smiley" on the Net is a good quick way to show a smile or frown; but I couldn't think of anything uglier in print than a series of symbols such as :-). So even in quotes, I've used them sparingly.

I wish Mark Twain were alive and cruising the Internet at 28.8 kilobits per second; I'd love to see how he'd have handled net.dialect.

David Rothman,
rothman@clark.net
Alexandria, Virginia

Acknowledgments

Alison, step to the front! Alison Andrukow, a graduate student at Queen's University in Kingston, Ontario, served as my chief researcher on this project—discovering a number of goodies ranging from Bianca's Smut Shack to arcane, Net-related policy studies.

Jennifer Basye Sander, my editor at Prima Publishing, working with associate acquisitions editor Alice Anderson and the project editor, Steven Martin, provided many suggestions, as did the publisher, Ben Dominitz. The latter promoted this book, so to speak, from *Digital America* to *Digital World,* and in time the title *NetWorld!* also came from Ben. Surprise, you guys! You thought you were getting a general book on computer technology, but wisely you let me get caught up in the Net. *Thanks!*

Bill Adler and Lisa Swayne of Adler and Robin Books, joined by Nick Anis, agented this book. Nancy Daisywheel Breckenridge was the transcriptionist.

Finally, I want to thank the many people who gave their time by way of e-mail or otherwise. Lest I forget some important ones here, I won't list any names. But by way of the references in the book itself, readers will learn the identities of many.

ONE

The Terrain

A color photo lights up my computer screen when I hit the return key, and, in big, bold Times Roman letters, I see the latest from the Internet:

*Playboy Is Traveling the Info Highway
Looking for Women for a Special
"Girls of the Net" Pictorial*

Sitting atop a pile of books, a most ungeekish model looks flawlessly nubile, as if part of a virtual reality tableau conjured up for Hugh Hefner himself. *Playboy*'s message is clear: What counts isn't mastery of Telnet, Gopher, Lynx, or other Net voodoo. Candidates should mail or e-mail "a recent full-length body photo in a two-piece bathing suit or less and a clear face shot."

The same day a famous hacker named Cliff Stoll goes on a Washington radio station to promote his book *Silicon Snake Oil,* which says the Internet steals too much time from true learning and life.

For better or worse—mostly better in my opinion, egalitarian that I am—the Internet has Arrived.

A quarter-century ago scientists dreamed up a predecessor of the network to let computers jabber to each other across the United States, even after a nuclear attack. Fearless professors followed with electronic talk on topics ranging from biology to poetry.

Now it's as if *everyone* is on the Internet—not just *Playboy* but *Penthouse,* some Arizona lawyers who love to inflict junk ads on the innocent, a Florida manicurist, ·Democratic and Republican stalwarts, thousands of college freshmen, punk teenagers, and elementary schoolers in London, Singapore, Minnesota, Nova Scotia—you name it. In one way or other, the Net ties in to smaller networks ranging from local, bulletin board–style systems to America Online, CompuServe, Prodigy, Delphi, GEnie, Bitnet, Bix, eWorld, and MCI Mail.

Fans of David Letterman and Jay Leno, the world's most famous talk-show rivals, are even duking it out online. The cyberspace section of *Newsweek* regularly lists the hottest attractions of the Internet—for example, the best sites on the World Wide Web, the multimedia area where you can see pictures and hear sound.

Hollywood is gambling on a movie called *The Net,* and *Time* and *Newsweek* have done several cover stories. Could the *Time* curse be at work here? Is everything else downhill, now that the Net has landed on The Cover? Not if you go by the stats. Internet demographers love to squabble about the exact number of people on the Internet, but at the very least, some 25–30 million can reach it by way of electronic mail; and in a few years, if the braver prophets are right, hundreds of millions may be wired in. For the snobs, of course, the old cachet is gone. A humor columnist says the Net is like citizens band radio with typing.

Is the Internet, then, about to become a 500,000-channel wasteland? Just what are all these millions *really* doing on the Net? Some politicians would have you think that a disturbing number of Netfolks are busy corrupting

the morals of minors, and shouldn't we ban smut from
the public areas of cyberspace? And if you believe some
American security bureaucrats, the Net might turn out
to be a haven for spies and dope dealers. "Shouldn't
Washington," they more or less ask, "be able to snoop on
pervs and subversives who scramble their messages?"

The counterrevolution has begun, and I feel grouchy.

Everyone is trying to reinvent the Internet in his or her
own image, even if, with these changes, the Net would no
longer be the Net. What's really pathetic is the ignorance
of the would-be meddlers. Censoring the Net would be
about as successful as trying to dam the Pacific. The same
decentralization that made the Net more nuke-resistant,
in the Cold War days, makes it harder to control. And how
can Washington sell the Net on Fed-friendly chips for
coded messages when scores of powerful encryption
products are on sale in Russia and the rest of Europe?

At the same time, certain writers are now attacking
the Internet as Cold and Heartless, or for other sins; some
are even Pulling the Plug, at least temporarily, to protect
their delicate brains against Information Overload.

"Don't make me go back!" J. C. Hertz recalls telling
her editors when they wanted her to log back on the Net to
wind down a book called *Surfing the Internet.* "Please,
don't make me go back there." Stephen L. Talbott, a computer editor and author of *The Future Does Not Compute,*
proclaims that he "immediately felt very good" when he
Unplugged. Bill Henderson of the Push Cart Press says
he'll publish a book with "cries from the heart about what
electronics has done to people."[1]

Perhaps a new literary genre is aborning—that of the
Snubbites, the new Luddites[2] who feel all Netted Up. The
definition might go something like this:

> *Snubbite:—n. One who, partly out of snobbery,
> partly out of boredom, partly out of sheer contrari-
> ness, snubs the computer technology that could help
> millions of others.*

A typical Snubbite is upper-middle class and very possibly Ivy League. Snubbites could afford computer and Internet connections—or more likely enjoyed them at others' expense—years before average people were even allowed on the Net. Often Snubbites live near large libraries or can catch up with books easily enough in other ways. Snubbites may have already used the Net to help stock up on their quota of friends and professional contacts. Most Snubbites are harmless and even charmingly eccentric; they worry me only when they start confusing their own needs and non-needs with those of society at large.

Cliff Stoll himself is very much on the Internet ("I still love my networked community") even now; to this day, I suspect, he truly enjoys seeing people home-brew their own machines. But in stretches of his book he could almost be mistaken for a Snubbite anyway, based on sheer fervor. "It is an overpromoted, hollow world, devoid of warmth and human kindness," Stoll writes of cyberspace, and goes on to say that nets address "few social needs or business concerns" and threaten "precious parts of our society, including schools, libraries, and social institutions." He complains, "No birds sing."

Have I been hallucinating? The Internet isn't Woodstock, the Vatican, or an aviary, but it is bringing together people for religion, education, business, love, and suicide prevention. Just what is Stoll writing about? Does the Net have an evil twin? Jews, Moslems, Lutherans, and Catholics—they are all using the Net to exchange prayers or electronic newsletters. Up in Canada an Anglican priest will even take confessions via e-mail. I doubt he'd agree with the author of *Snake Oil.*

Nor, I suspect, would the members of Walkers in Darkness. Walkers is a mailing list for people with chronic depression, and each week more than 300 messages whiz across the Net from Australia to Israel, from South Africa to California. I'm not depressed, but someone close to me is, and she spends hour after hour with her laptop, gazing at the blue-and-white on the screen, reading scores of messages, keeping up with the gossip about people and drugs, wondering what she would do without her Net connection. Being depressed is like kayaking or hang gliding: You won't die immediately if you skip the homework, but in a pinch you'll stand a much better chance if you've gone far beyond the basics. Walkers is in the grand tradition of the Net. Its members don't blindingly trust authority figures— their own shrinks—and they are reaching out to other patients and to an online psychiatrist. Tell us, Ivan, some Walkers ask, is Parnate as good a drug as it's cracked up to be? What about Nardil? Can you take it without your body swelling up?

"Ivan" is a well-credentialed psychopharmacologist in New York City who helps out for free. Dr. Ivan Goldberg doesn't prescribe drugs for people online, but he *will* report his own experiences with them after many years of practice. He has a knack for coming up with angles that patients' own doctors might miss. After months on Prozac, a man found his work slipping. Ivan Goldberg told him of a new way—successful here, it turns out—to treat the problem.

Goldberg is online two hours a day "as a way of paying back for the thirty-plus good years I have had from my work with depressed people."[3] After several years on the Net helping virtual support groups, he has won the respect of hundreds and perhaps even thousands.

Still, Walkers compare notes with each other and don't accept even Ivan Goldberg's opinions automatically. Just as if they were talking over the office watercooler, they weigh the validity of the information themselves. But what a collection of facts! When a new antidepressant shows up in Canada or the United Kingdom, Walkers learn about it many weeks before the news reaches the daily papers in the States, assuming that word makes their daily newspapers at all.

Many of the best conversations, however, aren't about drugs or the merits or perils of electroconvulsive shock treatments. They're about other Walkers. Remember the gay Walker in Iowa who was so quick to welcome newcomers and answer questions? Well, here's his obit: *Died of complications from diabetes.* How about the fellow on the East Coast, the programmer who never logs on with a name? Is he okay, after his last suicide attempt? Is somebody going to drop by to visit him in the hospital? What about such-and-such's cat? How's your new girlfriend? Is your landlord being reasonable? The questions and answers fly across the wires. Walkers may not be as famous a virtual community as The WELL, Echo, and similar bulletin board systems with Net and media connections, but it's hardly as if the luminaries of those places enjoy a monopoly on Caring.

Later that morning I hear Cliff Stoll push his book on WAMU radio. It's a slaughter; the call-ins run against him by at least five to one. I even feel a little sorry for him until I remember that the technophobes at many bookstores may outnumber the technophiles. The full title of the book is *Silicon Snake Oil: Second Thoughts on the Information Highway,* and it should be just the ticket for Luddites and Snubbites with spare change. I myself have Second Thoughts about his Second Thoughts. Early on in his book he says: "I look forward to the time when our Internet reaches into every town and trailer park." But his true emphasis comes through. Just how much of a technopopulist is he in the end when he claims that networks will "isolate us from one another" and "work against literacy and creativity"?

What's really freaky is that a woman from Walkers or a similar discussion group—out of all the thousands on the Net—calls up *The Diane Rehme Show* and ever so politely shreds the arguments that Stoll has made in *Oil.* A few years ago he wrote *The Cuckoo's Egg,* a wonderful book about his battles against errant hackers, and parts of

Snake Oil do ring true, but oh how wrong he is about the more cosmic issues. Confronted with the Walkers-style example, Stoll acknowledges that, yes, maybe the Net could be of use to people who need support. After all, the very anonymity he's assailed can work in favor of honest dialogue. Exactly. One of the glories of Walkers, however, is that depressed people can be as open or nameless as they want. What's more, they can even go Face to Face. Several Walkers near me, for example, will spend hours and hours talking in person with others dogged by this scourge of Lincoln and Churchill.

Dave Harmon is the man behind the Walkers list. He's a twenty-eight-year-old Harvard grad, bearded, bespectacled, and a little on the heavy side, as he describes it. I learn that he works as a programmer for a company that writes software to use with mice—the computer kind. His depression is moderate. Come the middle of the night, he may wake up in a cold sweat; he can also suffer flagging energy.

Several years ago Harmon was crouched in a Boston bus shelter, enjoying a break from a crowded but rainy New Year's Eve celebration, when he took out a notebook and wrote a poem. "I am the Walker in Darkness," it read in part, "I am the bringer of light." The next day Harmon called the company that had hooked him into the Internet—he wanted to start a list for depressed people interested in art and magic. "The thing that makes the Net so powerful is that you don't have to get into a big deal to start a minor newsgroup or a mailing list." The newsgroups and the mailing lists can precisely reflect Netfolks' interests, loves, and fears—much more closely than, say, CBS or the *New York Times,* or even niche programs on cable.

Newsgroups are a bit like local bulletin board systems except that some newsgroups reach hundreds of thousands of people around the world. Mailing lists are more intimate than newsgroups since you usually need

---

Oklahoma City and the
Ban-the-Bomb-Manual Panic

A citation for *The Terrorist's Handbook* popped up
on my screen a minute after I started a search of the
World Wide Web under the word "explosives." I apparently would be able to make "book bombs,"
"lightbulb bombs," "phone bombs."

Trying to retrieve the *Handbook* some weeks
later, I read the following: "Are you sure this resource exists?" Cute. The heat is on. *Handbook*-style
items caught the attention of the U.S. Senate after
sickos blew up a federal building in Oklahoma City
and killed 160 people. The response in effect was:
"Ban the bomb manuals—from the Net and otherwise!" and as of this writing, it looked as if such sen-
timents might end up as law. Still, a little problem
arose in the case of *The Terrorist's Handbook* on the
Net. The material was coming to me from Lysator, a
respected academic computer society at Linköping
University in Linköping, *Sweden.* Last I knew, the
U.S. Senate did not enjoy jurisdiction over its counterparts in Stockholm.

The Swedish computer that stored *The Terrorist's
Handbook,* however, contains megabyte after megabyte of valuable material on computing and other

---

to sign up for them electronically before you receive the
messages.

"The funny thing," Harmon says of freshly created
mailing lists, "is that you never know what will result.
What I found was that most depressed people couldn't
produce that much art and mysticism, but they were interested in supporting each other, and I looked at that and let
it go on its own."

subjects, and the electronic librarians didn't want to anger the university. So out of prudence, they voluntarily removed the bomb manual after hysterical stories appeared in the press. The *Handbook* wasn't worth the fuss.

Perhaps in other cases Washington will use diplomacy with other countries to unplug *Handbook*-style items. But no one should count on this approach working in the end. Inevitably the same material will be secretly making the rounds of obscure electronic bulletin board systems, as opposed to the Net itself. As if that isn't enough, Washington has unwittingly given out instructions for bomb-makers by way of the tax-financed *Blaster's Handbook* from the Forestry Service in the U.S. Department of Agriculture. Even *The Encyclopedia Britannica* has printed material on explosive making.

Most disturbing of all, Constitutional issues arise here. We don't need the government to restrain free speech. As writer Brock N. Meeks wrote in his *CyberWire Dispatch* newsletter, Senator Dianne Feinstein's proposal was "a break in the dike." It was "the trickle that could become a river of regulatory hammers meant to turn the rough-and-tumble, open and free-flowing online discourse into something with all the appeal and intellectual acumen of tofu."

A seventy-eight-year-old widow in the American South discovered Harmon's list. She was the first in her family, after several generations of mental illness, to seek psychiatric help. People from Singapore have popped up, too, reporting how they were stigmatized as lazy by people unable to understand the energy-sapping qualities of the disease. Walkers tell of spouses complaining about the loss of sex drive from depression or medications. Simply put, Harmon's list has not just helped people cope with a disease, but it has also helped those who can't understand it. And as shown by the Singaporean example, geography has been inconsequential for the most part. "When you're depressed," Harmon says, "it doesn't matter where you're from, you're still depressed."

What's more, Walkers can log on as often or seldom as they want. Frequently the depressed feel all "peopled up," so they may flee into their rooms and close the blinds when visitors approach. But with Walkers messages, all they need do is press the delete key. The Internet isn't just a medium of special benefit to the deaf; it's also one for the seriously depressed, many of whom, if made Netless, might try to do without *any* company offline.

As with thousands of other Net lists, people come and go, some of them overwhelmed by the sheer volume of messages; Stoll is right to characterize the Internet as like trying to drink water from a fire hydrant. But a core of stalwarts remain enthusiastically on Walkers, and along with Harmon and Goldberg, they're rather small-townish in cyberspace in the best of ways. I ask about the East Coast Walker with suicidal tendencies. Harmon says that by the time the supportive messages reached the man, the programmer had already called 911 and gone to the hospital to have his stomach pumped.

But, yes, Harmon says, Walkers has indeed saved lives. "A more usual situation is that someone is considering suicide and issues an appeal to Walkers for help. They'll say something to the effect that 'It's not worth it, and nothing I do ever works, and I'm probably bothering you with this note.' People respond to it and sometime call the person by phone if the number is available." If the number isn't, Harmon and other Netheads will try to use their knowledge of the Internet to track it down. "We don't breach privacy unless there really is a suicide threat, and sometimes people's accounts may be on services where we can't find them. More usually, various people may send their own phone numbers either privately or to someone or to the list, so that other members can reach them.

"The Internet," he cautions, "is *not* always a fast-rescuer—you may be lucky to get same-day service. In the programmer's case his note didn't even get *to* my list for an hour, much less get sent out to all the members. *I* found out about his note by getting a midnight phone call!"

Still, Harmon sees the Net as a godsend for ongoing support and as a crisis aid even if the help isn't always immediate. Goldberg agrees: "It's mobilized people to all kinds of interventions."[4]

"I'm sitting here with a knife in my hand," wrote a community college student asking for support from Walkers. "Don't worry, I'm not going to kill myself—just hurt myself a little. I just feel as though I deserve pain." She went on to tell how she had been in the National Honor Society in high school, gone on to an honors program at Loyola University for several years, then had been forced to leave. "I used to be strong, brilliant, and ambitious and now I am stupid and manic depressive. It just hurts so much. So I guess that's why I'm cutting on my wrists tonight." She told me when I wrote to ask about her condition—improved—that "I would be lost without Walkers."

A near-suicide in Santa Clara, California, aided by the newsgroup alt.support.depression, recalls: "I was so close it was amazing." Medical debts had overwhelmed him. He was a single father and his boss had put him on probation after child care gobbled up too much work time. In tears he began his note: "It doesn't really matter any more." A New York woman saw the note and begged people online to help. Hundreds of messages came over the Net from as far as Japan. Tracked down despite his unsigned post, the California man received help not only from a colleague at work but also from police. "Something snapped," he recalls, "and I just realized that there were a lot of people there who cared."[5]

Madness, another self-help group on the Net, is a mailing list for people who suffer drastic mood swings, hear voices, and see visions. Now, says Sylvia Caras, who runs the list, they can use the Net to carry on a dialogue with federal mental health officials. The Net offers a very *real* voice for those the world might otherwise ignore.

I could go on forever about support groups on the Net. Whether you're short or extra tall, anorexic or 300 pounds, a victim of cancer or of child abuse, the Internet teems with people wanting to share their experiences with you— a task made much easier through the efficiencies of the Net, which have brought the cost of electronic mail down so much. I bristle when I hear people talk about the Internet as worthless unless big profits await megaconglomerates. The activities of support groups and other virtual communities may not show up in any country's gross domestic product, but in the aggregate they're just as valuable as anything to emerge from AT&T or Time Warner.

May I emphasize that the Net is far, far more than a mental health clinic? It's a place, too, for political activists, boaters, golfers, motorcyclists, gun owners, gourmets, football fans, baseball enthusiasts, parents and teachers, writers and readers of many genres, pilots, airline passengers, amateur radio operators, and reggae lovers. All have their own niches, which is just what you'd expect with more than 12,000 newsgroups.

While the clueless are arguing over whether the Net has value, people like John Schwartz already know it does. Recently he wondered about lyrics by a singer and songwriter named Liz Phair. Just how did they go? Some of the biggest fun came from his hunt online. He tracked down at least five different Web areas—"digital fan magazines"—devoted to Phair. "Some had photos, some had biographical information, and a couple had song lyrics." And yes, he found the lyrics he wanted, and in their full, unprintable glory. "Useless? Probably. Satisfying? You bet." And Schwartz went on: "Think of all the stuff that you'd find in your public library if you pulled something off the shelf. A lot of it would be 'useless' for your own needs—tons of mediocre fiction, outdated information, and silly things. But would anybody say that it proves that libraries are worthless?"[6]

Other Net activities also suggest that *Snake Oil* is self-descriptive. A Michigan couple has started a virtual toy store complete with pictures of their staffers as children and service of the kind you'd expect from L. L. Bean; their first order came from Brazil (see chapter 2: "Business on the Net: From White Rabbit Toys to "Intel Inside"). Out in California two young techies are giving hundreds of young musicians a break through a much-needed project called the Internet Underground Music Archives (chapter 3: EntertaiNet: A Few Musings on Net.Rock, Leonardo da Vinci and Bill Gates, Bianca's Smut Shack, and David Letterman in Cyberspace). Just throw $100 their way and, for a year, you can post a sample of your music on the Net and perhaps stir up sales of old cassettes and CDs.

At the same time that Stoll grouses that the Internet is unedited, scores of dailies and weeklies are on the Net to one extent or another (chapter 4: Pulped Wood versus Electrons: Can the Print World Learn to Love the Net?). So's *Time* magazine. Random House, Macmillan, and Time Warner are there, too, posting samples from various books, and soon people at home will be able to send credit card numbers securely over the Net and dial up the complete texts of bestsellers and other books. Even now you just might be reading *NetWorld!* off a screen rather than from pulped wood.

Meanwhile, a digitized cadaver on the Internet may help revolutionize the study of anatomy (chapter 5: Wired Knowledge: When They Let a Murderer Loose on the Internet), and in Canada, leather-jacketed teenagers are using the Net to develop their reading and writing skills.

A Mini Jargon Guide

- Electronic Mail or e-mail. You can use the Net and other networks to send messages to your friends in Peoria or Melbourne—anywhere, in fact, where Internet connections go, from Alaska to the South Pole. An electronic mailbox is just like the physical equivalent. It's a little storage area where your messages pile up for you to retrieve when you want.
- File Transfer Protocol, or FTP. It's a means to send or receive files from one computer to another.
- Gopher. This program lets you track down information on the Net. The word *Gopher* also alludes to certain Gopher-style collections of computer files. Different Gophers connect to each other through items on menus. You might start looking at an article on water pollution from a computer in Washington, D.C., see a mention of an African river, click on that menu choice with your mouse or otherwise select it, and end up at a computer in Johannesburg.
- Internet Relay Chat. It's like a huge party line except that people are typing rather than talking. You can open up private areas, too, and reach just one person.
- Mailing Lists. To be a bit simplistic, they're just like regular electronic mail, except that a number

Also, the Net, in the opinion of many, is mocking Orwell's predictions (chapter 6: Governments and the Net: Making Sure Orwell Was Wrong). Some serious threats remain—such as the efforts of American bureaucrats to make the Net more friendly to snoopy cops—but 1995 is a long way from *1984*. What's more, the Internet doesn't offer just sex.

of people share messages, to which you can typically respond privately or with the entire list. Some lists, however, let only the *moderator* send out messages. Via Usenet, some mailing lists appear as newsgroups.

- Newsgroups. These are the bulletin board systems of the Net, in effect. Almost anyone can post messages there and potentially reach hundreds of thousands of people—far more than on most mailing lists, since people can read newsgroups without subscribing. The newsgroups are part of a service called Usenet, which reaches BBSs around the world, not just the Internet. No one owns this anarchy, and I wouldn't want it any other way.

- Telnet. Without leaving my regular keyboard I can operate a computer at Oxford University or the University of California by way of a procedure called Telnet. I'm remotely controlling the machines at the other end.

- The World Wide Web. It's the area of the Net that not only lets you read text but also see pictures, hear sounds, and even take in short clips from movies. Like Gophers, sites on the World Wide Web connect with each other. A program that lets you navigate the Web is known as a browser. Among the more popular browsers are Mosaic, Netscape, and Lynx (the latter, alas, won't let you instantly enjoy pictures).

Love, too, can thrive. The persistent may indeed find wives and husbands on the Net (chapter 7: The Electronic Matchmaker).

This all happens on my Internet—anyway the one I'll describe here. Let me offer an inevitable caveat, however: The Net is too vast for one writer to cover everything. So I won't bother with Internet Relay Chat, where you instantly see the other people's typing. As a temporary habitué of these regions, J. C. Hertz started to regard the Internet as "a Sartrean hell—too many people talking at one time."[7] Yes! Net chat brings Hemingwayesque accounts from witnesses to Japanese earthquakes or Russian coups, and I'm happy it's around for the aficionados, especially net.lovers, who can retreat to their own private channels; but I myself favor electronic mail and newsgroups, which I can read on my own terms without parrying incessantly with dyspeptic strangers half a planet removed. I promise, dear readers: I'll inflict nary a chat transcript on you.

Certain omissions, however, really pain me. Given more time, I'd have loved to cover the growth of the community network movement. For free, in many cities, you can open up an Internet account and tap into electronic libraries all over the world or receive electronic mail. Best of all, "communets" can bring communities together. The Net is one of the big lures to get people online, but once there, they may be able to fetch the schedule of their local public radio stations, find out about local charities, and talk back electronically to officials of city halls.

What's fascinating is the resemblance between these local nets and the Net at large. People on both would rather chat with other citizens than swap e-mail with the politicians or other celebrities. And why not? Communets are communities, just as the Net, serving so many interests, is a *series* of communities. Alas, Stoll does not appreciate the possibilities here.

Stoll is an astronomer, not just a hacker, and his *Snake Oil* makes me feel as if he is using a scratchy pair of binoculars to look for life on Mars. Fixated on negatives, he has downplayed even the obvious: the Net equivalent of Martian mountains. Has Stoll dropped by alt.music.chapelhill, or rec.arts.dance, or alt.christnet.christianlife, or the Dallas Virtual Jewish Community Center Home Page, or the American Ireland Fund, or the Voter Education Project?

And how about the thousands of other Web pages in which individual Netfolks can share with the world their love of families and pets, or gardening, or *The Catcher in the Rye,* or old Chevies, or whatever else they enjoy, at or away from their computers? Item by item, those are tiny, almost invisible slices of Netlife; but en masse, they rise up as mountains.

Yes, yes, sex *areas* thrive on the Internet. But it is that way offline, too; do snack-food stores turn millions each year off Chaucer or *Playboy?* Of course Chaucer himself could be randy at times, as could Shakespeare and Joyce and hundreds of other literary greats—an inconvenient fact for the American ayatollahs who hope to censor the Net.

The biggest irony here is that the Internet can actually promote Family Values and strengthen real neighborhoods. As George Gilder and others have noted, the new technology can serve people's exact needs rather than just dish out the standard sex and violence so beloved to TV networks. The Net is Example One in my opinion— especially The Barcroft School and Civic League page on the World Wide Web. Several thousand people live in the Barcroft area of Arlington, Virginia, near Washington, D.C. It's neither a slum nor a glitzy, status-crazed neighborhood, just a good place to raise the families that the ayatollahs love to extol. An old Methodist church has served as a community house. Now an electronic equivalent is on the Web, complete with a color photo of the church building; people can catch up with neighborhood news and learn of ice cream socials.

I'm writing this paragraph just before the Barcroft Fourth of July parade. The word from the World Wide Web is that Susan O'Hara Christopher will be the Grand Marshall. People can enjoy Nancy Tankersley's watercolors of past parades, or "Jim Lande's famous tree trunk sculpture. Games for the kids, no political campaigning, hot dogs and lemonade, the new Barcroft tee shirts and lots more!" The higher the percentage of Netfolks among the citizenry, the more Fourth of July bulletins we'll see in cyberspace.

Across the Potomac in D.C., the Internet is helping to reduce the number of hookers and drug pushers plying the Blagden Alley neighborhood. If the police catch you looking for women or dope, a man named Paul Warren will put your name on the World Wide Web. Thanks to his "Crimenet," residents no longer stand as much a chance of finding a hooker at work on the sidewalk a few yards from toddlers in living rooms. Not everyone would approve of the privacy implications here, but I myself love what Warren is doing. Like thousands of small-town newspapers that print the names of the arrested, Warren is just spreading around the public record. A notice reminds readers that "Criminal defendants are presumed innocent until proven guilty"; and he is willing to post an update for anyone exonerated. Warren isn't saying that prostitution should be illegal everywhere, just that it should not force young families out of Blagden Alley.

That, in fact, is how I feel about net.sex. If a fifth grader encountered alt.sex.bestiality whenever he or she flicked on a computer, why, yes, I'd join the ayatollahs. But the Net is not like the pre-Web Blagden Alley or daytime television. You normally don't find sex on the Net—at least not the truly kinky type—unless you seek it out. And the computer industry is working on software to reduce the chances of children accidentally running across alt.sex.bestiality. Even now, of course, the language in the average area of the Net is much cleaner than the words in the locker room of the typical high school. Trying to ban "smut" from the Internet would be like shutting down high school football because *some* sixteen-year-old tackles love to cuss at teammates and gawk at nude pictures.

Granted, the Net has problems, and rather serious ones. A Californian stole 20,000 credit card numbers from Net users; in New York some young men met through the

Net and figured out ways to order tens of thousands of dollars in merchandise illegally. Many Netfolks think it's too risky to send credit card numbers over the Net itself when ordering merchandise; better to use the telephone or fax. What's more, just as Stoll says, business on the Net is over-hyped. Meanwhile the Feds have reduced subsidies to the Net. Over in Australia there are already bothersome charges for use according to the amount of material transmitted, and people fear that the same could happen in the States.

Just as frustratingly, the technology isn't quite there yet. Pictures can take centuries to appear on my screen when I fetch material on the World Wide Web. I hook into the Internet by dialing up ClarkNet, a company in a barn south of Baltimore. This is one of the *best* services, but a good part of the time, in recent months, I've suffered a busy signal or worse when I try to dial in. Given the overcrowding of the Net, electronic mail takes longer to arrive than it once did. I believe Stoll when he says that in some cases the United States Postal Service will get mail from one place to the other faster than the Net will handle e-mail. That's the exception, but I'm disturbed to see it happen even part of the time.

I lament, too, the lack of commercial books available on the Net for free, in the public library tradition. Cliff Stoll is absolutely right to want better content, and my friend Jim Besser would agree with us. Jim is a journalist avid for new facts; he regrets that so much of the information on the Net is wrong or out of date. Beyond that, his Internet connection sometimes goes south when he is under a deadline.

Cures for the Internet's problems, however, are or could be on the way. Technology will make the Net safer to use and more reliable—lo and behold, the computers in the barn have behaved somewhat better these past few weeks. Over the long run, too, Netlife will improve. Popular programs in some cases, even now, are letting customers send credit card numbers online without the hackers intercepting them. Net businesses will take off when more people sign on and young hackers get jobs and families.

The Internet will even survive the reduction of subsidies from Washington. The price of the technology will just keep going down if past trends apply, and if the government doesn't let phone companies gouge people. Everything is faster and cheaper. Once the experts doubted that ordinary phone lines could carry signals at 9.6 kilobits, or 9,600 bits, per second. Today, even if I'm not IBM or the phone company, I can cruise along at around 28.8 kilobits per second, which is enough to receive a book in a few minutes.

If Cliff Stoll really wants electronic books, then computer networks can transmit them. When, just when, will Washington be brave enough to work toward a well-stocked national digital library offering commercial books for all; why should we replicate online the "savage inequalities" of our libraries and schools?

Netfolks aren't the reason why such a library for the Internet is so far off right now, and why we may well end up with a national digital bookstore as opposed to a true library offering books at no charge or at minimal cost. Even technophobic librarians—they exist, even if not in the same numbers as before—aren't the true villains here. *Lobbyists* are at fault. Bill Clinton's intellectual property czar, Bruce Lehman, is himself a former lawyer–lobbyist who acts as if he is still fighting for his old copyright clients. Members of his former law firm have donated tens of thousands of dollars to influential politicians. And in a five-year period people with corporate or family ties to a legal publisher, West Publishing in Minnesota, have given more than $738,000 in political contributions, some of which went to members of Congress influential on copyright matters.

With less eagerness to please lobbyists pushing for corporate business plans—rather than for the commonweal—the U.S. government could divert resources from bureaucracy to knowledge and pay publishers and writers fairly. How? Suppose Washington would link the national library with a focused program to buy hardware that schools and local libraries could lend out. In effect the Feds would prime the private market by encouraging mass production and by sending a message about priorities. Small, tablet-shaped computers with extra-sharp screens could eventually go on sale—much sooner than otherwise—for $99.95 at Kmart. And these same machines, although designed for reading electronic books, would be excellent for the Net or for filling out easy electronic forms; we could save tens of billions in money and time in the private and public sectors of America's $6-trillion economy. Needless to say, too, this affordable hardware could mean more eyes for retail businesses on the Internet.

Then high tech wouldn't pose such a problem to non-techie consumers and to computerphobic women and minorities. A study out of the Georgia Institute of Technology showed that 94 percent of the surveyed users on the Web were male and 87 percent were white. With less-threatening hardware and proper training of the right people, however, schools and neighborhood libraries could help bring a much wider segment of society on the Net. Cliff Stoll is aware of the possibilities here. He knew two years ago of my TeleRead proposal to improve the content of the Net, get many more people online, and spread the electronic books around from the very start. How much easier it must be for him to eulogize old wooden card catalogues and avoid a nasty tangle with lobbyist-cowed politicians and bureaucrats.

Bashing technology, of course, is hardly new. In 1854 a writer complained: "We are in great haste to construct a magnetic telegraph from Maine to Texas; but Maine and Texas, it may be, have nothing important to communicate." He said that "We are eager to tunnel under the Atlantic and

Touring *NetWorld!* Yourself—Via the Web

Webfolk, check out the Internet Underground Music Archive, White Rabbit Toys, electronic magazines, and many of the other Net delights I've described in this book. Just use your Netscape, Mosaic, or other browser to go to

http://www.webcom.com/~prima/networld.html

You'll find there a list of various Web sites mentioned here in the pulped wood *NetWorld!*—and perhaps some informal updates. You can reach the sites immediately. Just click on the hypertext links. People at the other end may change the links, but I've made them as up-to-date as I could.

If you would like Net addresses of *some* of the people mentioned in this book, go to

http://www.clark.net/rothman/pub/networld.html

Perhaps you'll also want to see a detailed electronic version of my TeleRead proposal for a well-stocked, cost-justified national digital library. It could let ordinary readers dial up the *entire* texts of copyrighted books from home for free without cheating publishers and writers. For more on TeleRead, check out the hyperlinked Net incarnation of my chapter in a forthcoming book *Scholarly Publishing: The Electronic Frontier* (Cambridge, Massachusetts, M.I.T. Press, 1995):

http://www.clark.net/rothman/pub/telhome.html

bring the Old World some weeks nearer to the New; but perchance the first news that will leak through to the broad, flapping American ear will be that Princess Adelaide has the whooping cough."[8] Henry David Thoreau was the writer and the words appeared in *Walden.*

Does their source, however, make them less dubious? Hardly. Imagine America without the telegraph—without an opportunity to forge lucrative commercial ties with the Old World, or to strengthen Texas's ties to Washington. As it turned out, Texas and the rest of the country had plenty to say. So did railroad employees talking to each other; companies could more easily use single tracks to handle traffic in both directions, knowing that the telegraph was there to handle scheduling.[9] In other fields, such as medicine, the telegraph undoubtedly hastened progress as well. It also helped friends and families keep in touch as the country was settled; today the Net does the same with people in this era of international travel. Technology, then, while ripe with opportunities for abuse, can do far more than recruit "Girls of the Net" or spread word of a princess's whooping cough.

Ironically, if the Cliff Stolls prevail, and if too many white hats abandon the nets as "devoid of warmth and human kindness," then his predictions *will* come to pass; the greedy will take over, confident that others won't mind so much.

Together with millions of other Netfolks, I'll remember the Great Spamming of '94. Laurence A. Canter and Martha S. Siegel, husband-and-wife partners in an Arizona law firm called Canter and Siegel, wanted to sell their services as immigration experts. So they splattered a "Green Card" ad—as if hurling spam against a wall— across some 6,000 newsgroups on Usenet. They didn't care if you preferred to read about baseball or UNIX; they wanted your eyeballs. The Net seethed. I myself disliked many of the tactics used against Canter and Siegel—was it really necessary to threaten death or favor them with a slew of unsought magazine subscriptions?—but clearly they merited some good, strong, healthy loathing. I complained to the American Bar Association, which, at the time, was spending hundreds of thousands of dollars on a PR campaign to upgrade the image of lawyers. You might say that C & S set the goodwill account back by several million.

My big regret is that I lacked more time to raise hell against Canter and his wife online and in other ways. The glory of the Net, this *series* of communities, was and is diversity; here C & S were dumbing it down to the broadcast model where one program served all. But Canter and Siegel didn't give a whit about the Net as it existed, about the outrage that so many unwilling people were bearing the costs of sending and storing their unwanted messages, about the fact that Usenet couldn't survive continued assaults in this vein, about the damage they were doing to the various forms of Net culture, a phrase that C & S would undoubtedly have dismissed as an oxymoron.

Canter and Siegel later added to the insult with *How to Make a Fortune on the Information Superhighway,* the 1990s equivalent of a guide to exterminating buffalo.[10] The book talked of selling to 30 million people, which was malarkey. Some Net demographers challenged the figure at the time—reality may finally have caught up— but more important, most of those 30 million could only send and receive electronic mail as opposed to using services such as the World Wide Web. And just how many people wanted to receive junk mail from marketers? Of course C & S might suggest mailing lists for the receptive—nothing wrong there—but without access to the right Net services, fewer people would know of the lists in the first place.

Does this mean that the Internet should be free of commerce? Quite the opposite. The challenge is simply to avoid letting the hardsellers overwhelm the Internet. Countless areas of the Net exist where people not only tolerate ads, they *want* to read them. Besides, the commercial and noncommercial can build on each other. When I put my TeleRead proposal on the World Wide Web—that is, my call for a well-stocked national digital library with copyrighted books included—I built in hypertext links[11] to

Web sites that could be useful. And several just happened to be commercial. The Minneapolis *Star Tribune,* for example, had done a Pulitzer-quality expose of the thousands of dollars that West Publishing had doled out in trips for some Supreme Court justices who passed judgment on copyright matters. Just why should I have avoided this superb material when a commercial publication was good enough to share it with the Net for free?

Electronic cafes, found in San Francisco, Seattle, London, and Hong Kong, among other locations, are another good example of how the commercial and noncommercial can strengthen each other. Cafes with Internet hookups can even help bridge the gap between Net and life. The Internet Cafe at 1363 4th Avenue in Prince George, British Columbia, doesn't just offer a coffee bar. Customers of the local Internet provider can pick up their e-mail there and wander around the Net, read "a good, old-fashioned cork bulletin board for community information exchanges," learn about local service agencies, watch resident artists at work, buy crafts from all over the world, and even get advice from a local psychologist, Russ Winterbotham, who just happens to own the place.

When Stoll writes about an Ontario bookstore with a water garden and three cats, it's easy to appreciate the potential charms of commerce offline. But clearly the Net itself can spice up a traditional business. In London, you can drop by the Cyberia cafe at 39 Whitfield Street and plunk down £1.50 for a large cappuccino and £2.50 for a half-hour on the Net. The word is that the cafe has drawn "more media coverage than a small war." I'm not surprised. Even if prices might be a bit lower by my standards, Cyberia is meeting a definite need. Of course Stoll would complain that the customers in the electronic cafes are "surrounded by people, yet escaping into conversations with distant strangers." Isn't he forgetting something, however: The way many Net aficionados love to meet the like-minded in person?

I'm also keen, needless to say, on the pioneering work that thousands of small businesses are doing on the World Wide Web itself—rather than posting in-your-face ads to nonrelevant newsgroups.

No, Web businesses aren't charities or consumer service organizations. But by offering details about their products and services, they are respecting our intelligence far more than does the huckstery on television. You wouldn't want to buy a new Buick or Volvo if you simply went by statistics and photos on the Web. But you just might learn more about gas mileage and safety claims than if you relied simply on the sales rep and brochures in the showroom. The more you shop this way, the more you'll encourage manufacturers to improve their products and services rather than just to shell out megabucks on more Super Bowl ads. Net business, major limitations notwithstanding, is indeed A Good Thing.

Our first stop in *NetWorld!*, in fact, might well be one of my favorite stores in cyberspace—White Rabbit Toys.

Business on the Net: From White Rabbit Toys to "Intel Inside"

Bob Lilienfeld worked for Procter & Gamble and the outfit behind the Muppets, and JoAnn Lilienfeld was a buyer at Bloomingdale's. Nowadays he consults on solid waste and other environmental issues. His wife, a neatly coifed woman who looks and dresses like an up-scale schoolteacher,[1] has started a toy store called White Rabbit Toys in honor of the character in *Alice's Adventures in Wonderland*. Bob enjoys technology. JoAnn herself is no slouch in that area. They are in their forties now but relish new marketing wrinkles just as much as when they were earning their MBAs from Northwestern University.

So Bob and JoAnn Lilienfeld have set up shop on the Internet, where, in a surprising but logical way that a mathematician like Lewis Carroll would have loved, their respective business ventures mesh.

Wandering through commercial listings on the Web, I discovered the virtual White Rabbit just as Christmas shoppers were crowding the corporeal White Rabbit up in

Ann Arbor, Michigan. Bob was a technohusband par excellence. He designed the toy store online, claimed just the right address on the World Wide Web (http://www.toystore.com), wrestled with the technical issues, and helped take orders from customers, the first of whom lived in Brazil. JoAnn would pay Bob in his favorite currency: teddy bears. The big question was: Will they make any money at it? I electronically hung around their virtual store and chatted with Bob on the phone as the season progressed.

He and his wife were among the thousands of small business people who were trying new marketing paradigms on the Net, where the denizens hated intrusive huckstery but might take to electronic catalogues.

Compared to most other business people on the Internet, the Lilienfelds were quick studies. You could type an electronic address into your computer and see a White Rabbit logo and a greeting from the toy store in several languages. Then you clicked your mouse on the proper area of your screen and opened up a colorful catalogue with not only blurbs but also pictures of tops and puzzles and wooden toy trains of the kind your parents might have bought for you. Most of White Rabbit's offerings were classics that you would never see at Toys Я Us.

Bob and JoAnn Lilienfeld wanted their business to stand out. Soon their electronic forms might let you type in the age of your child, information about his or her interests, your budget, and other constraints. You would instantly receive tips on what gifts to buy. Even now, you could order online without talking to a human—not as heartless as it might sound, if you simply valued your time and telephone money. The electronic forms could even calculate the postage.

White Rabbit intrigued me, and others felt the same way. Within a few weeks of my first visit, they got calls from the *Wall Street Journal* and the *Detroit Free Press*. Some reporters had caught on to the obvious: While

Hollywood and Washington were off prattling clichés about the overpriced medium called interactive TV—while Al Gore was cracking jokes on stage with Lily Tomlin during an entertainment summit disguised as an "information" one—entrepreneurs and Fortune 500 companies were trying ads on the Net. The Internet often narrows differences between large and small businesses. Even little ones can reach global audiences and, through well-planned Web areas, look like giants to customers in Rio or Tokyo. New cybermalls sprout up to get technophobic companies online by providing both technical and creative services. Corporations fight over addresses for the Net. Stanley Kaplan, a service that tutors students for academic examinations such as the Scholastic Aptitude Test, sued a competitor that stole the name kaplan.com. A writer for *Wired* magazine mischievously claimed McDonald's name, which the hamburger chain hadn't yet registered. Such oversights, however, were rapidly becoming the exception in an era when prime Web sites made the pages of *Newsweek.*

Even electronic hookers ("We go all the way") were on the Internet—in fact, operating under the name "Brandy's Babes." They plied their trade from Arizona, the same wild and quirky state from which Canter and Siegel enraged the Net. And yet, if you cast the usual moral questions aside, the Babes seemed to be exemplary citizens of cyberspace. Not just hypesters, they posted specifics like prices, bust, hip, and waist measurements, and preferences in men. "No beards," a Babe warned customers. "Employed men only."

Unlike the hardsellers, the Babes did not inflict unwanted ads on thousands of newsgroups. And in line with the two-way traditions of the Net, they solicited messages from customers—dirty ones that the Babes might charge good money to answer. You could even dial up Brandy's and see a live Babe at her computer with her impressive bosom exposed. The gig lasted several zany months. Fear of police raids grew, however, even before the ayatollahs

in the U.S. Senate ranted against net.sex. I finally saw just
a blank screen except for a laconic message alluding to
"bad links."

Separately a condom store was online as well. It offered medical information, supplied tantalizing odds and
ends on such topics as "The Size of a Man's Pony," and
wittily answered questions from appreciative readers.
Like Brandy's, it operated in a nonintrusive way.

The World Wide Web was also a virtual home for
thousands of more conventional businesses such as the
manufacturer of a toy gun that shot Ping-Pong balls, a
city's worth of bookstores, Godiva chocolate, and Ragu
spaghetti. None other than the Home Shopping Network
bought out a Net retailer specializing in computer equipment. Pizza Hut went online. And the United States was
hardly alone in this trend. The Singaporeans were competing in the cyberpizza race—Shakey's Pizza was girding
to take orders, via a fax-Net link, from hungry scientists
and students at the National University of Singapore. A
large Irish bank advertised on the Net. So did the Royal
Bank of Canada. It mounted a bilingual Web area for both
English- and French-speaking customers who, once past
the first menu, didn't have to clutter their screens with
material in the wrong language.

Some of the old technical barriers, of course, remained
even in rich countries: most hardware was still rotten for
doing home shopping. What the customers needed, and
what Silicon Valley could not yet provide, happened to be
small, affordable, sharp-screened computers that could
colorfully show off the merchandise. The main way to look
at the Net was through Mosaic-style programs. And even at
28.8 kilobits per second—the highest speed possible
through widely available modems—it took too long to go
from page to page of electronic catalogues. The biggest
problem was the software installation, which could be
tricky. Although software such as Internet in a Box simpli-
fied the matters, the Net was not yet TV-easy to use.

Even so, some companies were designing inexpensive gadgets, which could sell for mere hundreds of dollars, that would allow people to surf the Internet on their televisions. I hated the idea of anyone reading text off a blurry television screen. But at least the powers of the computer world were finally thinking of the Internet as a real, live marketplace. Just as important, Prodigy, America Online, CompuServe, and rivals were preparing to let customers reach Web sites from their proprietary networks.

Microsoft was planning point-and-click Internet capabilities for its Windows 95 operating system. And it had bought stock in a key Internet provider and would be linking its own network tightly with the Net. *Advertising Age* estimated the number of people able to access the Web itself—the best place for Net advertising—at several million at the start of 1995.[2] And that number might push past 11 million by 1998, according to a report from a Massachusetts research firm.[3] So, even if Internet merchants aren't advertising in the most consumer-oriented of places right now, they might well be awash in new business later on.

The existing denizens of the Internet were more technical than the people on, say, Prodigy or America Online. Some software companies used this to their great advantage. A good example was Cyberspace Development Company, which had created an extraordinarily useful program called The Internet Adapter, or TIA. Most Net people couldn't enjoy Mosaic-style viewers because their network connections did not allow this. But TIA let even Netfolks with $18-a-month accounts use Mosaic and other marvels. And to buy TIA, they did not have to go to a retail store.

If technically savvy, they could pick it up on the Internet itself. A digital key, transmitted via e-mail, allowed only authorized customers to use the publicly available files. Skeptics could try a test version of TIA for a few weeks before paying for it by check or credit card. Because of the low cost of distribution and, in my case, the lack of need for full consulting services, I spent just $25 on a product that might have cost a good $50–$75 if sold at the usual store. And by normally using a basic hookup with my Web software—as opposed to a deluxe, time-sensitive one—I could save hundreds of dollars a year.

The benefits of the Internet, for the Cyberspace Development Company and me, didn't stop there. Via discussion groups, TIA sellers kept us customers up to date, and just as important, we could share tips among ourselves. We could also use the World Wide Web to catch up with long documents; in fact, updated versions of TIA could travel to us over the Net. All of this, including the elimination of the need to go to the store, was taking place on commercial networks such as CompuServe. But the costs would have been greater for Cyberspace and customers alike if the company had to pay the usual commercial rates for electronic mail.

Among the wares talked up online were upbeat prognostications about the Net itself. For $3,500 you could buy a report from a California consulting firm that said annual commerce on the Net and commercials services such as CompuServe would reach $600 billion by the turn of the century. I was skeptical. Merchants like JoAnn Lilienfeld would have to sell warehouse after warehouse of stuffed animals or toys or whatever the offerings were. In fact, $600 billion was a good 8 percent of international commerce. On reflection, however, the estimate from Killen & Associates seemed possible. Through the Net you might find a buyer for shipload of scrap iron or an office building, not just a stray teddy bear in need of a child. I phoned Mary Cronin of Boston College, who had written a well-regarded book called *Doing Business on the Internet.* It teemed with examples from Digital Equipment Corporation and IBM and many other computer-oriented firms. And she had researched it before most business people grasped the importance of the Internet. Yes, she said, the $600 billion figure sounded credible if you counted business-to-business transactions.

Daniel Dern, an Internet consultant, had his own opinion on the statistics. He said the Net was like the highway. Just what did you count—all the goods that went over the road? The combined salaries of the people on the way to work? I could see his point.

Whatever the exact numbers, the demographics and technology might be on the side of the many retail businesses if they stuck it out on the Net and kept expectations realistic. Scads of people in Generation Net were about to marry. They would buy houses and cars and whatever else mattered beyond stereos and Internet-optimized computers. Just in the late summer and fall of 1994, the number of Net-related businesses on the Web had doubled, and a good many of the newcomers were not technical. Could the Net really, then, enrich business people without technical backgrounds? Was there indeed money in what had once been the province of cash-strapped college students and dreamy researchers?

Plenty of people thought that the answer lay in the case history of Grant's Flowers, which, like White Rabbit Toys, operated out of Ann Arbor, Michigan. Larry Grant had been a cover boy in an enticing article on the front page of the business section of the *New York Times;* the Internet pulsed with chatter about the electronic coups that he supposedly had achieved for just $28 a month. Excited Netfolks reported that he did not even have to type to his customers on the Internet; new orders just poured in on a fax machine with a Net connection. The California gold rush was almost a century and a half old. And yet, watching the Grant legend take off, I might as well have been among the boots and beards at Sutter's Mill.

So I talked not only to the Lilienfelds but to Larry Grant, the legendary florist himself. Many in the media were still enchanted with the Electronic Frontier metaphor, and I remembered the old films about Davy Crockett, the Tennessee frontiersman who loved corny jokes, bear-wrestling tales, coonskin hats, and Crockett-friendly news accounts—the grist for Walt Disney later on. What was next, a movie epic with a musical tribute to "Larry Grant, king of the Net frontier"?

A market might indeed be ballooning for cyber-retailers, as the hypesters said. But I still wondered about the present. What counted was not all the puffery about 30 million Netfolks, many of whom can only read electronic mail as opposed to *seeing* roses or toy tops or other merchandise. No, the real determinant was how often people dial up your particular site and bought. One well-crafted Web area, which advertised technically related goods, enjoyed just a handful of visits in six months without a single sale. This was an issue aside from the total amount of business done on the Net. Having talked with Mary Cronin and others, I hadn't any doubt about those giant commodity transactions and all the use of the Net by Big Business to automate the paperwork of commerce. But what about the small fry? Was the excitement about Grant truly justified? I'll answer those questions in the pages ahead, where I'll return to the Lilienfelds and to Grant, and where I'll examine the following:

- MCI, the phone company. It has provided thousands of miles of Net connections and now rents out electronic storefronts on the Net. MCI offers one of the slickest Web areas—complete with a fictitious publishing house (now evolving into a real one) that accepts manuscripts from real readers. *Advertising Age* has hailed the MCI site as "unquestionably the best Internet marketing effort to date." Frustratingly, however, while preparing to dispense advice on cyberspace, MCI in early 1995 was committing some of the very mistakes it should be telling its customers to avoid.

- Federal Express, whose Internet presence shows the potential of the Net for business-to-business transactions, not just the consumer variety. Ironically the people at FedEx in some ways were demonstrating more Net savvy than MCI was at the time, even though the Internet was more in the territory of the latter. The old values of customer service still reigned above all else. A smaller competitor of Federal Express, a shipper called Right-O-Way, was also making outstanding use of the Net. In some ways it was even staying ahead of the big boys.

- Intel, the chipmaker, which learned the hard way how good the Internet was for spreading news of flaws in products. The Net abounds with skeptical academics and consumerists with *fast* typing fingers.
- Other hazards of the Internet for business people. What if you set up an electronic storefront like the Lilienfelds' and then a manufacturer decided to cut out the middle people and sell on the Net directly or through a larger outlet? Security is another threat. While I was writing *NetWorld!*, most commercial areas on the Net lacked a way to protect credit card numbers. Hackers broke into General Electric's Web area and stole corporate secrets. Another risk is competitors looking over price lists and assessing the strengths and weaknesses of products.

Those caveats will end the chapter. By far, the Internet is a positive rather than a negative factor for business and customers alike. Wired consumers will reward good companies, punish the losers, and spur the winners to do still better.

Bob and JoAnn Lilienfeld: The Net as a Way to Promote Small Businesses

Thousands of miles to the south of Ann Arbor, home of White Rabbit Toys, Luciana Gores was reading a popular mailing list called Net Happenings. It was a kind of town crier. Each day from North Dakota a man named Gleason Sackman sent out informative posts on the many new services that were springing up on the Internet.

Gores worked as a network expert, and she was already used to buying technical books through the Internet, which offered a far greater variety than what she would find in her own city, Rio de Janeiro, Brazil.

She was also the mother of a seven-year-old named Lucas. So when the mailing list told her of White Rabbit, she checked it out on the Web.

People who visited the virtual store, or at least those with the right equipment, saw a logo with the rabbit from Lewis Caroll's imagination. They also conjured up a color picture of a real toy store with shelf after shelf of tot pleasers, a tiny table and stool on the floor, and a look of friendly chaos—in short, a shopper's delight for children and parents alike, which in fact the "real" White Rabbit was. The traditional store, the one at 2611 Plymouth Road, had thrived. Now Bob and JoAnn Lilienfeld were trying to woo virtual customers such as Luciana Gores. Their electronic White Rabbit just may have been the first full-service toy store—as opposed to one-product billboards or specialty shops—to open up on the Internet.

An ad on the opening screen helped set the tone for Luciana Gores and other customers of White Rabbit: "We specialize in high-quality toys that help children to create, learn, imagine, and explore. Our toys come from all over the world. We offer such international favorites as Brio (Sweden), Ravensburger (Germany), Primetime Playthings and Creativity for Kids (United States)."

Suitably equipped customers could actually see pictures of the toys, including a Ravensburger game called the A-maze-ing Labyrinth. "Travel the corridors of the enchanted labyrinth in search of treasures," read the carnival-like pitch. "But watch out! The walls shift, and the passages can close, leaving you trapped! For ages eight and older." Lucas was a year younger, but did it matter if the child was as bright as his mother, the network expert? "It seems to be an interesting game," Luciana Gores e-mailed me, "and it won a Parent's Choice award." And so she paid her $24.95 and shipping, which, given the light weight of the toy, was modest.

Thanks to the Internet, the Lilienfelds suddenly had the whole world as a market, not just customers living near by. The fact that White Rabbit was in a university town, with graduates all over the planet, could only help. So could the fact that the Internet was expanding overseas even more rapidly than in the United States.

White Rabbit also appealed to Stuart Lowry, another promising kind of customer—the computer jock turned family man. A Maryland resident in his late twenties, he wouldn't have made the pulses of marketers quicken several years ago; he was a grad student then at Johns Hopkins University and, like many people on the Internet, had more time than money. But that had changed. Lowry now worked at Computer Science Corporation, a large defense contractor, pulling down a salary in the mid-forties. He was married and lived in a townhouse, and four months ago his wife had given birth to a baby boy. And so, when Lowry was cruising the Internet from work and spotted a notice announcing White Rabbit Toys, he favored it with a virtual visit. He ordered a colorful toy top for $13, the Floor Spinner from Primetime Playthings.

Many people on the Web were young males more interested in pizza or condoms than in baby toys, but the Lilienfelds were looking ahead a few years when the same Net people would be parents. "It's an act of faith," Bob Lilienfeld said. "Today's demographics and selling a lot of toys on the Net may be out of synch. But today's college students are tomorrow's parents. Tomorrow's parents aren't going to consider ordering by computer any different from getting in a car and going to the shopping center."

Other trends might work in the Lilienfelds' favor. More and more Americans were time-short, with long commutes; Stuart Lowry himself spent forty-five minutes each way, and that actually was a quick trip compared to those in cities such as Los Angeles. In northern Virginia I knew of parents rising at 4 A.M. to go to jobs in Washington some forty miles away, and not a few of them were high-tech workers who would sooner or later end up on the Internet.

When I reached Bob and JoAnn Lilienfeld in the middle of November, White Rabbit itself had been on the Net maybe a week and had enjoyed around 1,000 virtual visits in that time. They were hoping that these numbers would multiply as Christmas neared. It was too soon to tell how many of these people would actually order. Back in June, though, the Lilienfelds had grown excited after reading about Larry Grant in the *New York Times* and elsewhere.

"I saw this figure of 20 million Net users," JoAnn said of the numbers du jour, "and thought there's definitely an opportunity here. But I didn't want to go about it in a half-baked manner. I thought there had to be someone who could combine knowledge of the Net with marketing experience." She checked out a local cybermall and found it wanting in the latter area.

That wasn't surprising, given JoAnn's perfectionism and eagerness to avoid easy but far-from-satisfactory solutions—whether in retail or life in general. She had grown up in a cash-short household where, more often than not, the children would get out the oatmeal cartons and construction paper and scissors and cobble together their own toys. And the same creativity had carried over to her Bloomies days as one of the resident experts on Christmas tree trimmings. According to the Lilienfelds, it was JoAnn who came up with the idea of selling leafless, white branches. She and Bob had moved to Ann Arbor because he kept flying off to the Midwest to consult for clients in Midland, and they felt that married people needed to spend more time together. JoAnn went about establishing the White Rabbit just as conscientiously.

Not finding the right toys for her own children, she studied the demographics of Ann Arbor to verify that a toy store could thrive there. She concluded that in a university community, many would love those wooden train sets and other classic toys as opposed to the trendier offerings that were touted on television and sold at Toys Я Us. Ann Arbor responded well. A local paper told how she blessed her store with a public bathroom—how she kept diapers and spare wipes around for the parents of children and emergencies. No need for toilets existed on the Internet. But even at this early stage, having read up on the Netfolks, she was attuned to the need to adapt to the culture of cyberspace.

JoAnn finally decided that her best savior, the requisite miracle-worker with both Net and marketing experience, lived right there in the Lilienfeld household. Those past few months her husband had been succeeding off a mix of garbage and the Internet.

To be exact, Bob Lilienfeld was advising clients about *future* garbage, the packing materials for consumer products, a major contributor to landfills. He hadn't anything against recycling. But thanks to his work at Procter & Gamble, he had concluded that the best way to cope with waste was to design packages to avoid it in the first place. Manufacturers and customers alike would win. Bob would go on to help put together a network of like-minded consultants, including William Rathje, a world-famous garbage expert at the University of Arizona who had co-authored *Rubbish! The Archaeology of Garbage.* Lilienfeld met Rathje at a press conference but also found himself relying on another source of contacts, the Internet. Again and again he had heard about the Net from professors at the University of Michigan, and he soon was in touch with other garbage mavens around the planet.

"I started sucking in information," he recalled. "I found out about mailing lists and newsgroups, and then I decided I would put my newsletter up on the Net and see what happened." The newsletter was a way to let clients know about his consulting company, the Cygnus Group. It helped Fortune 500 companies, other businesses, trade associations, educational groups, and others grow more sensitive to environmental concerns in activities ranging from packaging to marketing.

Just as JoAnn was careful to befriend Ann Arbor in the right way, Bob tried to honor the conventions of the Net—avoiding hucksterism in favor of helpful information. The announcements about the newsletter were low-key, and response was good. Soon he was sharing his articles with hundreds of Netfolks who asked such questions as: "I recently saw an article on compact fluorescent light bulbs in *Consumer Reports.* Why aren't more stores and utilities selling them?"

An "Ask Bill and Bob" column, cowritten with William Rathje, revealed that such lights "take at least eight times more energy to produce than old-fashioned bulbs. And they're heavier, so they use more energy during shipping." The column also told of an experiment that McDonald's was conducting in Albany, New York, with food and paper composting, saving perhaps 500–700 pounds per week of solid waste. Readers could learn, too, that a nut seller was moving from glass and plastic bottles to vacuum bags.

Bob Lilienfeld was hardly an eco-activist by the standards of, say, Greenpeace; Dow Chemical was among his prime clients, after all. But he was serving up information for people with many different viewpoints, and by way of the proper clicks with your mouse, you could travel from his Web site to areas of the Internet such as the Envirolink Network, or EcoGopher, or EcoNet.

His newsletter, known as *The ULS Report* (short for "use less stuff"), carried an item about CD-ROM disks. It described them as "an environmentally friendly way to reduce waste and save resources. One CD-ROM, including packaging, weighs under half a pound. The 22 books that it replaces weigh 70 pounds." Knowingly or not, he was helping to pave the way for the virtual White Rabbit—where the same principles applied. Via the Internet, White Rabbit could advertise to thousands without printing up catalogues for them. Oh, they might request catalogues later, but then they would have prequalified themselves, reducing the solid waste. Lewis Carroll would have approved of the reasoning here. What's more, unlike paper catalogues, Lilienfeld could update his electronic catalogue to change prices or play up the fastest-selling merchandise.

The World Wide Web was the main way to put White Rabbit on the Internet. Once merchants on the Net would have favored a service called Gopher (as in "go-fer-it") in honor of the mascot at the University of Minnesota. Gopher displayed text very well and needed less bandwidth on the Net than the Web did. But it lacked the pizzazz of the Web–Mosaic combination; that is, the ability to conjure up pictures and even sound so easily. Although Bob used Gopher for digging up scholarly works about the environment, it was like black-and-white television while Web–Mosaic was color and all the more alluring for commercial purposes.

Getting White Rabbit on the Web was surprisingly cheap in some ways. The Lilienfelds' network provider charged JoAnn just $50 a month, plus $2 an hour for when she was using electronic mail or handling other chores. That didn't include Bob's time, however. He knew at least the basics of the necessary programming language and didn't require the services of a consultant to the extent that others might have.

Lilienfeld himself put in most of the set-up hours. It took him a few days of programming to design the Web site and scan in the pictures of more than two dozen items—the train sets, the puzzles, the tops, the blocks—and like an old-fashioned art director he had to create within the limits of the medium. The big problem was photos. If they were too big to move over the Net quickly, then the peeved readers might give up and go on to another Web site. If too small, however, the pictures would lack enough detail to

Net.business, 3D-Style

You can't *touch* merchandise on the World Wide Web. But the next best thing may be in store.

Virtual reality will let you "walk" through Web businesses and see merchandise in greater detail as you get "closer" to the object on your screen. You can vary the angles, too. So you could use your mouse to tour a parking lot of automobiles. You could spot the Volvo or the Saturn of your dreams, and admire not only the outside but also the interior.

No, the Web will never replace actual shopping in most cases, but virtual reality will be increasingly good at helping you screen preliminary choices.

Keep an eye out, then, for WebSpace—the new 3D viewer from Silicon Graphics, the California company whose technology helped create many of the special effects in *Jurassic Park*. WebSpace will work as an add-on with popular Web browsers such as Netscape and Spyglass Enhanced Mosaic.

WebSpace-style technology, needless to say, is far too good to waste on shopping alone. Virtual reality software for the Web may also help you tour the National Gallery of Art, the Library of Congress,

show off the store or the merchandise. In many cases Bob would let readers click on pictures of bears to see larger versions of the photos.

He also had to worry about the software the readers used on the Internet—certain Mosaic-style browsers would show *smaller* objects first. Other challenges arose. What if technical standards changed so that only certain browsers would work with Bob's site? The real White Rabbit might be a victim of acts of God such as the ebb and flow of automobile traffic, and the virtual Rabbit needed to worry about patterns of Net traffic, but it also or Mount Kilimanjaro—not to mention Hong Kong or Rio de Janeiro.

3D technology could revolutionize the financial world. Small investors, not just high-powered stock analysts, could "see" stock market trends. Your screen might display a "Bulls' Corner" with a collection of corporate logos color-coded according to the improvement in the stock price. You could open up the logos and go on a tour of various divisions, wandering around them electronically with far more ease than you could with less advanced software.

Similarly, at the suggestion of your broker, you could tour a Bear's Corner and see why you might avoid or sell off certain shares.

Mind you, there are negatives. Corporations—whether stores selling merchandise or companies seeking investors—may use this slick technology to fool the public. On the other hand, the Internet is already a godsend for consumers and small investors. Via Usenet newsgroups and mailing lists, they can swap information, taking care of course to look for plants from companies trying to sway grassroots impressions.

could be subject to Jehovah in the form of macho software firms who wanted everyone on the Net to use their brainchildren.

Companies such as Netscape Communications Corporation actually gave away Mosaic-style products to us Netfolk for free, hoping to make fortunes instead off the software that merchants and others denizens on the Web would run. Netscape was the champ in late 1994, the one that let you go from page to page faster than any competitor did. Many people feared Netscape would be to the Web what Microsoft was to software; suppose Netscape used technical prowess and marketing skill to trample competitors, and maybe overcharge the customers.

A green monster named Mozilla came up on one of Netscape's welcoming screens, and pessimists wondered if the company itself might someday play the part. Marc Andreessen, the top software designer at Netscape, had led the team that came up with the original Mosaic at the University of Illinois. And then he had left Illinois to join a new company that, from the ground up, had designed the speedier Netscape product. The Web community mightily hoped that Mozilla and keepers would behave themselves. Suppose that Netscape joined Microsoft or credit card companies to build in special, billing-related features that users of other browsers couldn't use?

Netscape, however, seemed benign so far, and the browser's technical wizardry, was winning many friends. With a click of the mouse, for example, you could scoot smoothly from the Web to the usual newsgroups, and Bob Lilienfeld took advantage of this. He set up his computer system so that customers with the proper software could whiz directly from White Rabbit to child-related newsgroups.

One moment you could be shopping for toys; the next, exchanging tips with a New Zealander or Norwegian on how to cope with tantrum-prone babies. You could zip to misc.kids ("A great place to swap parenting war stories"), misc.kids.consumers ("Help with purchasing decisions"), or misc.kids.computer ("Enough said!"). Or you or your children could read odds and ends about wombats, Forester kangaroos, Tasmanian devils, fish, lions, dinosaurs, and other creatures at WombatNet; print out drawings of the human heart or the stars or hear a thunderbolt by way of the Franklin Institute Virtual Science Museum; and learn the population of Uganda or Afghanistan via *The CIA World Factbook*, a guide assembled by the real-life Central Intelligence Agency.

Fighting the companies such as AT&T and the big cable interests, many activists likened the Internet to a series of communities with opportunities for small merchants and citizen-to-citizen communications as opposed to couch potato offerings from the Fortune 500. Merchants such as the Lilienfelds were acting out the very models about which the activists waxed so enthusiastically.

Bob Lilienfeld understood that just as storekeepers in a small town would do well to join the Kiwanis Club, virtual storefronts should be part of Net life. JoAnn would soon go to a toy convention, and at some point, she might well share her impressions with the denizens of misc.kids and similar newsgroups, as opposed simply to touting her products. At the same time, yes, by way of a signature at the bottom of her posts, people on the Net could find out about the toy store. She might even start a mailing list for the receptive. Bob had already shown the success of this model by way of the list and other tools used to promote his consulting activities.

A toy-oriented list could be much more than ads. "Going shopping isn't just spending money," Lilienfeld observed, "its a social phenomenon. It's seeing people you know, it's being part of a crowd." And it's also picking up gossip and maybe even solid information. "Ultimately the toy store will be bigger than just a toy store," he said. "We might be providing information on child development, of the appropriateness of certain toys or coloring books. If you're a model train hobbyist, we might be able to help you hook up with model train users groups."

In fact, by way of the mouse-activated links from White Rabbit to newsgroups and other Web sites, he was already offering much more than just a store. The line between merchants and information providers was blurring in the case of Bob and JoAnn; the higher the quality of the information at White Rabbit, the more it would be a virtual gathering place for people on the World Wide Web. I wasn't surprised to hear some people say that librarians might be the star sales reps of the future. It wasn't hype. Information, not just prices and selection of merchandise, would be what drew Netfolks to sites such as the Lilienfelds'. Of course Bob Lilienfeld might want to be choosy about what links he listed. If he listed too many of the mediocre ones, then he would simply be replicating the function of the powerful search programs on the Web and adding to people's "information overload," to use an ever-popular phrase.

Software already let sophisticated Netfolks zero in on items of interest. Merely by typing in the word "toys," for example, I could find scads of listings—from mentions of adult sex toys to the Web site advertising the gun that fired Ping-Pong balls. And these programs would soon be simple enough for even technoklutzes to use. So the Lilienfelds had better offer something that the software could not supply: Their judgments about which Web sites, newsgroups, and mailing lists were the most fun or most informative.

All through the Christmas season, JoAnn kept refining her Net-related plans. "We need to ask, 'Have we chosen the right items?' " she said. "The draw of our toy store is, it's an exciting place to shop. We have to do the same on the Internet. If we add more items, it will approach a catalogue more. Right now our competition is mail-order catalogues, and we have a lot of items that they're not offering. Maybe we'll be reaching people not on the traditional catalogue list. They could be more occasional toy buyers than frequent toy buyers."

Thanks to a computerized inventory system, JoAnn's corporeal store carried more than 6,500 items. Bob made a mental note: He might want to put more of them on the Net so customers would enjoy a wider selection. JoAnn talked about her suppliers: "My goal was really getting this up and going for Christmas. When I get to the toy fair I'll discuss this with the national sales managers and see if I can't get discounts for advertising to so many people, and then we're working probably toward next Christmas. We'll be working toward fourth quarter of '95."

That was a healthy attitude. Even toward the end of the season the number of visits didn't go past 2,000 a week, and only a handful of actual sales resulted. The only customers were Luciana Gores; Stuart Lowry, the computer jock turned family man; Michael Wolfe, a West Virginia professor studying Internet commerce, who ordered half a dozen stuffed toy caterpillars; a second academic, in the Midwest, who bought a Ravensburger Snail's Pace Race game; a Massachusetts woman sending three customizable dolls to her sister ("I'm testing business on the Net—aren't you lucky?"); and David Fry, the operator of a cybermall nearby who was curious about the White Rabbit, and who bought First Blocks.

Not that the Lilienfelds had completely wasted their time. As of Christmas, a *Wall Street Journal* story hadn't appeared, but the Detroit paper and others had gone ahead with articles, and customers poured onto the floor of the real White Rabbit, one even buying the giant polar bear that Bob had been hoping to give his nine-year-old son. The publicity may have brought in some $20,000–$25,000 in extra sales by Bob's estimates, on which the Lilienfelds may have netted around $2,000–compared to $750 gross and $75 net from Net orders. Bob told me that other merchants on the Web were also reporting a low number of sales. The week before Christmas the number of visits to White Rabbit itself actually declined; many of the prospective customers had been logging on from school or work, and now they had partly emptied the Web along with their dorm rooms and offices.

From a get-rich-quick perspective, then, the virtual White Rabbit had been a zero. Bob and JoAnn were smart marketers with MBAs from a Big Ten business school, and he had a real feel for the Internet, which he had successfully used to expand his consulting business. But even

the Lilienfelds could not score right away. Oh, how tantalizing the gargantuan numbers had been—the tens of millions of users said to exist; the million by which the Net
was supposed to be growing each month. And yet in the
end, when the time came for customers to key in the
credit card numbers, the market had vanished like the
Cheshire cat. That didn't mean the Lilienfelds were fool-
ish; just a week or two after Christmas, a wonderful twist
happened. The number of visits to the toy store fell off. But
sales leapt up. By mid-January White Rabbit was moving
an average of a toy a day—not a Kmart volume, but an improvement. Bob explained the difference. Now White
Rabbit's first screen told customers that the store could
often get toys not mentioned online.

Encouraged, Lilienfeld added yet another improvement, an 800 number. Now customers could ask their
questions the old-fashioned way if they preferred, and
they could also order by voice if they didn't trust the Net
with their credit card numbers.

With enough tweaks like this, the virtual toy store
might eventually flourish as the number of Web users
grew. Just like the characters in many children's stories,
the White Rabbit would keep on changing—adding ever-
more-intriguing links to newsgroups and other Web sites,
putting in the software to help novice toy shoppers choose
just the right ball or train set, figuring out new ways to use
the interplay between the Net and the traditional media.
Sooner or later, the Netheads would reproduce, and when
they went looking for rattles and Lego sets, Bob and
JoAnn would be ready for them. The story of White Rabbit
Toys, like that of the Internet itself, was far from over.

The Electronic Billboard: Grant's Flowers

Larry Grant just might be doing better at the moment
than the Lilienfelds were. He was selling flowers, and

what better merchandise existed for grad students who were alone at the keyboard in a dark office at two o'clock, and who had forgotten their girlfriends' birthdays?

A newsletter publisher named Rosalind Resnick—a former staff reporter for the *Miami Herald* and the author of an Internet business guide—was grossing more than $20,000 a year in subscriptions and expecting to do much better in 1995.[4] And her media-oriented newsletter helped pave the way for a lucrative consulting business. I also knew of a network expert named Gordon Cook who was able to jet to a three-week research expedition in Moscow at his own expense, and who lived satisfactorily on the revenue from *The Cook Report on Internet* and related activities.[5]

Grant's Flowers, however, was more of a typical business. Larry Grant wasn't a writer. And his work was not as network-related as that of Resnick and Cook; unlike the latter, he hadn't evolved into a net.personality on some key mailing lists. Instead the word was that Larry Grant just paid his $28 a month to an electronic mall—a collection of stores that shared a common subarea of the Net— and sat back and watched his fax machine spew out orders. Grant might not be Davy Crockett in terms of action, but certainly in terms of fame he was coming along. He had appeared as a success story, after all, on the front page of the *New York Times* business section.

As I wended my way through the Net to Grant's Flowers, I passed through an area called Branch Mall. A logo with a tree branch greeted me. I saw listings for enterprises ranging from cosmetic sellers to H & H Logging and Timber Company. Under "Flowers, Gifts, Foods," I didn't see just Grant's listing. I saw White Dove Flower and Gift Shop, Flowers on Lexington, Exotic Flowers of Hawaii, Bonsai Boy of New York, and half a dozen others. Bob Lilienfeld was skeptical about cybermalls, and right now I could see why. With all this competition, could Grant's make money off the Internet?

Lilienfeld had reminded me that traditional malls and the cyber variety were different, and I understood. If I wanted to shop for books, I could brave traffic to reach Springfield Mall, a large collection of shops maybe ten miles from me in the suburbs of Washington, D.C. Springfield would be worth the drive. I could visit four stores right within a five-minute walk of each other—Brentano's, B. Dalton, Walden, and Crown.

The Net, however, was also different. I didn't have to drive anywhere. I could just use a powerful search engine such as Lycos, key in "bookstore," and watch name after name pop up on my screen. Lycos demanded just a little technical savvy. But easier alternatives would come along. As if that weren't enough, Netfolks put together lists of activities on the Internet, and often they included commercial categories. I'd found White Rabbit not through advertising but through the Yahoo list out of Stanford University, on the other side of North America. Distance just didn't matter. So could the shopping mall metaphor truly work out to the benefit of merchants such as Larry Grant?

Branch Mall at the very least had set Grant up in style. The opening screen was attractive and helpful to buyers, with such basics as: "Different areas of the country sometimes have different prices or may be unable to supply certain flowers. For example, New York City has high rents and costs of doing business, so flowers are more expensive there..." And then below I saw a list of the offerings—for example, "One dozen boxed long stem roses. A fragrant classic. $49.95 to $99.95." In the virtual version of the White Rabbit toy store you couldn't rattle the toys, and in Branch Mall you couldn't smell the roses, but like the Lilienfelds, Branch Mall had been generous with pictures of the merchandise. I loved some little touches. Branch had given Grant a reminder service into which you could key your spouse's birthday or some other date, before which an e-mail note would be sent to jog you to do your duty.

The selection was varied. You could order everything from the roses to "a get well soup cup containing button mums, daisies, mini carnations, standard carnations, monte casino, statice, and a package of chicken soup. $26." All in all, I felt that this area was even better laid out than White Rabbit Toys, where the opening page, though far, far above average, didn't communicate quite as much information as I'd have liked. As with White Rabbit, you could order online by filling out an electronic form.

Missing from the virtual version of Grant's flower shop, however, were the customized links that helped give the White Rabbit Toys its personality and made it a true part of the Net. If Larry Grant had been as at home in cyberspace as Bob Lilienfeld was, he could have added links to love-oriented discussion areas or to poetry—perhaps even the Shakespearean variety.

But instead this Web page was serving just as an electronic billboard with an ordering mechanism. I didn't even see a photograph of the store. When the *New York Times* published a photo of a Mosaic screen, it had superimposed a picture of Grant amid his flowers and dressed in an apron with an FTD insignia. Couldn't a similar photo have adorned his Web area?

For that matter, the store didn't even offer an electronic mail address, just a phone number for customers with questions. This isn't to criticize Larry Grant. He was not an honorary techie as Bob Lilienfeld was. Like Lilienfeld, however, Grant was an intelligent, diligent Midwest businessman who saw the Net as an opportunity.

Wild talk *about* Grant notwithstanding, he wasn't a braggart—simply a proud family entrepreneur. I learned that Grant's Flowers was actually part of a mini local conglomerate. "We've been here since 1947," he said, "and my folks started farming and selling produce by the side of the road off a kitchen table. We're now a million-dollar business and have many facets. We have a flower and gift shop, and the front of the building is beer and foods. We farm 131 acres." Two brothers were in the business, and so was his eighty-year-old mother. "She runs the flower and gift section, and I run the rest of the retail sales and my brothers do all the growing and production. We've got two acres of greenhouses growing plants for spring sale or gardeners. It's a very diversified operation."

Grant clearly wasn't making a living off the Internet alone, despite a good start. "We got online in February just before Valentine's Day and we received forty orders that week. In the first ten days we had over 2,900 look in on our electronic storefront. Then it dropped to one or two orders a day, and then we got to Mother's Day and had a high of forty in one day. Currently we've increased from one or two to six, in that range."

When I asked what his current Net-related gross would be per year, he roughly estimated it at perhaps $15,000 or $20,000. That was enough to make the Web area well worth his time, but this was hardly a tale of instant riches. I remembered a magazine ad—for would-be providers of Internet services—that showed a mustached man beside a Rolls or Mercedes. Larry Grant was a Web merchant, not someone hooking people up with the Net. But I wished that the get-rich-quickers of all stripes could see Larry Grant as a realistic example of the Net's promise. The gold might come eventually, and it was worthwhile to chase after it by going online, but, for most people, the big money wasn't there yet.

What's more, costs for newer customers of Branch Mall were higher. Grant had been the first merchant there and enjoyed a break. Now Branch was charging thousands a year for Web areas that included elaborate programming and creative work. [6]

Larry Grant, in any event, believed in the Net and in the Mall itself. His virtual operation wasn't costing him *that* much, and I suspected that even with somewhat higher expenses, other tenants might do fine in the end if they were in the right business. "Number one," Grant said, "we don't have to take and buy more inventory. Number two, we don't have to have a bigger facility. And number three, we don't need a sales staff. We can do with the staff we have in handling these orders. It's a neat way to find new business. I don't have to handle any of the products directly. The customer does all the ordering through the company in his area and it's shipped from the company to them, and I get my commission check at the end of the month." He liked the concept so much that he started a Fuller Brush franchise on the Net. The same key principles applied: No inventory to worry about and no sales staff, just some dealings with Branch and orders emerging from a fax machine.

Merchants like Bob Lilienfeld might fare well without a cybermall involved—they knew how to spread word about themselves on the Net by way of newsgroups and mailing lists—but I could also see the possibilities for people such as Larry Grant as long as they kept their expectations to a reasonable level. Grant himself didn't view the other flower shops at Branch Mall as direct competitors; he depicted himself as more of a general florist than the others, what with their specialties in Hawaiian flowers and the like. Certainly a good cybermall, like the brick-and-concrete version, needed a good tenant mix—with a toy store not appearing on the same screen as, say, a *sex* toy shop.

If that right mix wasn't around, why have the mall in the first place? While it was true that the Net shrank distances, it did take time to move from screen to screen at typical modem speeds. And yet, reflecting, I could indeed see a future for malls: Even when search engines were easier to use, people might still not avail themselves of them—preferring to browse instead. So the mall concept might well endure to the advantage of people like Larry Grant.

All kinds of people itched for their percentages of the cybermall business. Jon Zeeff, the mall operator who had set up Larry Grant with his electronic billboard, had once

written medical software. David Fry was a Harvard Ph.D.
in computer science, came from a family in the printing
business, and ran an offshoot called Fry Multimedia. Ann
Arbor wasn't Silicon Valley, but just in that one university
town, at least three local business people were on the Web
in a serious way, if you included Bob Lilienfeld. Like him,
Fry wisely thought in the long term. Drumming up business from well-known brands such as Ragu spaghetti
sauce, he did not promise an instant audience in the millions. He urged companies to go on the Web, experiment
with interactive advertising, and make their mistakes *before* the Net became a truly mass medium for Madison
Avenue.

Some get-rich-quickers, of course, also were jostling
for virtual tenants; even Canter and Siegel showed up by
way of an area called Cybersell, and I enjoyed the irony.
C & S had carpet bombed thousands of newsgroups with
the same message—while encouraging other merchants
to ignore conventional Netiquette—and yet now they were
also relying on the more focused approach of a Web area.

Phone companies, too, wanted to run malls on the
World Wide Web. And that created problems for some.
While the Net might use their phone lines, many of these
corporations felt out of place in an anarchistic environment over which they had far less than the accustomed
amount of control. In the mall business they would be
competing against nimble entrepreneurs like Zeeff and
Fry. Still, phone companies could take advantage of their
existing networks to one extent or another, and if the
Yellow Pages were going online in a new incarnation,
then the Baby Bells and AT&T wanted their share of the
business. Of all the mall-related efforts in early 1995, the
most ambitious may have been from a phone company,
MCI. It exemplified—as I soon discovered in the most direct of ways—both the best and the worst of Big Business
on the Web.

MCI's Giant Cybermall and the Search for Darlene

MCI and the Internet had A History. The Net used phone lines from many companies, but MCI had long been one of the major players here; some 40 percent of the Internet traffic in the United States passed over its cables, and nowadays the senior vice-president of data architecture was none other than Vint Cerf. As much as anyone he was Mr. Net, one of the founding fathers. MCI also employed the head of a standard-setting body called the Internet Engineering Task Force. Unsurprisingly, MCI marketers were coming out with statements in the vein of: *When you think Internet, we want you to think of us.*

I asked a product manager how much of the Net-related commerce he could envision involving an electronic marketplace from MCI. Well, he said, MCI had around one-fifth of the long-distance business in the U.S.—and why not the same share on the Internet?

Clearly, however, if MCI wanted to woo the Larry Grants of this world, it faced a major marketing problem. Just like Jon Zeeff, it would have to sell business people on the Net as a vehicle for their messages; and that meant *lots* of education, not just hype. MCI, moreover, was offering a range of services far, far broader than Zeeff's. In an MCI-perfect world, you would advertise your business by way of marketplaceMCI. Prospective customers on the Net could browse through a giant online directory and follow a link to your electronic storefront. MCI would cleverly lure them to its area. People would be able to retrieve voice phone numbers in far-off cities and enjoy other information services for free.

On MCI's planet, you'd of course use internetMCI for your electronic mail and your Web browsing. You also could hold video conferences during which people saw not only each other but the same contract or spreadsheet, which they could jointly modify even if they were thousands of miles apart. You could even receive updates on your pet news topic by way of MCI—just the ticket for keeping up with competitors or with a favorite athletic team.

Not all of MCI's new services related to the Internet. But like marketplaceMCI, many did. And even with 30 million people hooked in by way of e-mail if nothing else, public ignorance was massive. Larry Magid, a computer columnist, observed that even a single TV show such as *Home Improvement* could attract greater numbers. If MCI wanted to enjoy volume befitting a phone company, then, it had better prepare for some major evangelizing—about both the Net and non-Net services. MCI tried the broadcast model in the most traditional of ways. Splashy commercials aired on national television. They starred a fictitious publishing company, Gramercy Press, whose president, Peter Hoffman, had a *big* crush on MCI. Whether the service was video conferencing or electronic mail, Hoffman was itching to open his wallet for it.

Darlene Davis was the character with the most air time, the hip young receptionist who was waging a valiant battle to get Martin Banks, the resident technophobe, online. If this portly old crank of an editor wanted to read the latest memos from Darlene, then he had better plug in his computer. Curtiss Bruno was the sales manager with his heart on his quotas and Darlene. MCI's electronic services could allow him to achieve at least the former goal. Nowadays Darlene happily used e-mail to help stay out of flirting distance with him. Ellen deRosset was the resident intellectual snob and a Net browser. Reginald Gales used MCI's news feature to keep Martin up on cricket scores. Marta Dragelov was an info junky in keeping with her duties as a fact checker.

In a country where fantasy and reality often turned into one big mush, where O. J. Simpson movies could go into production before the end of the murder trial, where legions of commercials aped news programs, where the Speaker of the House would soon be hosting a cable TV showing of *Boys Town* after having touted orphanages as a major solution to the welfare problem—in a nation like this, it was as inevitable as a $1 million book deal for O.J. that the mythical Darlene would draw job offers and marriage proposals from people wanting to be part of the fun.

"These were breakout and breakaway characters that took on a life of their own," said Mark Pettit, the MCI public relations man who was handling Gramercy matters. What's more, the company's advertising agency, MVBMS, hadn't just tried to make Gramercy real in the real world; the agency people had also made the characters real in the *video* world by way of an introductory commercial that looked like a preview of a new fall series.

Having conquered TV, then, and with the Internet a main focus of the ad campaign, how could MCI *not* have opened up a Web area to ballyhoo the same services that Darlene was pushing on the tube? The commercials had whetted interest in the characters. And now MCI would see if it could satisfy this curiosity while also passing on more details about its new line of services. "People wanted more than thirty seconds of information," Pettit said, "and it can be hard to give them more on TV. What if we turned this into a real place that they could go visit? And that's how it came to life." By MCI's own estimate, more than a million people visited the "real place" in the first six weeks or so. Even Bob Lilienfeld dropped by. He was an MCI stockholder and wanted to keep an open mind despite his skepticism about the mall concept— maybe he could do business with pros like MCI's. Lilienfeld filled out a form that offered a two-month trial of Net-related services, and waited.

I first visited the Gramercy Press around the same time that Lilienfeld did. The site popped up on my screen with

color photos of a perky-looking Darlene and friends. I saw a
red logo, too. A small "GP" appeared between "Gramercy"
and "Press," a nice little touch that a real publisher might
have tried. I wondered what ambitions MCI had. Might it
turn the fictitious GP into a commercial publisher someday? The screen said Gramercy was "The World's First
Virtual Publishing House," and across the top I saw color
photos of Darlene and friends, all looking as real as ever. If
I'd been impatient for a hard sell, I could have clicked immediately on items such as "networkBusiness" or "MCI
Telecommunications, Inc."

But like the rest of the cosmos, I was more keen on
reading some virtual gossip from virtual humans. In a
primitive way, reminiscent of many a best-seller, a teaser
led me on. I learned that the people of Gramercy were
"working on secret projects, curt memos, random
thoughts, Machiavellian power plays," and that I might
"even browse a clandestine love letter or two about to be
sent via e-mail across the corridor."

So I clicked, with much anticipation, on "Gramercy
Press." Against a dark, purplish-blue sky I saw a semi-
ornate, low-rise office building, the same one featured in
the TV commercial. Not to leave anything to chance, a
caption told me about tweeds and patches and old pipes
and the fact that "every one—from the receptionist to the
president himself—is online via networkMCI Business."
Despite the clichés such as the stereotypical reference to
tweeds, this site was clearly showing far more imagination than the usual WWW area did.

"Now," the screen told me, "click on any window and
you'll start to get a feel of the inside workings of a major
New York publishing concern."

I chose a pane on the top floor and saw Darlene near
her keyboard, smiling away and looking as if I'd caught her
in the middle of an intense gossip session. The screen suggested that I click for audio. I did and downloaded a short
snippet. "I love technology," she said in a high-pitched,

girlish voice, and giggled a little nervously as if to tell the world, "Hey, I'm a real person, not an actress taping an ad."

The text on the screen was credibly self-promotional: "I'm a combination of a staff psychiatrist, gopher, organizer, coffee maker, ruffled-feather soother, astrologer, party organizer, invitation sender, flower orderer, delivered-lunch acceptor, and philosopher. Oh yes, I also disseminate messages. A job made infinitely easier thanks to e-mailMCI. I threw out those little pink message pads. e-mailMCI is so much more efficient. I just click on my computer and the message gets to the right person instantly. Whether they call back is up to them. Hey, I can't be their conscience, mother, and etiquette professor too. I wear enough hats. And I have many aptitudes. For instance, I was college skiing champ. You didn't know that about me. Nor did you know I have a master's degree in medieval literature. Or that Ellen deRosset is going to need an editorial assistant. Of course, she doesn't know it yet either."

I moved on to Darlene's e-mail by clicking on, yes, her monitor. And suddenly I was getting another pitch from MCI in the cleverest of ways—I saw a screen shot of a menu from e-mailMCI, complete with such commands as "Compose," "Forward," and "Reply."

Beneath the menu appeared a message list:

E. deRosset	Short Story Submissions
C. Bruno	Excellent Proposition
R. Gales	Cover Art Submissions
M. Dragelov	Interesting Facts
P. Hoffman	Free at Last

I opened the e-mail. Ellen deRosset was complaining that "My office has more manuscripts than the Library of Alexandria—I'm running out of room for me. Could people submit their stories over the Internet instead of through the mail?" Reginald Gales wrote that he'd sent out a fax to computer artists, asking for submissions; and in fact MCI was offering to post the works of electronic artists, not just writers. Under the subject line "Excellent Proposition," Curtiss Bruno asked: "Hey Darlene, want to come by and check out the romance section of our newest catalog?" Funny. The TV commercials had led me to believe he might be tiring of the chase. Marta Dragelov passed on some funny trivia from a book she was researching. Peter Hoffman announced that he would be out of the office the next week but would be keeping in touch with electronic mail.

So, yes, I could read the same e-mail as Darlene could. But that still wasn't full interactivity. I wanted a two-way, and the "Compose" command intrigued me; perhaps I could e-mail the crew behind the Darlene character. I wrote that I was a real writer, working on a real book, for a real publisher; could they please tell me what kind of responses the people at Gramercy Press were getting over the Internet? *And how about Darlene?*

"What's she like?" I was thinking. "How'd those people choose her? Does she enjoy computers? Has she been on the Net?" Once I established contact with the virtual Darlene's keepers, perhaps I could find out.

Having already snooped at Darlene's e-mail, I went on to the offices of the other characters. Ellen deRosset, a dark-haired woman dressed in black, confided that she had corrected her seventh-grade teacher's grammar. "I read *War and Peace* when I was fifteen. The complete works of Balzac before I was twenty-five. I think you get the picture. So I am not happy that I was given the assignment to edit this 'women in sports' book. I dislike sports rather intensely. The only sport I know anything about, really, is fencing. But one must be flexible these days, and the MCI Business software makes this assignment easier to handle, if not more palatable."

Reginald Gales told me how MCI's e-mail and conferencing services came in handy. One of his authors lived on a caboose in Wyoming, while another wrote from a houseboat in Florida; "he once had a shark bite off his TV antenna."

Marta Dragelov, the fact checker, was an avid user of MCI's news-flash service, which crammed her computer with such items as, "India Asks Phone Firms to Set Up Local Factories"—actual news stories that I could see while clicking on them. Peter Hoffman was away at home and working in his pajamas. Martin Banks, the technophobic editor, said he was "being tutored on the wonders of MCI electronic office ephemera by none other than Miss Ellen deRosset." He hoped that she would notice his new pair of wing tips.

The real payoff for readers was in Curtiss Bruno's office. Wearing a striped shirt and a tie and looking like an incurable office politician, he nevertheless held a hand over his mouth as if to say: "Maybe I'd better shut up before I spill too much." Oh, Curtiss, why bother? I could tour an electronic version of the not-quite-completed winter catalogue—with listings of fiction, visual arts, poetry, and nonfiction.

All categories carried dates older than the Web area itself—MCI was apparently relying on imaginary contributors to prime the pumps. "Ivana diTommaso's" background just seemed too *New Yorker*-ish. She had "grown up in Bologna, Italy, and Grosse Pointe, Michigan" and had "developed from a quiet film student" to "one of America's fine short story writers." If she existed, the electronic catalogue at the Library of Congress had yet to note it when I made a short detour by way of my software's task-switching capability. Not that I trusted the catalogue. A branch of Random House had published my first book, *The Silicon Jungle*, yet it was missing from the LC catalogue that day; and for all I knew, maybe the librarians had also neglected the accomplished Ms. diTommaso. I charitably allowed for the fact that she just might exist.

Her story, "The Legend of Wendell County," told how a county records keeper had become a community grandmother who, not content to record births, deaths, and divorces, tried her hand at marriage counseling and other social workish pursuits—until one day she lost her way in winter and turned into something else, a ghost. The bottom of the page carried an authentic-looking "© 1994 Ivana diTommaso."

I moved on. "The Tree House" was a story from Katy Rudder, a member of "the first Peace Corps class ever assigned to China, where she is teaching English at Leshan Teachers College in the Sichuan Province." Based on what I was reading, MCI's artistic tastes—or its ad agency's—were corporately wholesome. And so were its contributors. I doubted that Gramercy would have been the best place for the young Burroughs or Kerouac.

Perhaps this would change, maybe Gramercy would grow more adventurous with time, but right now I wasn't sanguine in that regard. The nonfiction area was a real loss with just one title, of a harmless, theological type. I doubted that this would be the place for, say, Seymour Hersh or Robert Caro. Like the writing, the art looked competent and maybe much better, but, again, safely within corporate parameters.

The most cautious contributors were MCI's lawyers, or whoever else had written the legalese for one Web site. All writers and artists had to send in releases saying they wouldn't sue MCI for using accidentally similar material. The lawyers warned, "All work that is submitted electronically over the Internet needs to be accompanied by a hard copy of the release form, sent in separately by postal mail. We will not look at any work placed on our server until we have received the hard copy of the release form. All files on the server older than 14 days, for which we have not received a release, will not be reviewed. . . ." I remembered the essay on theology. It was uninspired enough for an attorney other than Scott Turow to have written it, and sure enough, the author's note said he was "happy with the practice of law."

Despite the less-than-striking short stories and the soporific essay, I loved the sparkle of Gramercy Press as a whole. I recalled an area on the Web known as Bianca's Smut Shack. Its creators let you get inside the head of a virtual woman, let you know what books she read, what movies she watched, what records she listened to, and you could add your own opinions. At the time I'd told the Shack crew, "Watch out, folks. Don't be surprised if a big company creates characters in an ad where *everyone* buys the right products." Well, it had happened. And MCI and its advertising agency had done many good things that people with their resources could more easily accomplish.

Building Notre Dame, thousands of workers had pieced together the stone, fashioned the gargoyles, assembled the stained-glass windows. And the MCI Web area, while hardly art, was somewhat like a cathedral. The area's masterminds had bungled in some ways, but they had used sheer staff power to toil over countless details.

I was sorry when Mark Pettit told me that some Real People in Publishing had hated Gramercy Press. Didn't they get it? Granted, the publishing company was stereotypical to the point of being self-satirizing. But so what? I was no more expecting MCI to be a first-rate publisher than I was expecting Random House to lay fiber-optic cable.

As a display of the Web's potential to attract a mass audience, of course, the Gramercy endeavor had triumphed. For consumer business on the Net to take off, ads would have to be a complete departure from those on television, and MCI had done just that—even if it was able to benefit from characters from the older medium. Many small-timers could never have discovered an actress as perfectly suited to play Darlene as Katy Selverstone was. This was a real coup. MCI was brilliantly drawing in a big crowd through a skillful interplay of television, print, and the Net.

Selverstone herself had become a living ad for MCI, drawing stare after stare as she walked down the Manhattan streets. Her Gramercy role was a real tribute to her acting ability. *Entertainment Weekly* described her as not "much of a gadget-head. 'I've got a 12-inch, black-and-white TV that emits a faint gaseous odor,' she says. 'And I have to change channels with a pair of pliers.' " The word from MCI was that she'd just bought a computer and would herself be on the Net. Advertisers hired models today on the basis of looks and I wondered if, in the future, they would consider the ability to give good chat online.

A major problem, however, arose with this scenario in MCI's case. While I hadn't asked for an interview or e-mail from the real Darlene, I had yet even to hear from her handlers after six weeks. These people had wooed me with a first-class Web area and encouraged me to write in, and yet they had then ignored me except for a little boiler-plate from their Darelene-bot, who said she was busy coping with "emergencies." The MCI media crew reinforced my skepticism; only after a series of phone calls was I able to pry basic information. On a day when Pettit solemnly promised he'd talked to me, he was off holding a press conference for the *Wall Street Journal* and the other usual suspects without alerting me about the postponement. Clearly this was a big company focused on other big companies, and I wondered if the small merchants in the Web area might suffer if they entrusted their fates to MCI. I myself was not just a writer. I made it clear that I was also a customer of MCI Mail, an electronic mail service to which I had subscribed for a decade. Perhaps someday I might even want a Web area through MCI. And this was the treatment I got?

If MCI slighted me—a writer–customer who spoke out in print and on the Net, and who had many friends there—how would it treat the Larry Grants of the future? I thought of the elusive, virtual character who had asked me to write to her. In a metaphorical sense, small merchants might futilely spend their days searching for Darlene. Now I wondered about Bob Lilienfeld. How was he coming along with his own information request? Was there *any* chance that White Rabbit might end up in an electronic mall after all? Lilienfeld, albeit not a mall booster, was in many ways a good prospect since he was so Net oriented and could appreciate a good deal. Why, he even owned stock in MCI.

Efficiently, however, MCI had alienated Bob Lilienfeld. Just like me, he had not heard a peep out of the company, even after filling out a form for his two months of trial services. He had followed up with three e-mail notes to an address set aside for prospects like him. I told MCI's media people about this mini-debacle and was assured that someone would contact Lilienfeld. But after several weeks, no one had. MCI was nicely apologetic, of course. Mark Pettit and colleagues reminded me of the huge number of people who had replied to the Gramercy Press ad. They said, too, that MCI technical people were busy at work answering questions, while creative types handled the correspondence for Darlene. But they were missing the point. This was a massive advertising campaign, and they should have planned for success as well as failure.

The issue *should* not have had anything to do with corporate size. MCI could have requested zip codes and states and sorted out Darlene's e-mail in that way—for area sales reps to answer if her handlers in New York were swamped. In fact, the form that Lilienfeld filled out did ask for his postal address. It also inquired, "What interests you?" so that, during the two-month trial, MCI could mail him news stories through the new automatic clipping service. "You can choose any topic: your competition's advertising, the future of your industry, or southwestern cooking, anything," MCI had assured him. And yet, after six weeks, he hadn't received a single call or piece of literature.

As if that weren't enough of an outrage, MCI's fees might overwhelm many small business people. MCI wanted to charge some $2,000 a month for getting them on the World Wide Web—or at least several times what many independent malls would have billed. Yes, MCI talked about adding value through its brand name and through customer draws such as directory services for the Net and for voice. It would even line up copywriters for the storefronts. But what good would this do merchants whose volumes simply did not justify such expenditures? Pettit reminded me that a quarter-page listing in a phone directory cost $2,000. But that wasn't true in many areas, and most merchants did not take out that much space anyway. Even then the typical business person might hire an extra clerk, and perhaps have money left over for advertising with a smaller cybermall. That, of course, was projecting into the future. After all, even Larry Grant wasn't grossing more than $15,000–20,000 a year at the time, and the Lilienfelds had a long climb ahead to reach that level.

Perhaps MCI would learn. I still loved the sparkle of the Gramercy area and hoped that it would thrive in the end. Regardless of my doubts and frustrations, I hadn't anything against the people of MCI, especially Mark Pettit, who, despite his absentmindedness, had actually been more helpful than the others. MCI wasn't Canter and Siegel. It hadn't disrupted Usenet. As long as it paid its own way and did not take advantage of its Net connections in ways that stifled competition—Washington needed to monitor MCI closely—then it could actually help the average Net user. The greater the volume on the Net, the greater would be the virtual pipeline and the lower the cost for everyone. So, far from disliking MCI's interest in the commercial promise of the Net, I still saw plenty of potential here. MCI simply needed to understand the obvious. If its electronic marketplace were to succeed, then the company must price its services more realistically and not keep customers searching for Darlene.

Federal Express and Right-O-Way: Absolutely, Positively on the Net

A FedEx woman called me up and asked what the people in Memphis could do to retain my business, which had plummeted to almost zero volume. "You've given me great service," I said, thinking of all the foot-to-throttle occasions when FedEx had picked up manuscripts on deadline. "But you see, I'm on the Internet nowadays. *Everything* for my current book project goes ever the wire." I was working on a guide telling how to lobby for one's political beliefs online, and the publisher had even received the book proposal via the Net. Lots of people were doing the same, not just with the Net but with commercial services and fax. On legal lists, some lawyers were debating the validity of electronic mail for business matters, but the new technology would quiet the discussion soon enough when foolproof, digital signatures could establish the identity of the sender.

No one needs to weep for FedEx, United Parcel Service, and the rest, however. The typical computer is a medium-sized box full of parts that come in much smaller boxes, such as a disk drive or a modem. And, as shown by the thickness of *Computer Shopper* and other magazines that cater to computer users buying from afar, FedEx and similar services are thriving. That is just one example. High-tech companies, especially the network kind, want reputations for reliability and fast turnarounds. They love the FedEx slogan: "When it absolutely, positively, has to be there overnight." Courier services are godsends for corporations that rely on just-in-time delivery to reduce inventories of spare parts. If nothing else, this principle appeals to manufacturers with slim inventories. Also, more and more people are working at home. At the same time, upscale consumer magazines abound with ads touting merchandise via express, everything from steaks to flowers.

The real question, then, isn't how to downsize but rather how to cope with the deluge of business in small packages. And Federal Express views the Internet as among the more promising of many possibilities.

For years, FedEx used its own network to set up computer links through which high-volume, Fortune 500 companies could request pickups, track shipments, and receive invoices. First, FedEx communicated with mainframes. Then it began supplying some customers with personal computers; eventually, some companies shipping as few as three packages a day could qualify. "We started with the biggest customers first and then extended that service to smaller and smaller companies," said Robert Hamilton, a marketer at FedEx dealing with information matters. The next move was supplying tracking software through which people could use their own machines to dial up FedEx. Step by step, FedEx was working to get almost *all* customers online to its computers—even the operators of small home businesses.

The Internet could play an important role here because it is the closest thing to a universal computer network. By the mid-1990s people in the air freight business caught on to the advantages of the Net over the proprietary networks in many cases. The Internet reached scores of countries, no small advantage in an internationally oriented business, and planners could use the Net's volume to help slash the costs of telecommunications *and* improve service to customers. Right-O-Way, a freight forwarder in Tustin, California, was among the Net pioneers. Back in 1992 the company had figured out how to use customers' personal computers to print out bar code labels.

With portable radio-frequency scanners linked to the firm's mainframe, Right-O-Way's workers could track shipments for customers—could, in other words, offer the same services that Fed Ex could. Right-O-Way's customers dialed up the company directly rather than through the Internet. But in 1994, Martin Hubert, vice president of information systems, hooked Right-O-Way into the Net for customers wanting to use it. He spent just $1,000 on additional UNIX software, modems, network setup charges, and programming time, and $350 a month in Internet-related bills.

"Some customers have tried it already," Hubert said. "We have sales people use the Internet to access shipping data. Our advanced overseas partners can access our computer directly for e-mail, tracking, and tracing. Customers like BMW, ClothesTime, and Packard Bell access our computer and save money on long-distance charges from overseas."[7] Those companies could reach the Right-O-Way computer directly, getting immediate answers while they were online. Using the Net, they could even schedule shipments. Right-O-Way told me that it protected account numbers by requiring customers to use passwords that they received through sales reps and ways other than the Internet.

What's more, the company served even customers having only the most basic of Internet connections. Yes, you could Telnet into the Right-O-Way computer system on the Internet—could issue commands as if you were at a keyboard at headquarters. But if you lacked Telnet capabilities and didn't mind the delay, you could also send electronic mail messages in the appropriate format to track shipments or issue pickup orders.[8]

Around the same time, FedEx and other industry giants were gearing up to do business on the Internet. The Net, of course, wasn't the only possibility. Federal Express by then was an old hand at using its own network, which at the time accounted for more than 50 percent of the packages shipped. It was also distributing Windows and Mac software to enable tracking through the FedEx net. Just the same, in December 1994, after having earlier

experimented with the Net for the distribution of press releases, FedEx turned to the Internet's World Wide Web as
a way for customers to track packages. Within FedEx's
Web area, they could key in the number of the package
and get the latest information.

I checked out the Web service. At www.fedex.com I
saw "FedEx" in big purple and orange letters, along with a
short, easy menu that led me to electronic forms. A detour
offered "Interesting Facts about FedEx!" It was the "world's
largest express transportation company," had 1994 revenues of $8.5 billion, employed "more than 505,515 world-
wide," served 191 countries, owned more than 400 aircraft
ranging from 32 Fokker F-27s to 5 Airbuses and 13
McDonnell Douglas MD-11s, operated "more than 32,560
vehicles, and shipped an average of more than 2 million
packages each day." Another menu item could tell me
about pickup availability. If I typed in the time I would have
a shipment ready to go, my zip code, and the destination
code, among other items, then FedEx would tell me how
soon it could deliver the package using Priority Overnight
Service or alternatives.

Right now, however, I wanted to learn the where-
abouts of a test package—containing nothing more than
Robert Hamilton's business card—that went out under
airbill number 50044562. It was a no-brainer. I chose
"Select Track a FedEx Package" and keyed in the number.
Almost immediately I learned when a courier had picked
up the package and when it had left Memphis. And eventually the Web would pass on other facts such as the name
of the driver at the destination, the delivery time, and who
signed for the package. An idea hit me. When you filled
out an express form in the future, perhaps you could give
both your recipient's e-mail address and your own. Via the
Net, a service could tell the other person that a package
was on the way—and after it arrived, you'd automatically
receive a receipt.

Even as the FedEx area existed now, however, it was serving customer needs well. Yes, I appreciated the flash of MCI's efforts, and I understood why Darlene and friends were attracting many more people than the courier company was right now. But compared to MCI, FedEx left me feeling *better*. Those modest little electronic forms, the ones that would let me track packages and check out Fed Ex's service availability by location and time, treated the customers as individuals and responded in seconds. MCI, however, ignored Bob Lilienfeld, who, disgusted, later sold his stock.

On top of everything else, MCI, which had vastly more programming talent than FedEx did, had missed out on some major opportunities for interactive software. I could imagine a small company keying in a description of its telecommunications and network requirements and getting a series of at least basic recommendations. On a package-by-package basis and in the most private of ways, FedEx was doing this already—since its forms queried you about your shipping needs of the moment and then told you what services were available. The people at MCI weren't dumb. They could turn around their operation in a flash—they might have done so by the time you read this—but in terms of customer service FedEx was clearly the winner right now.

"Five years from now," said Robert Hamilton, "35 or 40 percent of the customers connected to FedEx could be using the Internet." His company stood a good chance of saving millions in annual communications costs and the expenses of staffing phones. "The big factor is how individuals are connected today," he said. "With Compu-Serve and America Online galloping in the direction of the Internet, maybe that will happen sooner rather than later." FedEx would let customer usage, not official corporate policy, drive its use of the Net, and that is exactly how it should be. One way or another the Net would definitely figure in its plans. The only question was, "How much?"

The big need now, of course, was for customers to be able to key in their account numbers and get immediate pickups. FedEx did face some challenges here. FedEx needed to blend the Internet into its existing network of computers, and this complicated the security issues. FedEx wanted to make certain that a cyberthief couldn't go on a joyride with an illegally obtained account number of a customer. So it was evaluating security-enhanced software from CommerceNet, a California organization that helped put businesses on the Net. Meanwhile, we customers could not use the Net to schedule shipments through Federal Express. FedEx had offered a temporary solution: we could at least download software that let us call up the company directly, or we could reach FedEx via America Online or another commercial network. That would do for the moment.

Mulling over what I'd seen and heard up to now, I could not escape three conclusions. First, it was clear that computer networks could be a help, not a threat, to delivery companies that were trying to upgrade service. No longer would I have to wait for an operator to schedule a pickup or check on shipments from FedEx. The second conclusion was broader: The Net often could be good for corporations of *all* sizes, not just Fortune 500 firms like FedEx. Right-O-Way had staked out its own place in cyberspace by going for the simplest solution—Telnet and electronic mail—rather than worrying first about the World Wide Web. The company could add the Web later. On the Internet, with its inherent economies for the Right-O-Ways of this world, "smaller" didn't have to mean "backwards."

The third conclusion about these case histories resulted from my comparisons of MCI and the courier companies, and it transcended the fact that they were in different industries. Even on the Internet, good customer service would have to be a company's first priority and counted even more than the technology per se. Oh, you could use electronic forms. But unless you programmed the forms to provide the right services—rather than simply trying to sell The Product and awe the customers—you might actually alienate the people you were trying to befriend. MCI didn't understand this sufficiently. FedEx and Right-O-Way did.

Intel: How the Net Helped Turn an Advertising Sticker into a Warning Label

The Internet, of course, can hurt as well as help business. Well populated with skeptical academics—whose postings often find their way onto the screens of equally skeptical journalists—the Net is a good place to learn about scams. Legitimate companies, of course, needn't worry: They will benefit as word of their successful products spreads, and the Net excels as a conduit for rumor control. Should there ever be another Tylenol scare, you can bet that publicists will use the Net to get the truth out. Even legitimate businesses, however, can feel the wrath of the Net if they err—as Intel, the chip maker, found out in the ugliest of ways after it released the Pentium chip.

The Pentium chip was the new flagship product, the speedster that would let PCs impinge on minicomputer territory. But that wasn't all. Intel envisioned the Pentium as the perfect chip for computers aimed at the home market. No longer would Mom, Pop, and The Kids poke along with computers weaker than those at the office. Thanks to Intel, they would enjoy glitzy cartoons, educational programs, and other multimedia offerings in full glory on their machines at home. Intel launched a major TV campaign and persuaded scores of computer makers to adorn their boxes and ads with "Intel Inside" stickers. Intel was looking ahead to millions of dollars of Christmas-related sales. At the time, I suspect, the Internet didn't figure that prominently in Intel's plans. Its Net area was hardly as dazzling or as ambitious as those of many other companies. That would change.

The trouble started when a mathematics professor in Virginia found that under certain conditions, the Pentium chip would make mistakes in arithmetic. There at Lynchburg College, Dr. Thomas Nicely couldn't believe his screen. To his amazement, he was able to verify that the chip, not the human, was at fault here. In October 1994 the professor's "Bug in the Pentium" memo went out over the Internet. It circulated rapidly from mailing list to mailing list, from newsgroup to newsgroup, as well as on commercial nets such as CompuServe and Prodigy.

Pentium-hostile messages flew back and forth between scientists, corporate executives, consultants, and other influential people, who, thanks to the Internet, could share complaints more efficiently than ever. Intel tried some damage control via the Net and in press statements. The heat reached the point where the head of Intel asked a underling to issue an apology and a technical explanation. The message betrayed corporate panic, pure and simple. "I am posting from my home system," Richard Wirt, Director of Software Technology, prefaced a weekend note. And then came an "I am truly sorry" message from Andy Grove, President of Intel. In various statements Intel assured customers that the average computer user would typically run across the problem once every 27,000 years. The official line was that nontechnical people needn't worry. Intel announced it would replace chips *if* people could show that the defect could harm their work.

That still didn't placate the Net and the media. Netwise reporters at papers such as the *Washington Post* and *New York Times* and at *Newsday* warned the thousands of Christmas shoppers who were about to buy $2,000 Pentium machines. Billions of dollars were at stake here.

Computer makers had already moved millions of Pentium machines, and IBM came out with a statement saying that it would replace defective chips—even though Intel kept claiming that the nontechnical need not worry. It didn't help when shoppers learned that Intel knew about the Pentium's defects as early as June.

What most threatened the Pentium, however, may have been the humor. It started on the Net and, via mailing lists such as On-Line News, reached major newspapers. David Letterman started cracking jokes. Politicians and chips had something in common. If still quite alive when Letterman ridiculed it, the Pentium was headed toward the emergency room afterward—given the speed with which the story was traveling around. On the Net itself, and on the front pages, typical Pentium humor went something like this:

Q. "How many Pentium designers does it take to screw in a light bulb?"
A. "1.99904274017, but that's close enough for nontechnical people."

Q. "What do you get when you cross a Pentium PC with a research grant?"
A. "A mad scientist."

Q. "What's another name for the 'Intel Inside' sticker they put on Pentiums?"
A. "The warning label."

Maintaining to the end that this was more of a marketing problem than a technical one, Intel relented. It agreed to replace chips for free without interrogating the public. What's more, Intel expanded its presence on the Net. It now offered a nice area on the World Wide Web with items ranging from product descriptions to job announcements. Still, this fiasco aside, Intel had a good reputation for quality control, and by not shrinking from the Net community, it was responding correctly.

Another major lesson should also have sunk in among marketers of all kinds—beyond the obvious fact that the Internet could spread news of flawed products. Customers throughout the world could use the same channels to find out about geographically based price gouges. If a software firm charged reasonable prices in the United States but boosted price tags for Europeans, then the Net would spread the word. Software companies might not appreciate this immediately, but sooner or later they would. This was especially true of companies sending their products over the Net. The Internet Adapter, the product that had proven to be so good to my wallet, would have cost me $25 even if I'd lived in Antarctica or New Zealand. I wondered how long it would be before the traditional vendors of shrink-wrapped software would understand this lesson and stop squeezing customers outside the United States. Even with the expenses of middle people and translation factored in, the prices of some American software products were too high in Europe. Consumerism on the Net just might make the marketplace more sane.

Other Hazards for Business People

Not surprisingly, the old sixties people saw the Internet as a victory of smallness over big corporations. Little companies could use the Net in new and imaginative ways and woo prospects thousands of miles away. Some enthusiasts promoted the Net as a powerful weapon for individuals who hated life in sluggish, bloated corporations.

Still, the Net might not always be a Nirvana for small entrepreneurs. Consider the Lilienfelds. What if toy companies decided to sell on the Net directly, for example? The Lilienfelds themselves could still fare well since they were working hard to become known for personal service. For example, if a toy weren't shown online, Bob might even scan in a photo from a wholesaler's catalogue and e-mail it to an interested buyer. And he and his wife were planning to make themselves a conspicuous presence in relevant newsgroups, while respecting netiquette. But not all of the small merchants would be as astute and dedicated. I suspected that many bankruptcies lay ahead.

Other problems might hit large as well as tiny companies. Many customers refused to give their credit card numbers online; in fact, many stores didn't even *want* them. The Net wasn't entirely secure. Theoretically, snoops in a number of locations could intercept orders and pick up the MasterCard or VISA numbers with software that looked for common data associated with credit cards. I regarded this as a temporary problem. Lilienfeld had dealt with it nicely by letting people—at least those in the United States—phone in their credit card numbers for free. The numbers would remain safe in White Rabbit's computers, ready for future transactions. Besides, as Lilienfeld pointed out, it wasn't worth the trouble for thieves to keep a tab on small stores like his.

Bigger businesses, however, were right to worry, and solutions were on the way. Popular browsers such as Netscape, for example, were coming with security features. Customers would be able to effortlessly transmit their credit card numbers in encoded form.

What about the problem of customers without sufficient funds to pay for merchandise? Some Web merchants could almost instantly verify that a customer had enough money in a credit account. The process would be even easier if companies such as Microsoft followed through with plans to team up with credit card companies. But that still left another worry for customers—privacy.

If you use old-fashioned paper money, your transactions aren't traceable. With electronic money—or with regular credit or conventional debit cards—they might be.

What if you were a gay woman, lived in a small Arkansas town, and enjoyed lesbian literature? Or suppose that in the future you were caught up in a divorce and your wife employed a cyberdetective to snoop on your spending habits? DigiCash, a company in Amsterdam, thought it had a solution in the form of anonymous electronic money that you could spend without being traced. Only your digital banker would know for sure. The possibility, of course, gave fits to tax collectors throughout the world. It was one of the reasons why bureaucrats in the United States had lobbied so hard for industry to adopt the Clipper chip, which allowed federal snoops to break its codes. Clearly, however, the Clipper effort could *harm* U.S. companies. Suppose foreign governments used a similar approach—making it easier to steal commercial secrets from American-owned multinationals?

Still another threat to business is from people who might spy on or change data on corporate systems. Hackers got into General Electric computers containing secrets. The solution to these electronic thefts, in many cases, was stronger "firewalls"—electronic gateways between public and private areas. In some instances, however, the threat was exaggerated. Yes, in theory, hackers could turn your home phone into a pay phone or make off with your corporate password or spy on your electronic mail. And some hated commercial activities on the Net and were ready to act. But by far, these were exceptions: most of the better hackers were benign—they saw themselves more as scholars than as snoops and saboteurs. Indeed, old-timers would not use the word "hackers" to describe the malevolent; no, they were "crackers."

Ironically, on the Net, the real worry isn't hackers but snoopy competitors, who, without necessarily breaking the law, can find out information about prices and new products much more efficiently than before. A rival phone company has paid thousands and thousands of visits to the MCI area on the Web. This must be going on constantly.

Earlier, Digital Equipment Corporation offered software demonstrations over the Net and found that its competitors were tying the machines up. More scrupulously, companies could use powerful searching tools such as the Lycos on the Web to seek out files mentioning rivals' products. They could also send the names of rivals to a computer at Stanford University. And then whenever a company was mentioned in a major Usenet newsgroup, an electronic clipping service would send the information back to them at no charge. A careless engineer or marketer could jeopardize thousands or millions in investments. The answer, of course, is to educate people about the risks.

Not so controllable is the risk of companies using the Net to troll for unfavorable mentions of rivals—grist for negative advertising. There is only one solution: make better products or give better service.

• • •

Of the goods and services discussed here, a major kind is conspicuously missing so far: entertainment. Some of the best is free. Just ahead you'll find a favorite of many Netfolks—the Internet Underground Music Archive, from which you can download free samples from top hits as well as surprises from new musicians.

THREE

EntertaiNet: A Few Musings on Net.Rock, Leonardo da Vinci and Bill Gates, Bianca's Smut Shack, and David Letterman in Cyberspace

Don't count on the Ugly Mugs pushing Billy Joel off the charts, or even showing up at your closest record store.

They're zany, avant-garde musicians whose work is a cross between Frank Zappa and freakish, carnival rock—not the stuff of the Top 40. But Jeff Patterson, a thin, pale guitarist with a fondness for old jeans and green-topped sneakers, can still spread the word about himself and the other Mugs. Their music is on the Internet. Fans as far off as Turkey and Japan can dial the Internet Underground Music Archive run by Patterson and his "co-czar," Rob Lord. Hundreds of musicians are suddenly in cyberspace. For just $100 a year they can pay IUMA to post cuts from their music, complete with information on how you can send away for the CDs and tapes. In fact, some have even posted complete songs to the Net for free.

Tens of thousands of Netfolk a week dial up IUMA, making 200,000 page-accesses—perhaps a third of the attention that *Playboy* gets, but still one of the best numbers on the Web. That's no small feat: The archive more or less started in a tiny room with a bare lightbulb dangling from the ceiling, and it is still a low-budget operation run by two information science majors.

IUMA is just one of many delights on the Net for techies and technophobes alike. Entertainment and culture are taking off in a major way in cyberspace just when clueless Snubbites are deriding the Net as artless. I can enjoy gifted but unheralded performers, from reggae artists to banjo players. The New Zealand Symphony is online with a digitized rendition of the national anthem down there. Imagine the possibilities for fans of classical music in the future—the chances to hear live performances of Tchaikovsky directly from Moscow, or enjoy classical Chinese music from Peking or Taipei. Net.radio is already here. WYXC, for example, a station at the University of North Carolina at Chapel Hill, sends rock music into the ether twenty-four hours a day.

Running software called RealAudio, owners of deluxe home computers can hear top-ten rap from an Internet site in South Korea, astrological forecasts from England, and selected programs from ABC News, National Public Radio, the C-SPAN cable network, the radio version of the *Christian Science Monitor*, the National Press Club, the Canadian Broadcasting Corporation, and a wealth of other draws whenever they want—even weeks or months after the original broadcasts.

Just a mouse click on the right Web address conjures up a Daniel Schorr commentary, or a feature about the Illinois reporter whom the mob supposedly buried in concrete, or scads of other NPR offerings that I wish I could have enjoyed when they first aired. I don't have to bother with tricky downloads of files containing the sound. This happens on its own.

RealAudio sounds rather muffled right now, at least on my computer, as if the technology is a throwback to

1920s radio. But sooner or later it will make FM stereo seem antediluvian.

Consider, too, the diversity of programming from grassroots people who can broadcast at a fraction of the costs of even peanut-whistle stations. Thousands of mom-and-pop sites—unencumbered by the Federal Communications Commission, unless the nanny faction wins out in D.C. and cracks down on the Net—may be online in the next year or two. What happens when unpopular political beliefs spread around this way? Will the Oklahoma City tragedy be invoked to squelch RealAudio and equivalents?

Cheerier possibilities may arise. Someday you might go hiking in the middle of the Rockies and be able to tune in performances and talk shows from all over the world through a net.satellite link; never mind the limits of the local radio stations.

Even video transmission will be routine over the Net or a successor. And then what? When Michael Moriarty, a TV actor, appeared in a public Q & A session on Prodigy, the possibilities made him wonder if network television would go the way of vinyl records. "Television," he told the *New York Times*, "might become the $33^{1/3}$ of the visual arts."

For the moment, however, the Net is Fan Central for television along with other media. David Letterman fans and those of Jay Leno debate the merits of their favorite talk show hosts, while major movie studios preview their megahits with video clips. Elvis is alive and well in an area on the Web. And just when we Netfolks are ridiculing the TV moguls' dream of 500 channels of *Terminator* movies, Hollywood has used our Net to ballyhoo *Junior*— a comedy starring the Terminator himself, Arnold Schwarzenegger. As if that isn't enough, Hollywood has just released *The Net*, a thriller with some evil techies; let's see what the marketers will post on the Web to push *that* one. Lower on the show business hierarchy, you can find model Danielle Ash replying to questions, in alt.sex.breasts, about her double Fs.

Netfolks with more elevated tastes can dial up the WebMuseum, Paris, or check out the works of new digital artists from Boston or New York or dozens of other big cities. Obviously the Net isn't the same as beholding a Rembrandt in Holland and gazing into the face of a local man or woman a few feet away. That's screamingly clear. Stoll, the near Snubbite, correctly notes that "Rembrandt painted real people—their facial features and mannerisms live on today in the Dutch population. Dressed in period costumes, I'll bet the security guard with his war medals and the young woman tour guide would look as if they stepped out of one of those incredibly detailed paintings." Moving and true. Imagine, however, the benefits of the WebMuseum to people without the Snubbites' ability to jet to Amsterdam or Paris. What's more, the Web brings its own glories to compensate; I can view Artist X's work, then call up text about the person or the times; if anything the Web can provide *more* context than do the skimpy handouts available at most museums.

Caviling away, Stoll also objects that computers can't reproduce the art exactly. But colors and resolution will just keep improving. The Snubbites who rant about lost details remind me of the foes of electronic books; incorrectly, given the ease of digitizing everything, the foes worry that new technology could kill off distinctive typefaces. But we shouldn't preserve art and literature just by attending to the detail work. Culture also needs a place in the public mind; da Vinci-class art should be free, or close to it, by way of the Net. That is surely the ethos of Nicholas Pioch. An ex-Microsoft intern now studying economics in his native France, he is behind the WebMuseum, Paris, the new name it bears, now that bureaucrats won't let him say, "Le WebLouvre."

Within Le WebLouve—there, I'll say it anyway—I saw such da Vincis as *Mona Lisa* and *Virgin and Child with*

the Infant John the Baptist and St. Anne. I went on to look
at Rembrandts, van Goghs, Cezannes, Dalis, Klees, and
Manets, among others, and to read two warnings. "If you
think the law prevents you from viewing these exhibits,
you should stop now and do something more interesting,
such as flying to Paris and touring live!" Pioch wrote.
"Some companies may be trying to get a monopolistic
grab on arts and culture," he said elsewhere, "developing
a pay-per-view logic, shipping out CD-ROMs while trying
to patent stuff which belongs to each of us: a part of *our*
human civilization and history."

How right Pioch was. Bill Gates has just bought a
notebook of Leonardo da Vinci, and let's hope that like
some of the old robber barons, Gates will habitually share
his acquisitions with the world. But a major difference
shows up here. Andrew Carnegie and the rest did not
make their money off art and entertainment, part of Gates'
master plan. For Bill Gates to give away great paintings
and manuscripts will be like Carnegie giving away steel.
His motives may be the most ethereal, and with a $10-bil-
lion net worth, he can afford many a donation; but a con-
flict will forever arise between Gates the businessman
and Gates the philanthropist. Just which side will prevail
when he dies? If not in life, then in death, by way of his
lawyers, will he have the decency to turn *all* his old masters loose on the Net for free viewing? No judgments here.
Perhaps that day will come. He has already agreed to loan
the notebook to a museum.

Old masters, of course, are far from the only Culture
on the Net, and I doubt that Bill Gates will be interested in
buying some of the other kind—especially Bianca's Smut
Shack. Don't ask me if Bianca exists. The Shack's "trolls"
swear that she does. If so, maybe a good many Netfolks
know her at least slightly. They can click on a picture to
flit from room to room of her virtual apartment on the
Web, leave notes on the walls of her virtual bathroom,
enter her virtual music room to take in the latest jazz or

rock, or engage virtually in sex acts with strangers in Argentina or Brazil or San Francisco or wherever else hormones fuel technology.

Bianca's proud trolls have not sold out their mascot; the virtual Bianca lives on the Web for fun, not direct money making. But sooner or later, elsewhere on the Net, if this has not happened already, an ad agency will create a fictitious character who buys CDs, foods, books, video tapes, automobiles, and other products only from hidden "sponsors"—not open, MCI-style ones (as described in chapter 2). I'll hope that day is far off. The FCC has had problems enough regulating children's TV; imagine what could happen if supposedly educational areas knuckled under to Madison Avenue. I'm not sure if laws are the solution here, but it would behoove Net providers to come up *now* with rules against that sort of thing.

In the fun areas of the Net, other dangers lurk for the vulnerable. Millions of Netfolks enjoy role-playing in imaginary worlds known as Multi-User Dungeons, where they can be knights or damsels, regardless of gender— sometimes men assume women's roles to win more attention. At the risk of sounding like Stoll and the Snubbites, I have mixed feelings about the worth of MUD-style diversions.

A real potential exists for cocaine-heavy addiction— far more than just regular Netsurfing, where you're not competing to rescue a fair maiden or dodge alien attacks. Stories circulate of role-players who have kissed off good grades and careers. Up in Canada, one player got so wrapped up in his game that my researcher found him amid wall-to-wall trash as he struggled to balance his schoolwork and role-playing.

Just like online groups for depressed people, however, MUDs and similar areas can bring shy Netfolks together face to face. I heard of several romances, in fact, that the games led to. Risks notwithstanding, games do more good than harm if players just know when to quit. Like it or not, among millions of Netfolks, MUDs and cousins are as much a part of the Internet as the Web and @ signs.

Of all the entertainment on the Net, however, the musical and video kinds could most intrigue the masses as the technology takes off; with just a modem, a reasonably powerful computer, and a $100 sound card, you can hear the offerings of IUMA and similar areas. You don't even need programs such as Mosaic or Netscape if you know what you're doing. People with cheapie dial-up connections and no frills software can download rock albums and the rest. Granted, the technology as a whole could be better, and even using IUMA can tax the wallets and patience of some. In most cases you'll spend more time downloading the music—from a remote machine to your own—than you will hearing it. Fidelity on some setups may be just this side of a tin can. But that's now. Wait.

Transmissions in the future will zip along through cable TV connections to the Internet, or through ISDN[1] phone connections. Then you'll truly be able to use the Net as a jukebox and *hear* what you click on with your mouse. What's more, even now, with the right software, you can enjoy almost CD-ROM-quality fidelity from areas such as IUMA. Audio was the next step up after text, of course, and, yes, video is on the way. Techies already have mounted gigabyte after gigabyte of amateur videos on the Net. Sooner or later, directors of little films will enjoy a monster-sized IUMA-style archive. Perhaps Rob Lord and Jeff Patterson, those co-czars of IUMA, will run *it*, too.

If you think that the $10-billion-a-year recording industry is a little nervous, you're right. In early 1994 Lord told the *San Jose Mercury News:* "We want to kill the record companies." He and Patterson have backed off since then; they've even helped Warner and other giants set up Net areas of their own. IUMA's own 500-act selection is pathetic compared to those at the largest record stores. Still, think about the long run: The IUMA model just might jeopardize the seven-digit salaries of top recording executives. After all, if the Net can advertise music and even be used to take orders—perhaps with electronic forms—just what becomes of the big studios? They themselves will sell music directly over the Net, but with heavy competition.

The bypass-the-middle-man idea could apply in other ways. What about radio hosts, for example? Suppose they can reach people all over the world through the Internet, and perhaps ultimately through wireless connections based on the Net. Will they need CBS or NBC or ABC or equivalents as much as they do now? I can already download snippets from, say, the Canadian Broadcasting Corporation. Too, just what will be the fate of art dealers if so much of art goes digital and people can discover artists on their own without leaving their living rooms? Publishers of newspapers, magazines, and books, of course, are in a quandary—see the next chapter on electronic publishing.

In some ways I don't envy the big guys. IUMA is clearly wired into the Internet, while companies such as CBS, at least at this point, are fumbling in some respects. Many of the amateurs on the Net are actually coming up with better offerings than are the professionals. When I dropped by, the official Letterman page on the WWW was far from an abomination, and yet at the same time it showed the problems here.

The page indeed was full of odds and ends about how to get *Late Show* tickets, Letterman's upcoming guests, his top-ten lists (the one for the April 13th broadcast was on "Ways CBS Can Raise Money," with number one being "A two-hour paycheck freeze on Letterman"), and the rest. But where were the connections with the rest of the Net, especially the many Letterman fans out there? How about the fans' Letterman pages? Or relevant mailing lists or newsgroups? Perhaps they were there but hidden, but whatever the case the cyberspace Letterman was less hip than the one on The Box.

To Letterman's credit, he didn't fake things. He publicly confessed he was ignorant of data ways. But in my opinion, his Web people could have done better.

Moving on to the CBS home page, I saw an offer for me to "Join the EYE ON THE NET club. That way we can send you more information about CBS and its programs. You can also take part in special previews and other interactive events. Fill out the following registration form and we'll give you a special CBS screen saver just for joining." Oh, boy, that was just why I was on the Internet—to end up on marketers' lists. I didn't blame CBS for trying; some of Letterman's fans would like the free software. But surely the network could have done better.

Aaron Barnhart, who put out a good little electronic fan newsletter called *Late Show News,* defended Dave's people on the Net. "I think it's great," he said of the official Letterman area. "All of these large entities are trying their best to integrate with the interactive age. A lot of e-mail gets passed that you never see, so don't assume that just because there aren't any bulletin boards . . . there is no interaction happening."

Perhaps he was being kind to his sources for his newsletter—I hadn't any idea. What was clear was that he'd made a second career of Lettermandom. He devoted twenty to thirty hours a week to Letterman-related activities. Much of his newsletter was a review of reviews ("Frank Rich of the *New York Times* wrote one of his standard pitiless columns last week on the Oscars broadcast, and we quote, 'in which the belly-flopping David Letterman demonstrated just how large a bullet he dodged by not moving his own show to L.A.' "). Barnhart also served as owner of the Top 10 List ("60,000 subscribers and booming").

So what was Barnhart in it for? He was freelancing for the *Village Voice,* and I could see where some attention might do any writer's career good, but if Barnhart even wanted to be on *The Late Show* itself, he did a pretty good job of concealing that. "Attention is great," he said, "but it doesn't pay the rent." Did he send stuff into the show? "No." So why was Letterman so popular on the Net? "Demographics." Well-off computer owners just liked that kind of program.

I checked out the Letterman page maintained by Jason A. Lindquist, an electronic engineering student at the University of Illinois, Champaign-Urbana, a self-described "Statistician, Smart-Ass-for-Hire, and Mac Programmer." I found references to newsgroup postings on such items as "Dave instigates the feud with Bryant Gumbel with these words," "The great Stevie Nicks controversy of 1986," "Madonna—Your first choice to date your son," and "No inside stuff on the strong guy or the fat guy here." And I saw mentions of the newsletter, the Frequently Asked Questions List, and at least two Letterman-related newsgroups. CBS ought to hire this guy.

It was time to move on to alt.fans.letterman. I did a search within Netscape for the word "Leno" in the subject header and found a post from an apparent Leno fan on the attack: "Everyone knows that Jay Leno is way better than ugly gap-tooth Dave!"

"Oh," replied one of the faithful, "you say that Jay Leno is still on the air? Is it true that they use a wide-angle lens to photograph that lantern jaw of his? Just wondering."

"Letterman has more comedy in his little pinkie toe than Leno will have in his wildest dreams," said another Davite, "and if Letterman is so ugly, who has all the models and top actresses flirting with him and asking him to go out—it certainly isn't Leno."

That, not the official Letterman area, was the true Net. Just what might await the world if the inmates actually ran the asylum and themselves mounted a major entertainment effort rather than trusting the corporate world. It had happened with the Internet Underground Music Archives, and I liked the results.

IUMA

The normal story is that IUMA began when Rob Lord and Jeff Patterson, the co-czars, met in a newsgroup devoted to supermodels. Both liked Kate Moss, a waify Calvin Klein woman; strutting down the runways, she was lost amid the big, bosomy knockouts favored by so many young men on the Net. It turned out that Lord and Patterson were both from Valencia, California, a far-north suburb of Los Angeles. They knew each other slightly from William Hart High School, both had worked in record stores while teenagers, and both had both been attending the University of California at Santa Cruz. That's the story, and it's true.

IUMA, however, in another way, may have started not on the Net but in the corporeal United Kingdom.

Thousand and thousands of Brits were dancing to synthesized *bleeps, conks, cooonkks, clunks, bomb-bombs* and *tssss-tsss-tssses,* and odds and ends that I could never even come close to reproducing here. The name of the music was Rave, as in "raving mad," and by the time Lord was in high school in the 1980s, the craze had found its way to Los Angeles.

Middle-class white suburbanites, Latinos, Blacks, they were all *bleep*ing and *conk*ing together, thousands of them, risking the wrath of the fire department, overcrowding the halls, going at it from 11 P.M. on, some dancing twelve hours on into the morning.

"No place in Los Angeles," Lord said of the Rave halls, "had such a peaceful coexistence as between these three groups. They didn't say anything. They shared the beats and feelings and the technology. And on the Rave scene, the person in charge is the DJ, and they're sort of the cultural funnel. The DJs were in charge of finding these odd records that would come from Belgium and from the UK and from Chicago, and there were some made-in-

Los Angeles things. They were hard to find, but the DJs were responsible for scouting them out and bringing the very latest *bleeps* and *conks* together."

"So," I asked, thinking of IUMA and Lord's chance to bring the world to his listeners, "you liken yourself to those DJs?"

"Yeah, yeah!" Lord said enthusiastically. "I believe IUMA is my personal implementation of Rave's calling. I just love working with technology and all those kinds of things, and what Rave culture espoused was that there's a new revolution going on, an information revolution. You know, one of the biggest stars of Rave music was a band called Dee-Lite. And one of the first lines was, 'From New York City in the age of communication.' And that means all kinds of communications, a shrinking world, Internet, it means ideas and the convergence of ideas."

Returning to the subject of his younger days, Rob Lord told me how much he hated the Depeche Mode music that was so popular in upper-middle-class neighborhoods like his—the kind the record stores were selling. He wanted his music from the clubs, from the 100-copy pressing, not from the megaconglomerates offering the likes of Depeche. "The lyrics were terrible, and the emotions were feigned." I'm sure Depeche fans might disagree. The point, however, was that Depeche music was much more readily available at record stores than Rave was, and Rob grew unhappy with the distribution system.

Jeff Patterson, working at a music store, just like Rob Lord, was equally disgusted. Patterson and co-workers "would sit there and talk about who's making all the money." CDs cost $15–$17 at Music Plus, his employer. Elsewhere they were around $12–$13. "And you know, we were thinking like, 'Where is that extra $4 being pocketed?' You know, after all the costs were taken out, then their manager would get paid, the record company would get paid, people on the tour would get paid, and then the band would finally get some money after all that, and it was usually a very small check. So the artists that were actually continuing to be artists were the artists that were making money; so it was, like, this level of superstardom that was consistent and the barriers of entry were extremely high."

That was true in all kinds of creative endeavors, especially in writing. I myself was amused when lobbyists representing industries such as music and publishing would rant on and on about the need for "creative incentives." If business people at the megaconglomerates really understood incentives, they would cut out their caviar, sell off the executive jets, and spend more than a modicum on garden-variety artists—not just the Mailers and Madonnas. When, even as a teenager, Jeff Patterson started asking where the money was going, he was laying some of the more important underpinnings for IUMA.

An "A" student who would later graduate near the top of his class, Patterson wrote a school paper on another major issue: censorship. Back in the 1980s, Tipper Gore, Al's wife, had helped start a group called the Parents Music Resource Center, which wanted to rate music and keep the more nefarious offerings out of the hands and CD players of young people. "I was a big fan of Frank Zappa and he was basically taking it upon himself to challenge the PMRC." The Senate held hearings. And Patterson recalled that PMRC deemed a Zappa recording, "Jazz from Hell," to be sinful. The album lacked lyrics and the cover just showed Zappa's face. "It was obvious," Patterson said of Tipper's group, "that they weren't actually listening to the content or caring what it was. They just kind of labeled some artists as being bad, and therefore were trying to prevent stores from selling many albums." I asked if that made Patterson think later on, "Let's go on the Net so we don't have those bozos to worry about." "Yeah, yeah. That actually had a big part in it."

From the start, it was clear that Patterson's own music wouldn't exactly please the conventional. In high school he played guitar in speed metal bands, which are "usually a lot faster, a lot more angry sounding" than heavy metal. When the Ugly Mugs found each other at William Hart High, Patterson rejoiced in his friends' weirdness. The style in this case was Dada, a form of random art.

"Who cared if anyone liked listening to it," Patterson said. "We just wanted to play it. We were using mainly guitar and keyboards and bass. However, we wouldn't always play them in the normal standard ways. Like, we'd use guitar for percussion or something, and we had also used a vacuum cleaner and things like that. A lot of times we just recorded sounds of things that were just laying around." Their big gig was at an interpretative dancing class at a community college where teacher and students loved Dada-style mime.

The Ugly Mugs was a life, not just a band. Except for an Egyptian guitarist, whose hair stubbornly kept turning into an Afro when he let it grow, all the Mugs sported long locks. In a dark, ratty, poster-ridden room, they would talk politics and philosophy, standard teenage fashion.

Lord ended up at the University of California at Santa Cruz, and Patterson himself went on to the University of California at Berkeley, where he studied computers, his fallback field. He had made music on them in high school, and, in fact, at Berkeley. "I started changing my major to be a combination of music and computers. Two years into it I really got frustrated with the high pressure and decided to transfer to U.C. Santa Cruz. It's right on the beach, a laid-back community. Everyone drives, like, five miles under the speed limit." Beyond that, members of the Ugly Mugs had moved there, and in Patterson's opinion, the school itself was "really great."

David Huffman taught there. In a certain niche of computerdom, Huffman was famous as the creator of

Huffman coding, a compression routine that software products such as Stacker use to double the space available on hard drives. Music isn't exactly a low-bandwidth use of the Net. Compression routines of one kind or another are de riguer for the transmission of high-quality sound—not just because of the space that the material require, but also because big files take longer to transmit.

At the time Patterson moved to Santa Cruz, he wasn't using Hoffman compression on the Net or posting CD-quality sound from hundreds of musicians through an IUMA-style operation. But like other techies, he was posting files in the synthesized MIDI format. "The stuff I put up there, it sounded like a bad Casio keyboard playing our songs. It really wasn't very representative at all. I'd just sit there at my computer, compose 'em on the computer, and upload 'em on the Net. I posted them to a couple of news groups, like alt.binaries.sound and things like that and basically got no response at all."

Jeff Patterson was reading the supermodel newsgroup when he saw a posting from Rob Lord in favor of Kate Moss, the model that so many of the regulars considered too bony. Patterson replied. "We were both huge Kate Moss fans." Lord sent him some e-mail talking about how Kate Moss should be the "queen of supermodels." People on the Net have a custom of leaving "signatures" at the bottom of messages—places where they may post their address or phone number, or an I-don't-speak-for-IBM disclaimer, or quote somebody to support them or deride them—and Patterson took quick notice of Lord's ".sig." It alluded to "MPEG Audio Compression, 16 to 1 CD Quality."

"And," Patterson recalled, "I was like, 'Wow, what's that?' So I e-mailed him back talking about getting together some Moss pictures, and in passing I asked him about MPEG compression." MPEG stood for Motion Picture Expert Group—engineers who set standards for audio and video compression. Growing curious, Patterson downloaded software so he could play MPEG through his sound card. The results delighted him, and he spread the news to the other Ugly Mugs. Hey, guys, Patterson said in effect, what if we put our music on the Internet? "They thought it was a pretty good idea. So we decided to chip in together and go ahead and buy the software that we needed to compress MPEG files, because you could get that player for free, but the compressor cost $100. Rob came over to my house, and I told him we were putting our band on the Net, and he was all excited about the whole idea of creating this archive of bands on the Net." But of course! Rave-think could reach cyberspace.

Something was evident here, something obvious to me, but perhaps not to all the bluenoses and prudish, power-fixated bureaucrats. Patterson and Lord were proving the old wisdom that hormones could drive technology on the Net, or at least the applied variety.

The wizardry of MPEG would be useless if people didn't use it. And it took a meeting of Patterson and Lord in the supermodel group—not one devoted to Bible study, or to paeans to Bill Clinton or Al Gore, or to the mandarins of Singapore—for IMUA to give MPEG one of its biggest boosts on the Net. Why, horror of horrors, Patterson and Lord just may have wanted to scan and swap *copyrighted* photos of Kate Moss. One way or another MPEG would become important on the Net, but thanks to people like these two, it was happening far faster than it would have otherwise. Technology was at odds with the vested interests of record companies, and they knew it.

At around the same time IUMA was getting under way in fall 1993, lobbyists for the companies and performing artists were fighting for laws that could lead to onerous pay-per-listen schemes—while publishers were trying to lay the basis for pay-per-read. Indeed, business people and creators should receive fair compensation, especially the creators; but in the zeal to protect major political contributors from the entertainment industry, bureaucrats and lawyers could imperil technology in the most lethal of ways. Bruce Lehman, Bill Clinton's intellectual property czar, would prove it later with a stunningly oppressive proposal called the Green Paper, a technophobic lawyer's wetdream, a techie's nightmare.

The first song the Ugly Mugs put on the Net was called *"Arbeit Macht Frei"*—German for "Work will make you free." A punky carnival song, it sparked an instant debate on free speech.

Asked about the title, Patterson told me, "It was kind of born out of our frustration of, 'In order to have the money to do everything that we want to do, we have to work, but if we work, we can't do anything we want to do.' So it was kind of like commenting on people's attitude of, 'If you work you'll be able to do what you want to do,' when actually you won't be able to do what you want to, because you'll be working.' Actually it wasn't a smart song title. It was a phrase that was over the gate on the way to the Auschwitz concentration camp in Poland. Unfortunately, people took it to be this Nazi song, which is actually completely the opposite of what we meant.

"We got responses from people who flamed me because they thought it was extremely cruel to be using this as a name for a song and taking it all lighthearted when it actually meant something serious to a lot of people. Whenever anyone actually wrote to me, I usually sent them back the lyrics and explained our stance, why it was called that. It definitely created enough of a stir among the few people who heard it. You wonder if a label would ever take a chance with something like that."

On the Net, however, *"Arbeit Macht Frei"* would find its audience. A man from Turkey asked for a full demo tape—unavailable—and more songs. Other Netfolks wrote in from Texas, Florida, and elsewhere in the States, some of whom said more or less: "You know, wow, I'm a Zappa fan and I can hear the influence. It's pretty cool." The Net, in character, was blurring distinctions between artists and fans and helping the two groups mix. "We realized we had something," Patterson told me. "Like, 'Jeez, we got these responses to a band that had never played anywhere and didn't have a tape out.' So we started grabbing a couple of our friends' bands—like my roommate's. And we put Rob's roommate's band up there, and we just kind of kept grabbing bands to put up. And slowly everyone was getting one or two responses to what they had posted. And we needed a place to actually keep all this music. There were like four bands maybe at that time."

Patterson, however, quickly filled up all the disk space available to him at his commercial Internet provider, Netcom; so he and Lord contacted their university and asked if they could store the music there. "Well, it turned out that the guy who was in charge of running the FTP site was a musician—he was in four bands—and he said, 'Sure, go for it.' And we put his four bands up there."

The technology would have seemed infuriatingly hard to the world at large. You couldn't just hook into the World Wide Web, point and click your way to the IUMA archives, and choose the song you wanted; no, you had to do FTP, short for File Transfer Protocol, threading your way through the big hard drives at Santa Cruz, until you reached the subdirectory with the music. And then, with most software, you had to type out the file names. Patterson and Lord didn't even start out with postings on Gopher (which, to be grossly simplistic, is a more primitive version of the Web).

Even back then, however, the two were thinking about the Net equivalent of album covers or of the J cards that record companies used to tout cassettes. In other words they didn't just post files of sound alone. They also pondered the use of files with pictures that music fans could download.

"At this point," Patterson said, "it was still just a fun project. We didn't think about making it a money-making venture at that point. We were just like, you know, 'Let's put bands up and see what we can do to mess with the record industry.' We had this attitude like, 'We'll cut out waste in the industry.' At that time there was, like, no press about us, so we weren't really vocal, but we had those attitudes. We were kind of like naive and rebellious."

Then an event happened that was almost as significant to IUMA as was the discovery of MPEG. Lord discovered the World Wide Web. "None of us," Patterson recalled, "had any clue what it was. I think it was in December of '93 that we got a hold of a copy of Mosaic." They tried it out in a faculty lounge at U.C. Santa Cruz. "There wasn't really much content on the Web at all. It was pretty much, like, weather satellites. We realized from that point on that we could really do something with taking the music and the pictures and using the World Wide Web as the way to present everything. People would be able to look at the album cover, read the text, see 'play' buttons. You know, press the play button, hear the music, and all that sort of thing.

"So," Patterson said, "we called up the guy we knew from maintaining the FTP archives at U.C. Santa Cruz, and asked him what he knew about the World Wide Web." Overnight he learned how to set IUMA up on the Web. His name was Jon Luini, and he would become a partner in IUMA, the co-czars' "Kaiser."

Meanwhile IUMA's popularity kept growing, and soon the archives landed on SunSite UNC, a big digital library sponsored by Sun Micro Systems at the University of North Carolina at Chapel Hill. IUMA would even make it to servers in Europe, so that people there could enjoy the music without tying up the trans-Atlantic connections. Other big companies, such as Silicon Graphics, took an interest in IUMA and donated computers and other gear.

But how were Patterson and Lord—and their musicians—going to make money off the Internet, where "free" was a religion and where commercial audio might be pirated? I loved the many legitimately free pleasures of the Net. It was truly for sharing. IUMA, of course, was offering lots of music at no charge. Via the World Wide Web, I my-self was giving away a book chapter I'd written for a forth-coming information science collection; and I hoped that at least some material from *NetWorld!* would be retrievable without any money changing hands. But what to do about the darker side of "free?"

Sympathetic to the cash-short but clearly a realist, Lord told how casually kids copied computer games for each other. "There's a complete underground going on," he said, and he told how young hackers had secretly turned the IUMA archives into a site for stolen software. The mischief was hard to spot just by doing the usual check of the storage area.

"We deleted their stuff," Lord recalled, "and left a note saying, 'Leave us alone, you Rug Rats,' because it was clear there were 13-year-olds doing it. Some of the biggest pirates in the world are younger than 15."

His words rang true. Adolescents in the States were no match for the best pros abroad, but the teenaged pirates could still be awesomely well organized. One group of teens might crack the software. Another group might craft a slick screen telling who had defeated the protection. Lord told of a 13-year-old making $24,000 a year writing and selling shareware; and although the business was le-gitimate, this example showed the energy and brains out there among the young—in other words, the difficulty of fighting rip-offs.

Lord and Patterson were thinking about releasing IUMA offerings with digital identifiers that would make it easier to track down thieves. And yet another tack could be to design the music files that you could play only with the right digital keys. IUMA's owners were of GenNet; they were more interested in relying on technology than law to thwart pirates.

Piracy is one reason why major record companies feel uneasy about the Internet. Unable to ignore so large a mar-ket, they want help in getting their message across to the strange, young denizens. Warner paid IUMA to put short samples of music online, along with pictures and information about the artists. It was similar to what Patterson and Lord were doing already.

Now, however, like many others, the two were looking ahead to new business models. Lord had a bunch of possibilities in mind.

One was that people would pay if they liked what they heard, and maybe even give in advance. Another was that they would receive little gifts—maybe clay cats?—for making donations.

Patterson, however, offered some models that were more conventional. Gasp, his comments even sounded like an actual business plan.

First, he said, he and Lord would take orders for CDs and tapes online for companies such as Tower Records. Then IUMA would go the next step. It would sell files of music electronically. Fans would be able to use Web browsers like Netscape to encrypt credit card numbers so hackers couldn't intercept them. Eventually IUMA would sell music for instant listening without customers first having to transfer it to their hard disks. "There could be some kind of royalty treatment," Patterson said. "You might pay two cents every time you listened to a song. Or you could just buy an album." Some good possibilities existed here as long as no one gouged. If people could hear music with just a tiny investment up front, that might benefit new performers.

More immediately, IUMA was helping fledgling musicians and others by way of an informal support network. Sue Few, a Santa Cruz woman who'd formerly worked for record companies, went online with a newsletter called *Sound Check* and offered a stream of tips on subjects such as copyright law, musicians' unions, royalties, and lining up bookings. "Booking people aren't so bad, are they?" she wrote. "If they enjoy your tape and feel you'll fit well with their customers, you'll get booked—simple as that.

So they don't return your telephone calls—keep calling until you talk to a live person and still keep calling until you get an answer and a date from them."

IUMA itself was a calling card of sorts. Record companies and clubs could cruise the archives looking for bands to sign up.

Most important of all, however, IUMA helped potential fans and musicians get together. At the time I toured the IUMA area you could check out offerings by "Last 15 Bands" just uploaded to the archives, by artist, by label, by location, and by song title. Or you could click on a database with a number of options. I myself wanted to know more about Scott Brookman, who had written "When I Die You Can't Have My Organs," and who, as a result of IUMA, had been on National Public Radio.

A digitized photo showed him to be a bearded man with glasses. Something white was against his face, though I couldn't quite discern the shape. I hoped it wasn't a stray from an anatomy lab.

Messages on the screen said IUMA would let Netfolks listen to Brookman's "Organs" in stereo or mono. I clicked on the latter option and watched the bottom of my screen as it showed the number of bytes passing over the wires from a computer in California to my 486DX-class machine. Within 45 seconds I'd received a 119K file. In size it was equivalent to maybe 60 double-spaced, typewritten pages even though this was music not text.

"When I die," the lyrics wafted out of my stereo hooked to the 486, "you can't have my organs, though you think that you will need them . . ." If I'd had the right software on my machine, I could have heard several minutes' worth. The song was good even if, with my primitive sound software, it wasn't even AM in audio quality. My rather untrained ears picked up a Loudon Wainwright-ish edge to the music. I made a mental note to myself. When I was off my book deadline, I'd do what I should have done in the first place and install the MPEG software whose existence had helped make IUMA possible. I had heard only a little cut in another format. With MPEG I could have enjoyed three minutes' worth, and in better fidelity.

In the IUMA area Brookman said, "Organs" was "from my latest cassette release, 'They'll Nickel and Dime You to Death.' " He thought of his music "as a bizarre mix of stylistic parody, satire, self-referential, and meta-songs, full of clever guitar riffs and daring vocal harmonies. I write about personal heroes, local history, teenage memories, bits of folklore, and sometimes I make fun of rock music (lovingly, of course). Usually the result is intentionally funny . . ."

Brookman's inevitable pitch for money was reasonable enough. "I hope you enjoy the song, and I really think you should get yourself a copy of 'They'll Nickel and Dime You to Death.' Send a check for five bucks (no charge cards) made payable to Loser Records. That's a full 60 minutes of awesome music for only $5. Where else, other than a used record store, can you find that kind of entertainment bargain? Here's our address: Loser Records, P.O. Box 14719, Richmond, Virginia 23221." Hey, I'd already enjoyed a bargain, his delightful little fan area. I would remember the name Brookman.

People could leave feedback and I brought up some. "My colleagues and I agree—what a scream!!" read a note from Virginia, where Brookman lived. "I think we're going to track down your CD. Congrats on a nifty tune! It's good to hear a local band 'make it big.' " An Australian wrote in: "Heheheheh. Nice sense of humour." None other than Jon Luini, Kaiser of IUMA, said of "Organs": "I cannot get this song out of my head! The sincerity around this song is a great combination with the odd nature of the lyrics, especially when combined with the folk feel of the music. It makes me feel like it should be included whenever people first get their driver's license."

Brookman's electronic mail address was online, of course, together with those of listeners who had offered feedback. Anyone wanting to start a fan list focused on him would already have some names and e-mail addresses handy.

This was what the Net was so good for—not displaying Canteresque spam on behalf of Green Cards or pitches from CBS to join its fan club.

Small business actually enjoyed an advantage here. To CBS, fan mail must have been a nice a way of gauging the market. But the Brookmans of this world could go far beyond that and establish good rapport with fans, one by one—something for which the people at the CBS site would never have had time, given its volume. Small worked in other ways for Brookman. He or Loser Records (were they the same?) could do a short run of CDs and spread the news with minimum investment. Pressing a thousand CDs costs less than $2,000 nowadays. Combine that with the Net, and the music world just might be a little kinder to a young performer than it was in the days when Lord and Patterson were toiling away in the record stores back in Valencia.

Granted, a place in the IUMA archives was hardly a guarantee of success. A musician with the band Black Watch told me that she and her colleagues normally heard only from a fan or so a week. IUMA would *not* make a band instantly rich. On the other hand, she loved the feedback and encouragement that arrived from all over the world; and, we both thought, wasn't that important, too—not just the money? The music was finding its way to those who loved it. Besides, in the end, all the small fry might add up. Lord said that instead of one Madonna there might be fifty—"Maybe it will no longer make sense to have even one."[2] Perhaps, I hoped, the money instead would reach the Black Watches.

Once Lord had predicted that in several years IUMA might be "a one- or two-digit percentage of the $9 billion music industry."[3] I didn't know what would happen. Major record companies would surely be doing plenty on their own. And when I talked to Lord in April 1995, IUMA's annual revenues were still in the low six figures. But that could change, quickly. No matter what happened, IUMA was brilliant for a niched world in which millions were rebelling against the any-color-if-it's-black mindset.

We want just the right friends and spouse; the right home; the right coffee; the right newsgroups, now that they existed for all; and, yes, just the right music.

• • •

The same nichization is happening in the world of publishing—the Internet is home to hundreds if not thousands of electronic publications. So what's a hometown paper to do? Just how is *Time* magazine responding? And in such strange times—normal times, actually, once they've been around long enough—what becomes of books, especially when you consider the digital piracy issue. In the next chapter I'll lay out the problems and even suggest a few solutions.

CHAPTER

FOUR

Pulped Wood versus Electrons: Can the Print World Learn to Love the Net?

ran across A. C. Snow on the Internet the other day, and old memories poured forth.[1] A.C. is as low tech as they come. He writes a Tar Heelish column with jokes and stories about church picnics and football and beach trips, and yet there he was online with the folksy prose that I remembered from eons ago. The *Raleigh Times* is gone now. A.C. works instead for the bigger *News & Observer,* a sister newspaper that thudded against my dormitory door when I was in college. Weekday circulation is around 150,000 nowadays, and many state legislators wake up each morning to the *N & O*—it just might be the most powerful paper in North Carolina.

Millions of people on the Net, however, would question the need for the three-story tan brick building, the fleet of delivery trucks, and the recent decision to invest $36 million in color presses.

You can't update the ink on pulped trees the way you can move around dots on a computer screen. "Aren't

newspapers obsolete?" scads of techies are asking.
Besides, the Raleigh–Durham–Chapel Hill area has
changed. Thousands of locals swap e-mail addresses at
cocktail parties, while many schoolchildren grow up
reading off computer screens as well as from books. IBM
and other Fortune 500 companies are in Research
Triangle Park outside town.

Still, like the Raleigh area, the *N & O* has evolved. In a
nearby building, a small crew is putting out electronic
newspapers on the Internet and on a bulletin board system. This isn't just a pulp-and-ink-era newspaper company. It's also an Internet provider. Aided by two phone
companies, the *N & O* gives out free Internet service to
teachers and students to find out what the latter would
like online in the future. It's offered Netfolks a colorful,
multimedia tour of the state. Tens of thousands drop by
the *N & O* area each week. "The Internet is like the real
world—unorganized, unruly, and filled with more happenings than any one person can possibly track," says
Frank Daniels III, the paper's executive editor. "It's growing at a fantastic speed, and its citizens are literate. An opportunity for editors!" [2]

Not everyone on the print side feels as he does. When
a *Washington Post* writer did a gossipy little item on Cliff
Stoll's net.exposé, the journalist said book editors were
looking forward to reviewing *Silicon Snake Oil* as "confirmation of what they hoped was true all along." [3] That may
or may not have been a joke. Whatever the case, a war is
going on between pulped wood and electrons. Can commercial publications, from newspapers to book publishers, learn to love the Internet, and what does this mean to
us readers?

"There is no doubt in my mind that the Net will force a
transformation of newspapers," says Peter Lewis, a cyberspace writer for the *New York Times,* "but demise? That's
what they said about radio and television as well." [4] Just
the same, a headline in *Wired* magazine said online news-

papers "still suck." Many newspapers are too enamored
with the traditional models where editors and writers inflict whatever they want on the unsuspecting public. They
don't give their readers enough of a chance to speak back
online or communicate with each other. Still, the best electronic publications can indeed be two way. And more and
more of them will be packaged for the medium. You'll be
able to read summaries of stories, for example, and then
summon up longer versions with a click of the mouse.

Even ads may improve. "Think of the typical print tire
ad," says Teresa Martin, an online expert with the Knight-
Ridder newspaper chain. "*Yawn.* But what if touching each
tire bought up detailed specs about it, or the sizes in which
the store currently has it in stock—or even some really
cool car careening around a racetrack with the voice-over
'speed rated'? The ad can be like a window to a store, enticing the reader in to look for information."

I know—computers are too hard for many technophobes to learn, too big to use in bed, and often too blurry
or flickery to read off of; and batteries are forever eager
for their next charge. But life will get better. It will happen faster if governments worry less about smartening
up TV sets and more about smartening up schoolchildren
with programs that drive down the cost of book-friendly
computers. Much, however, is already going on. Xerox,
for example, has experimented with a computer screen
whose output is as sharp as printing on paper. It's a
power hog, but less hungry screens are coming. Writing
in *Digital Media,* Martin says the right hardware could be
a mere six years away.[5] I myself think—based on my
monitoring of technical publications—that her estimate
is conservative.

Besides, even now, electronic texts can at least comple-
ment the paper kind. For example, they can increase the
variety of newspapers, books, and magazines available.
After U.S. Senator Jesse Helms joked that Bill Clinton
would need a bodyguard to protect him from angry service

people who resented his military policies, I did not rely just on the *Washington Post* for details. I called up the story directly from the *News & Observer* hundreds of miles away. What's more, it's easy to wander from one electronic publication to others when you are after facts on the same topic, or to search back issues of newspapers and magazines. Even novelists are discovering the possibilities of the new media. Readers can choose their own endings or pass on suggestions to the authors of works in progress.

Adventurous media people are trying to adapt to this online world as gracefully as they can, and the Internet is oh so enticing to many. The cost of the technology has fallen to the point where a bare-bones newspaper can go on the World Wide Web by investing as little as $5,000–$10,000 up front. Publishers needn't divvy up revenue with a commercial online service, such as America Online or CompuServe.

Compared to pulped wood, the Net looks better and better—the price of paper shot up some 30 percent between the fall of 1994 and the spring of 1995. Environmental regulators are forcing the pulp mills to quit sullying the air and the water, and new mills can cost half a billion dollars each to build. "Like the rest of us," writes Jonathan Seybold, publisher of *Digital Media,* "the paper company executives read all of the press stuff about the Information Highway, the rise of online services, and the decline of paper-based publishing." And he says they are now asking, "Why should we invest in a new paper mill?" The result? Newsprint shortages and higher prices. "The fear," Seybold says, "creates its own reality."[6]

More than 100 newspapers either are on the Internet or are planning to be there. The *New York Times,* for example, has used the World Wide Web to transmit a fax edition condensed from the normal paper. A full-grown *Times* may be on the Net now. The *San Jose Mercury News* in California not only is online, it offers a service called News Hound. For just $10 a month, the Hound will automatically scan a mas-

sive database from Knight-Ridder papers and additional
dailies, then e-mail you the latest articles on the cover girls
of *Sports Illustrated*, on Afghanistan, on the Chicago Bears,
on Bill Clinton, or on any other topic that quickens your
pulse or makes you reach for your Valium. From the
Halifax Daily News to Poland's *Gazeta Wyborcza*, newspapers are trying the Net. Even a strike paper, published by
reporters of the San Francisco *Examiner* and *Chronicle*,
made it into cyberspace.

Some Netfolks preferred the strike daily to the electronic spin-offs of the regular ones, and I wasn't surprised. What applies to business applies to newspapers:
The Net is a great equalizer in some ways; a small newspaper can reach as far-flung a readership as an international daily. In fact, the first paper on the World Wide
Web just might have been the *Palo Alto Weekly* from
Silicon Valley. South Africa's *Mail & Guardian,* a 30,000-
circulation weekly, finds the Internet a much cheaper
way to reach people overseas than air-mail. Devoted to
Russian news, the *St. Petersburg Press* uses the Internet to
serve an English-speaking audience throughout the
world. The *London Telegraph* has shown up on the Net
with some striking graphics. No longer is the Internet just
for little magazines published by techies and smart young
English majors.

Time Warner has put *Time, People, Entertainment
Weekly*, and a shelf full of other magazines in a colorful,
well-done area of the World Wide Web. Readers can
praise and flame the editors and each other. Hearst magazines have their own area. *PC Magazine,* one of the
giants of the Ziff-Davis chain, enraged many Netfolks
with clueless articles suggesting a rather thorough ignorance of the Internet and its reasons for existence. But
guess what. Now Ziff-Davis has a wonderful Web area
with generous samples from its magazines, including *PC.*
The German newsmagazine *Der Spiegel* is on the World
Wide Web, too, complete with some news in English;

from Japan, specialized publications serve Net audiences ranging from gays to office workers.

I learned of the most dramatic use of cyberspace by a magazine just as I was finishing this book. *Omni,* the popular science publication, said it would forsake monthly paper editions in favor of a version on America Online, augmented by just four print editions, one each quarter. It expected to save some $4 million a year. The newsletter *Interactive Week Publishing Alert* raised some valid questions—copies of back articles from *Omni* were too hard to locate—but even if the grand experiment failed, the model was out there. A major publication was more or less forsaking pulped wood in favor of computer networks.

Book publishers are catching up with newspapers and magazines. Time Warner, Random House, Macmillan, and McGraw-Hill use the Internet for promotion, and they will distribute more and more of their books this way. Free classics like *A Tale of Two Cities* have been a staple of the Net for years, thanks to voluntary efforts such as Project Gutenberg. And now you can pay a few dollars to download a short story by Stephen King or works by many others.

Meanwhile, however, some old-fogey publishers view the Internet as an unfathomable virus transmitted via cable. That's especially true of the book business. People in it fear a massive bootlegging of their wares. Using the Net, you can even pirate paper books; there is no technical reason why machines cannot scan the latest from Philip Roth or Tom Clancy, convert their novels to bits and bytes, and zap them to your friends in Juneau. Software-based copy protection could help safeguard electronic books. But I myself think there are other solutions as well—for example, a national library fund to make free or low-cost books practical and reduce the incentive for bootlegging.

Paper publishers also complain that if electronic books are cheaper to create and distribute, manuscripts will receive less editing. With a good library system in effect, however, a way would exist to highlight works of merit—marketers would enjoy less clout and we'd see fewer best-sellers on astrology and more on history. And without the distribution costs, more money could go to writers and editors.

Other obstacles also exist in the minds of publishers eyeing the Internet. Some worry about finding a market for text offered through a global network. And certain people in the book industry also dread the competition from the many gigabytes of free material that the Internet offers. Didn't Samuel Johnson know best?—No one but a blockhead ever wrote except for money. If nothing else, many word people are captives of their senses. They hate reading off computer screens; they want to hear a newspaper thunk against their doors, hold Section A in their hands, hear it rattle, sniff the ink.

Going in the other direction, many people on the Internet love to bash the print world as benighted and even a little worthless. Who needs publishers when you can post your own books and little magazines for the world to read on the Net? That's simplistic in many cases; I've got a little more faith in the editors at Knopf or Viking than I do in the proofreading gang from the Department of Chemistry or Joe's Literary Bar.

People on the Net, however, are right to criticize the print media's ignorance of electronic publishing and computer networks. If nothing else, many traditional publishers fail to grasp the potential here. Looking at the old, underpowered machines that clutter their offices, they may believe that computers won't progress from there. An intelligent staffer with a publishers group— someone I respected on other matters—didn't understand the promise of computers for reading e-books. I shared this story with Robin Peek of Simmons College, who coedited a book on electronic publishing for the American Society for Information Science and the M.I.T.

Press. She told me that many book publishers just hoped that computers wouldn't improve until the publishers died or retired. Computers keep stubbornly getting better, though; blurry screens and fragile hard disks won't always be the order of day.

More amazingly, a popular magazine misinformed some of us Netfolks that we were "netgods." Didn't our Internet addresses end with a prestigious ".net" rather than ".com" (the designation for a commercial site) or ".edu" (for a school site)? Strange. Anyone can pay $14 a month to ClarkNet or many other services and automatically get an address like rothman@clark.net. So much for my godliness.

Zeuslike, however, I'll hurl thunderbolts at Harper-Collins and Doubleday. The former published the book that the immigration lawyers in Arizona used to justify the off-topic ads that they had inflicted on thousands of newsgroups. The Canter and Siegel guide was in the same class as astrology books. It talked about spending just $.0333 per thousand users per month to reach 30 million people on the Net. Most of the people, however, can only use e-mail and aren't on Usenet or the Web. Doubleday erred in other ways. It let Cliff Stoll smear cyberspace as "devoid of warmth and human kindness." Devoid? A rather all-encompassing word. In both cases the paper publishers were entering an unknown world.

To give another example, a *New Yorker* article lamented the destruction of library catalogues without really telling how electronic libraries could do the job better. The article went on about the handwritten annotations on the cards, and I could see the point here. Couldn't a card for a Civil War book include an informal recommendation for a book on Antietam or Gettysburg? Must all cross-references be official? So I could appreciate writer Nicholson Baker's worry about the fate of those beautiful wooden cabinets. What he played down, however, is that technology can let electronic librarians create quick paths from one work to another.[7]

Far from being exotic nowadays, this technology is the essence of the World Wide Web. So if you looked up a general item on the Civil War, you might see some annotated references to an item on Antietam, and go there instantly with a click of the mouse.

Just as wrongly, an article in the *Atlantic Monthly* of September 1994 said future electronic books could perish because they used many disk formats. "The End of the Book?" asked the headline over T. J. Max's doomsaying. But CD-ROMs and books on floppy disk are just transitions. Unless legislators interfere in the most ham-handed of ways, computer networks should be the natural homes for electronic books. They could reach us more cheaply, and in greater varieties, without the bottleneck of physical bookstores. So disk standards should be just plain irrelevant in the end. The true raison d'etre for the Internet is its ability to let many kinds of machines share information without the least worry about floppies or magnetic tape. Must of the time I don't know if my no-name IBM clone is talking to a Mac or a $5-million mainframe. Besides, we mustn't preserve books just physically; in a videocentric era we also need to help them survive in the minds of readers, particularly those outside the elite. We should spread books far and wide, then, and make the technology as friendly to words as possible.

But tell that to Max. In his eagerness to put down electronic text, Max depicted the *print* version of *Wired* magazine as hypocritical. He wrote:

> *Although* Wired *communicates extensively by e-mail with its readers, conducts forums, and makes back issues available on-line, its much-repeated goal of creating a magazine—currently called* HotWired— *that is especially designed to exist electronically*

remains fuzzy. For the moment this is no open
democracy, and Wired *is no computer screen—its*
bright graphics would make a fashion magazine en-
vious. Wired *celebrates what doesn't yet exist by ex-*
ploiting a format that does: it's as if a scribe copied
out a manuscript extolling the beauty that would
one day be print.

Strange. Just what's so odd about using old technology
to spread word of alternatives, especially the dazzling
e-magazines that already enliven the Web? When Nicholas
Negroponte published *Being Digital* (New York: Knopf,
1995), a bestselling collection of his lively *Wired* essays,
some Generation Xers bought it not for themselves but for
their parents—which was exactly what Negroponte wanted.

Max is especially off target about *HotWired*. Today,
just months after he wrote of the publishers' "fuzzy" goal,
the magazine is one of the most successful on the Net with
far more than 100,000 readers. It makes massive use of
hyperlinks—the technology I described by way of the Civil
War example. Within discussion areas, readers can create
links from their posts to text, pictures, and sound elsewhere in the World Wide Web, including their own electronic pages—they needn't confine themselves to tiny
letters to the editor. Simply put, *HotWired* both praises and
exemplifies the new medium.

I couldn't care less, moreover, if this electronic magazine runs long articles that have come out in print or
could have—just so *HotWired* also gives me new material.
Not everyone on the Internet reads the printed *Wired*. One
of joys of the Net, moreover, is the ability to offer greater
levels of detail for those wanting it. What a grouch Max is.
He might as well be a monk lecturing Gutenberg about
the glories of calligraphy.

Even *PC Magazine*, one of my favorites, at times can
be all wet about the Internet and related topics. A columnist suggested that most people on the Net be forced to pay

for each letter sent out; supposedly, Netfolks were too quick to e-mail each other. Excuse me. Such an approach could kill off many of the mailing lists through which academics and nonacademics swap ideas and research notes en masse. A very small fee based on actual costs and Net congestion? Maybe. But not one designed to minimize use. To the columnist, however, the Net's role as a petri dish may count less than its promise as a corporate mailman. He misses a major point. The Internet is one of the planet's cheapest ways to transmit knowledge, including the kind that might cure cancer or give us a 150-mpg automobile. While commerce on the Net is laudable, we need those mailing lists as well—and not just for professors but public schools, libraries, charities, psychological support groups, and activists of all ideologies, to name just a few of the better examples. The economics of the Net will make this possible, especially as bandwidths increase to accommodate greater use of audio and video—text just won't cost that much. Alas, the columnist in this instance failed to understand the Internet and its possibilities.

I myself won't claim omniscience about the Net. Once I saw a message on a mailing list from someone pushing for a huge National Knowledge Foundation to benefit educators, librarians, journalists, and investigators. The post mentioned international topics, among others, and flares went off in my head. I posted some sharply critical, journalistic questions, wondering if the post had come from a CIA type. Some people on the list cheered me on while I pressed for public answers. It turned out that the post *was* from a former Company man, and as I persisted in querying Robert David Steele about his funding and motives, he sent me a colorfully worded note that might have made a Paris Island drill instructor envious. I quoted his e-mail, as I would have done if writing this up for a magazine. What a way to justify my fears of the intelligence establishment playing too powerful a role in determining the content of material online. I remembered the valuable exposés that the press had done of the CIA years ago; we need to separate U.S. journalists from spies, lest impartiality of the news media suffer. This debate I would win.

But I didn't. In fact, I suffered a major debacle; flame after flame from bystanders assailed *me*. Even though I told Robert Steele I wanted public answers, people felt that I had violated the traditional prohibition against quoting private posts in public, at least with names attached. Some of the bluntest Anglo-Saxonisms came from luminaries on the Internet. People wanted perfect freedom to speak their minds in messages deemed private, just as professors and students in class would want to be free to say outrageous things without ending up on the front pages of the local paper. I, on the other hand, had applied journalistic expectations to the Net. A reporter might end up with a better story if a celebrity exploded during an interview and this fact came out in print. But on the Internet, the freedom to be outrageous in private mattered more than the freedom to quote, even with advanced warning. Yes, I had questions about this custom. What if people took advantage of this Netiquette to engage in sexual or racial abuse, or just abuse, period? Should rules really be hard and fast? Just the same, in Net terms, I was the loser here because I wore my Writer Hat at the wrong time.

Luckily the story ended happily. Robert Steele and I, while disagreeing, made our peace. I went to one of his conferences and shook his hand. Later I happily discovered that he shared my hatred of the Clipper chip, the loathsome White House scheme to make it easier to snoop on citizens' communications. He was far more open-minded than I'd originally expected. Even without that consideration, however, a feud just didn't make sense here. Canter and Siegel may claim you can reach 30 million people in one swoop, but as I say repeatedly, the Net is a *series* of communities, some of them rather small-townish. Within our somewhat overlapping circles, it would have been mutually harmful for Robert Steele and me to squander time and reputations on a protracted flame war.

Other kinds of clashes take place between Internet culture and that of traditional media types; in the eyes of many people on the Net, print people are not the only villains. *Dateline NBC* ran a story about children using computer connections to locate recipes for making bombs. The children, however, could have done the same at bookstores or public libraries. *Dateline*'s episode reminded one Netizen of the time NBC secretly used a hidden ignition system to show that an automobile could explode. Just as bizarrely, in print and on the air, some journalists love stories about the Internet as a playground for child molesters. If we on the Net were a religious or ethnic group, we could start an antidefamation league and keep it forever busy.

By Net standards, the media bumble in yet other ways. If you're a newspaper or magazine journalist, you may have been reared to neuter yourself about The News; no opinions online, please. On the Net, however, many people are suspicious if you do *not* join the crowd and speak out. They dislike net-thropologists; that is, media people and others who study the Net rather than contribute to it. Among some journalists the standard modus operandi is to post questions for an article, then vanish without sharing anything with the Netfolks.

Happily, this is changing somewhat. In fact, you can find a few journalists from the *New York Times, Wall Street Journal, Washington Post*, and other major papers speaking up online about matters dear to them. Recently a reader flamed the *Post* for its Internet coverage ("what those idiots at the *Post* write isn't worth minimum wage"). Alluding to software that can screen out messages from offensive people, reporter John Schwartz punched right back: "It's bozo filter time." He had been using online services for years, and here, it showed. The old stereotype, in which all members of the major media are clueless, just doesn't fly any more. Not too long ago somebody shared a *New York Times* article—discussing some other people's proposal for a national digital library—with hundreds of a members of a list devoted to law in cyberspace. He did not ask permission from the *Times*. A pithy reference to copyright law then emanated from none other than Peter Lewis, who had written the article and was a regular on the list.

So how are Netfolks treating Lewis nowadays? He e-mailed back an answer in prose worthy of a discussion group on the Internet itself:

> *It took me a while to get used to being flamed by pencil-dicked geeks who hide behind their terminals, saying things I'm sure they'd never dream of saying to my face. But now I've become something of a connoisseur of flamage, and while I regret that it is widespread on the Net, I regret more that the quality of flaming is almost uniformly weak. I now savor good flames and ignore the rest. On the other hand, it took me almost as long to get used to having instant feedback, often pointed and critical and right-on, to my writing. While there is a danger of a "chilling effect" from flamage, perhaps subtly influencing reporters to back off a subject in anticipation of a flood of "Dear Clueless" letters, I think the overall benefit of instant and widespread reader feedback is a Good Thing. Perhaps all rookie reporters should be required to write a Net story just to let them know that they do not write in a vacuum, whether their beat is the Internet or the police station or sports.*

Like the police beat, the Internet comes with its set of rules—as my experience with the CIA alum vividly showed. Some on the Net attach a statement to every post saying it's copyrighted. Others just worry that the wrong set of people may read and quote their more outspoken messages. Lewis considers list and newsgroup posts to be public: "My mother once advised me, long before she knew I would be a journalist, 'Never put anything on paper that you wouldn't want to see on the front page of the *New York Times.*'"

Still, Lewis normally catches up with the writers of posts he plans to quote. "However, the reason has more to do with verification than with netiquette. In cyberland as well as in the real world, as you know, the fact that someone's name and address appear in a letter does not guarantee the identity of the writer." Lewis reminded me that "half a century ago some newspapers forbade reporters from quoting sources contacted by telephone on the same rationale: How do you really know that was Mr. Doe on the phone if you didn't see him? In cyberville, not only can we not see our sources, but neither can we hear them." And then a few sentences later came the electronic signature, "Pete (at least, you *think* it's Pete) Lewis."[8]

Other challenges exist online. When reporters use e-mail for interviews, they take away the element of surprise—often the surest route to the best answer. "Also," says Jordan Green, a Canadian freelancer who relies heavily on e-mail, "there is no body language or voice intonation in e-mail. We do have our various symbols to >>>highlight<<< and _emphasize_ WORDS and feelings :-) but there is far more which cannot be picked up."

In the end, however, computer networks will make the press better informed, not worse. Via Lycos, for example, a searching tool on the Web, I can track down files written by just the right person to interview or find background information that someone archived from the relevant newsgroup. Besides, who says that all interviews are confrontational? Often e-mail is just right, and I can always use the telephone to fill in gaps. "I used to ask, 'What's your fax number?' at the end of a phone interview," says a magazine writer named Peggy Noonan.[9] "Now I also ask, 'What's your e-mail address' because it's often much faster to post a question or send a draft for approval via e-mail than by another means." Some journalists might object to showing drafts to sources. But Noonan clearly sees the networks as a godsend for other purposes as well.

Another believer is Arik Hesseldahl, a young reporter with the *Idaho State Journal* in Pocatello who, like many journalists of his generation, grew accustomed to the technology in college. "Remember that flesh-eating bug scare a few months ago?" he said. "I got in touch with a doctor in England who debunked all the rumors and media hype, which is what it was—hype. Just today I am looking for an expert on nuclear fuel reprocessing equipment who is untainted by the Department of Energy and the rest of the federal nuke bureaucracy. Already I've gotten five suggestions for experts."

I myself see other advantages for people in the pulpedwood world; via the Net I don't just approach editors—I hear from them out of the blue when they like my postings. Other freelancers have also benefited. Steven Sander Ross, a professor at Columbia University, uses the Net to communicate with European magazines that pay better than those in the States. Just as the Net creates global markets for florists and sellers of teddy bears, it multiplies opportunities for the best writers. That is true for newspaper and magazine writers now and will be increasingly true for authors of books. Mind you, there is a downside, too. The Net may actually *hurt* the worst writers as they face more competition, whether from professionals across the planet or from the free material that Netfolks share with each other.

Here are three case histories that should be of interest to writers, editors, publishers, and the rest of the cosmos:

• Case History 1. The *News & Observer* has used the Internet not only to reach the denizens but also to get existing readers and advertisers on the Net. In an era when so many greedsters hope to charge outrageous fees to consumers for online information, the *N & O* is hoping that ads will pay much or even most of the freight.

- Case History 2. Time Warner, as noted, is putting magazines and book excerpts on the Internet, and it's doing so in ways befitting the medium. Many of the same concepts carry over from online newspapers, which is why this section and the next will be much shorter than Case History 1. In fact, so far, an *N & O*-style business model seems to be influencing Time at least somewhat.
- Case History 3. Laura Fillmore runs an online bookstore that not only sells books but *gives them away* on the Internet. She even used the Net to promote a pulped-wood book that has sold hundreds of thousands of copies. Fillmore's ideas are significant because she is working hard to reconcile publishers' needs with those of society at large, and I commend one of her business models as an alternative to pay-per-read gouges. The ultimate answer, in my own opinion, is a national digital library and a program to drive down the cost of book-friendly hardware. Using this approach—a mix of editorial and technical wizardry to add to the value of plain text—good publishers would flourish. Readers and writers would come out ahead, too.

Finally, I'll offer an update on the *N & O* and other publications on the Internet. When Frank Daniels described the Net as "unorganized" and "unruly," he might also have been talking about certain trends in his own industry. A surprising twist unfolded in the story of the *N & O*.

Newspapers on the Net: The Raleigh Experiment

More than two decades ago in a scuffy-floored room at the University of North Carolina, not that far from the *N & O*, I heard Professor Walter Spearman expound on the prickly question of uppity letters to the editor. What if a reader taunted, "You'll never print this"? The crux of Walt

Spearman's wisdom was this: *Don't go for the bait. If you don't want to print it, don't.*[10] He was teaching me to be, in modern parlance, a "gatekeeper"—to decide which news and opinions made it into print and which didn't. Only so many column inches existed on the editorial page, and we journalists were to watch over this space as if it were the Mona Lisa. Without the slightest apology, we should tell the public what to read, and besides lording over the editorial pages, we should inflict the same front page stories on everyone. The notion that each reader could write regularly for other readers, or that he or she could see wire service stories online, was as sacrilegious as it was science fiction–like.

By the end of the 1970s, however, at Duke, UNC, and N.C. State, hackers were paving the way for Usenet, a series of discussion areas on the Internet and on bulletin board systems that let *everyone* have a say—from Nazis to Maoists. Together with talk radio and with other forms of computer communications, Usenet could help Americans bypass the gatekeepers. Readers wouldn't see on their screens an appealing combination of headlines and Times Roman type. But no blue pencils would be around to scratch out the heresies of nonjournalists.

Usenet in the end wouldn't just carry alt.activism or comp.general or alt.sex; it would also be home to a nice little electronic newspaper called ClariNet, which in 1995 enjoyed 100,000-plus readers, and which each day let readers choose from among hundreds of dispatches from Reuters, the Associated Press, and more specialized services. My friend Jim Besser covered Washington for a string of Jewish newspapers. He could dial up ClariNet, other sections of Usenet, and the Internet at large and see material that might take days and days to wend its way into the *Washington Post,* assuming it ever got there at all. Usenet in the end was more of a wire service than a newspaper; that just may have been its real triumph. Some old print people hated ClariNet, seeing it as a threat to their gatekeeping. For a while, ClariNet sent out the columns of Dave Barry, the quirky but popular humorist enjoyed by thousands of Netheads. Then, however, his syndicate pulled him off the service. Illegal copies had wafted all over the Internet, and the bootlegging had surely outraged client newspapers—the main reason; but a second, minor one may have existed as well—the hostility between the Net and many members of the print media.

The Internet was partly why Michael Crichton, the author of the novel *Jurassic Park*, could shrug off newspapers and some other mass media as "tomorrow's fossil fuel." The Cable News Network and radio talk shows are not the only threats to the hegemony of the old-time gatekeepers. So are the Internet, CompuServe, America Online, GEnie, Delphi, and, of course, the more than 50,000 bulletin board systems run by hobbyists and others. "Newspapers," wrote the media critic Jon Katz, "have been foundering for decades, their readers aging, their revenues declining, their circulations sinking, their sense of mission fragmented in a world where the fate of presidents is slugged out on MTV, *Donahue*, and *Larry King Live*."

I was fascinated, then, to learn that the old *News & Observer* was on the Net now. Was the *N & O* serving readers better? With the above in mind I spent several week talking to the Raleigh people on the phone and via e-mail, and studying the electronic versions of the newspaper, both the free samples on the Net and the version for paying customers.

My conclusions were positive, though not entirely. Katz, the author of the "Still Suck" article in *Wired*, would have disliked some aspects of the *N & O*'s electronic efforts. *Wired* had asked, "How can an industry which regularly pulls Doonesbury strips for being too controversial possibly hope to survive online?" And, sure enough, if you were on the Internet by way of the *N & O*'s service in fall 1994, you couldn't subscribe to the alt.sex string of newsgroups. Moreover, unlike the *Time* areas online, the *N & O*'s BBS had not sprouted hundreds of messages from free-spirited readers and editors. Truly controversial postings were rare. And yet the editors were clearly moving away from the traditional gatekeeping role. Meanwhile, the *N & O* was enriching the Internet by way of well-written news stories and features—many available for free. Flaws aside, this was a fine example of how the print media could befriend the Net and the young people who favored computer screens over pulped wood.

Frank Daniels III, the executive editor, tinkered with computers himself in high school two decades ago, and as early as the late 1980s he was using Macs to shuffle around stories on the pages of a magazine that his family owned in Charlotte, North Carolina. Working with a stock analyst, Daniels created a computerized database of the top fifty companies in the Charlotte area, and that, in turn, led to a newsletter. So early on, Daniels saw how high tech could spawn lucrative opportunities. He also saw the negatives. The owners of the *Los Angeles Times,* Knight-Ridder, and other organizations were experimenting with Videotext, which allowed news stories to scroll across television screens.

Such endeavors were brave. They were also premature. Videotext at the time cost the customers too much, and just as the Prodigy service would err later on in the same way, the newspapers failed to appreciate the fondness of many customers for typing to each other. Reading news stories and shopping from home weren't enough.

Many U.S. dailies would go on to flounder even on pulped wood. Whether Americans were watching videocassettes or hang gliding, millions had other uses for their time, especially baby boomers. Some 60 percent of the households in Wake County had once subscribed to the *N & O;* by the late 1980s, just 40 percent did. Newspapers kissed off much of the market, jacked up their prices, and began seeing themselves as a way for advertisers to reach at least the Oldsmobile set if not the BMW set. And yet, even by those criteria, the *N & O* was a slacker. Back then, as it does today, the Raleigh–Durham–Chapel Hill area boasted one of the highest concentrations of Ph.D.s in the country. Some 40 percent of the households now own computers, more than 10 percent can go online, and the average home price is well on the way to equaling that of some major metropolitan areas. Even five years ago, and long before, high tech was enriching the Research Triangle.

But would the *N & O* adapt to this new market, a harbinger for many other areas in the United States and elsewhere? Frank Daniels saw the newspaper as a change-proof antique, and he was ready to dump his *N & O* stock and sink the money into an online service.

Then Daniels got some journalistic religion at a news-paper seminar, the secular equivalent of a good Baptist soaking. To hear him tell it, he suddenly understood that "the relationship between a newspaper and a community has such a richness and history that communities shouldn't lose that." And he felt that online services could take advantage of those relationships with readers and advertisers. Today the *N & O* goes by this philosophy, not entirely but to a great extent. Readers can e-mail many of their favorite writers, while long-time advertisers can buy *X* number of column inches in the paper editions and re-ceive exposure in the electronic editions.

Something else, however, may have bound Frank Daniels to his paper as well—old family stories and the memories they stirred. The first Daniels landed in North Carolina several hundred years ago, and the family re-unions continue to this day. Frank III's great-grandfather, Josephus Daniels, purchased the *N & O* at a bankruptcy auction in 1894. He carried on as one of the state's more colorful and outspoken publishers, with a strong populist streak, and took time off in Washington to serve as secre-tary of the Navy under Woodrow Wilson. I ran across Josephus on the Internet, just as serendipitously as I had

found A. C. Snow. Through the American Memory Project
at the Library of Congress, I could *hear* Josephus honor two
naval heroes with a speech called "There Is No Rank in
Sacrifice." I passed on word of my discovery to Bruce
Siceloff, an online editor, and he played another Daniels'
speech for the clan while showing off the paper's marvels of
technology. Frank Jr., publisher of the *N & O*, tapped the
arm of a cousin who had just walked into the room. "That's
your grandfather," he said as the spooky old wax recording
crackled away in its new electronic incarnation.[11]

Josephus, though his racial views softened, reflected
the separatism of many Carolinians in the first half of the
twentieth century. The paper itself changed. It eventually
hired Claude Sitton, a Pulitzer winner notable for his civil
rights reporting in his days with the *New York Times.* The
N & O in some ways became the *Times South.* Reporters
fought racial injustices. Frank III portrayed the paper of
that era as never having met a cause it didn't like. What's
more, he said the *N & O*, although exposing politicians on
the take, was too quick to editorialize for local programs
that raised local tax rates. I myself favored the crusading
kind of newspaper—in fact, one risk of a high-tech orientation was that it could turn a newspaper into an uncritical
cheerleader for business if editors were not careful—but I
could understand Daniels' concern over government
spending. At any rate some felt that the *N & O* was losing
touch with many readers, and so Frank Jr. and the others
on the board of directors agreed to let Frank III serve as
executive editor in the wake of Sitton's retirement.

The contrast between the old and new editors couldn't
have been more stark. Sitton was a formal man who in-
sisted that his reporters wear suits and ties. Frank III relaxed the dress code. In place of a sign with his editorial
title, he stuck up one that said simply, "Frat Man." Old-
timers groaned that this young Duke alum lacked enough
journalistic experience. The man had been the newspaper's *operations manager.* Wasn't it apparent? For each

year of experience on the State side of newspapering, you could subtract two years of experience with the Church.

Even under Sitton, the reporters typed away on a modern publishing system for newspapers. But that was more or less all they did—write. Many could just as well have been pounding away on old Smith Coronas. They hadn't any desire to learn the technology, not when there were doors to knock on, vote counts to check, political corruption to chronicle, Ku Klux Klan rallies to report, and courthouse records to search the old-fashioned way. Young Daniels set to work changing all that, and with the most surpassing of allies. The news librarians almost instantly grasped the potential of computerized databases. So did Pat Stith, the senior investigative reporter. The *N & O* would go on to collect state records showing traffic or hunting violations, or others, and then seek out patterns. "We analyzed all the speeding tickets," said Daniels, "and found out what percentage of tickets were given at each mile-per-hour level. It turns out that if you go 63 miles per hour in a 55-mile-per-hour zone, you have less than a 1 percent chance of getting a ticket." Via the same quantitative techniques, the *N & O* could evaluate the programs of local government. By the time Daniels had effected his transformation, he had squeezed dozens of personal computers into an already-crowded newsroom.

A year or so after Frank Daniels III became executive editor, he first beheld the Internet over at North Carolina State. "An engineering student said, 'Have you seen this?' and he showed me Usenet. And about forty-five minutes later, while I was thirty minutes late for a meeting, I was speechless. I walked out. I was just buzzing with the possibilities." Daniels saw some engineering newsgroups and, yes, some sexually related ones. "I couldn't believe how many people I saw talking together, just following each other's conversations. The letters to the editor at the time were the only connection the *News & Observer* had with its readers.

"Our business is connecting people. Here was a whole world that existed without our knowledge. It was a small world and an elitist world, but it confirmed my earlier belief that computers were going to be ubiquitous."

Effortlessly Daniels understood that Usenet wasn't Videotext—people *wanted* you to talk back. So the Internet was at least on his mind as a possibility for the time when the numbers were right. Daniels for the moment pushed into less exotic areas; for example, he started a useful, lively, but expensive fax newsletter for the elite, *The Insider*, which covered North Carolina politics with a commitment to detail missing from the daily press. The *N & O* also offered sophisticated research services, using the databases it was amassing. And the paper let readers dial up stories over the telephone through a technology known as Audiotext.

The electronic action, however, really took off after Daniels hired George Schlukbier, a computer-oriented librarian who had worked wonders at the *Sacramento Bee*. Like Daniels the frat boy, Schlukbier flaunted a few eccentricities within bounds. An electronic signature at the bottom of his Internet messages identified him as "Chief Bull Goose Looney," a tribute to the giant Indian who terrorized Nurse Ratched in *One Flew Over the Cuckoo's Nest*, the Ken Kesey novel. Some, of course, might argue that the Internet is itself a virtual asylum with the inmates in charge.

Schlukbier and Daniels checked out Prodigy and America Online to see about getting on those networks and decided that the numbers stank. Yes, Prodigy-style services already had their networks in place, and the *Los Angeles Times* and papers in George, New York and elsewhere would go on to sign up. But the *N & O* concluded—rightly, in my opinion—that the online services would need the newspapers more than the newspapers would need the online services. Newspapers were the best source of steady, detailed news about local communities.

Each year the *N & O* spent $12 million covering mainly
local and state news, an amount that even a giant like
Prodigy could not replicate everywhere. "They've got their
view of the world that's defined by whatever technology
they adopted at the time they started their service,"
Daniels would later say. "We got uncomfortable with the
fact we'd be living their rules, and the customers would be
their customers."[12]

Some other newspapers felt happy with Prodigy. "No,"
said Mike Gordon, an editor with Cox Newspapers in
Atlanta, "Prodigy isn't taking most of the money." What's
more, his online edition could enjoy revenue from online
ads. Still, more and more publishers were turning to the
Internet rather than Prodigy-type alternatives, and the
balance of power changed. When Microsoft started a new
online service later, it offered newspapers as much as 80
percent of revenue—at least several times the amount that
Prodigy had offered the *N & O*. (The Atlanta papers would
themselves end up on the Internet eventually, not just on
Prodigy.)

Instead of relying on a Prodigy-style service, Schlukbier
started a locally oriented BBS with an Internet connection
and a strong emphasis on schoolchildren, not just the
adult readers of today. This orientation may have baffled
many. Some newspaper publishers were too myopic to see
past the next quarter, especially if they worked for the big
chains. Exceptions did exist, of course. Knight-Ridder, for
example, regardless of its public ownership and its
Videotext flop, was still pouring millions into the new
technology. As a family-owned newspaper, however, without security analysts breathing down its corporate neck,
the *N & O* was especially free to experiment. Schlukbier
believed that a decade would pass before 40 or 50 percent
of the homes in Raleigh were online, and by then the children would be of customer age.

"By focusing on third-graders," Schlukbier said, "I've
got ten years to learn from them what information they

really need and want."[13] What they hoped for, in many ways, didn't seem, like a newspaper at all. Rather they wanted their own tools. The bulletin board blossomed with imaginary worlds in which, for example, Frank Daniels was the owner of a fictitious newsstand. Children could wend their ways through cyberspace by using written descriptions and computer commands to tell where they were and what they were doing. George Schlukbier's young son, Shane, designed a mythical camp online with danger-ridden woods. Some may have wondered how this applied to *newspapers;* I myself did. And then it dawned: if newspapers would be increasingly two-way in the future, just like the Net, then didn't it make sense to see how the children interacted with each other, as they did in role-playing games? The children could change as they grew older, or moved away from the area when their parents packed up for another job with IBM, but the journalists could still observe the basic patterns.

The *N & O* put more than 6,000 children and 700 teachers online for free. NandOLand was the name of the educational service designed with children in mind; a mouse click on a cloud, for example, would take children to a NASA area on the Net. The students could send electronic mail to each other or type to each other instantly. "I have seen children who never cared what they wrote turn to a dictionary rather than send a letter to a key pal with misspelled words," said a teacher named Stephanie Toney. "I have seen a child with a severe reading disability sit for hours and concentrate on e-mail to another person on the other side of the world. His English teacher would have given her right arm to interest him in reading and writing for this period of time."

Granted, NandOLand wasn't the entire solution to the needs of children. Many couldn't spend much time on a machine at school and lacked one at home. But the program was much better than the alternative: expensive school connections to the Net or no Internet at all.

Like the children, the *N & O* itself was learning—about
the local schools and other institutions and the Net itself.
"How many newspaper editors and reporters get to talk
with students, parents, and teachers any time they want to
without making a big deal of it?" asked Daniels.[14] And so
the educational coverage was better. Rosalind Resnick,
publisher of *Interactive Publishing Alert*, wrote that the
N & O was "at the head of the pack when it comes to promoting interactivity between its readers and reporters."
By the summer of 1995 every staff member, including
those in circulation and advertising, would be able to go
on the Net from their desks. Daniels' own Net address
showed up on the paper's editorial page each day. The
N & O was publishing a dozen or two Internet items each
month, complete with a column called "Net Rider." How
different the paper was from a rival in nearby Durham:
"We don't print many Internet stories," a staffer there said
when I asked to speak to whoever covered the Net. The
words were spoken almost in a way to suggest that
"Internet" was synonymous with "*N & O*."

Not everyone was happy with the *N & O*'s Internet service. Around 700 people had subscribed commercially by
fall 1994, paying $20 a month, and some rightly com-
plained about the look and feel of the BBS and the busy
phone lines they had encountered during the summer.
When I posted a query on the Internet, at least half of the
replies were hostile to the online *N & O*. Some showed a
knee-jerk hatred because they disagreed with the paper's
politics. But others were right on target. The BBS incarnation of NandO.Net, the name for the commercial part of
the online endeavors, was more of a rutted dirt road than
an eight-lane information highway. Customers for some
months had trouble dialing up the service's modems for
want of enough phone lines. Other glitches arose. The service prided itself on the ability to whip people back and
forth between the local board and the Internet-related services without any effort. And yet in making the transitions,

customers suffered delays and software glitches that they might not encounter with a more polished service. Schoolchildren and BBS junkies were the best kinds of people to enjoy the wild ride and the scenery.

The online *N & O* responded with some technical improvements; the paper added many more phone lines and gave customers the ability to use Mosaic to point and click their way through the Web. Mosaic had a much smoother feel than the BBS software. By late 1994 the *N & O* was offering the public an electronic newspaper and the Internet at the competitive rate of $20 a month while helping to subsidize the educational side. And it was serving people with different levels of equipment. The BBS was designed to work especially well with less powerful machines and snailish modems that were far too slow for Mosaic.

On the Net, the people who answered my queries had another major complaint—the inability of NandO.Net to make alt.sex-style groups conveniently available. Frank Daniels made no apologies. However liberal towns like Chapel Hill might be, the state as a whole was of the opposite bent. And that included more than a few church-goers in Raleigh. "The community standards of our community don't mix with some of the sexual parts of Usenet," Daniels said, "so we edit them out." In addition, most subscribers were children. "I have a seven year old," he said, "and I don't want him delving into alt.sex.bestiality or those other places." Many of the Netheads would have said that one person's "editing" was another's "censorship." I myself, however, understood Daniel's worries. At least two other Net services were available in the same area, so it wasn't as if he were gatekeeping for the entire town; what's more, he said that when the software allowed, the sex-related news-groups would be available as an option. Just the same, the issue epitomized the clash between the gatekeeping ethos and that of the Internet.

More serious than the lack of alt.sex, to my mind, was Daniels' failure to appreciate sufficiently the political freedom of Usenet, the same service that had attracted him to the Internet in the first place. I complained to him that his own BBS included far, far less in the way of political discussion than I'd have wanted, and I contrasted this to the robust debates of Usenet. "To be honest, David," he said, "I think one of the least useful pieces of the Internet so far is their political discussions. They're not very good ones. There's a lot of flaming. The political discussions aren't very productive. I follow mainly the local ones here. These people discuss national issues and never have a policymaker looking in there. So why discuss it if it isn't going to have an impact on policy?"

While Daniels was worlds ahead of newspaper editors at large, he was showing the vestiges of the gatekeeping mindset that the new technology had made obsolete. I myself disliked unmitigated flaming. And yet there were times when harsh words were called for. The *N & O* didn't wimp out when the editorial board attacked the Ku Klux Klan or the more outrageous statements of Jesse Helms, the right-wing senator. Why should people online be any different? And although it might be nice for a policymaker to read my public messages as soon as I sent them out—and, yes, I could recall hearing out of the blue from the White House after one such posting—that was hardly necessary. Democracy isn't just a citizen writing to a congressman. It is also citizens communicating with citizens, educating, proselytizing; and with the economies of Usenet, more citizens could reach their peers for greater enlightenment. And then, if a consensus were reached, political action might ensue, such as letters to Congress. So why must politicians be involved from Day One? Daniels was out of touch here, and I hoped he'd catch on.

Admittedly NandO.Netters could hook up with the Usenet political areas, even if the *N & O* played them

down; but the newspaper didn't really promote political
debates on the BBS itself. And it was not just because
Daniels believed that the readers disliked flaming and ex-
tremism—it was also because he felt that real, live politicians were not ready for online appearances yet. "When
we can get commitment from the politicians and policymakers, then we'll make a push at it. But not until it becomes something where our community can have really
productive discussions. I don't want to train them not to
like them. What happens is that the people on the Net are
trained not to like them. Extremists and flamers love
them." I supposed there were a lot of us undesirables,
however; for alt.activism and similar areas were among
the more popular newsgroups on the Net—no match for
alt.sex, but certainly not small time.

If Daniels had had a complete set of Net values, he
would have understood the benefits of debate online, and
not just the political action but the *education.* I myself was
liberal. And yet when discussing information policy, I
could learn at times from the most zealous of Libertarians
and Objectivists. Some were among the most advanced of
the technologists. In fact, their technical backgrounds may
have led to their hatred of regulation—they loathed the
bureaucrats who could not fathom the direction in which
computers and communications were headed.

To his credit, Daniels at least was not calling for censorship of Usenet; he was merely saying that he wanted
his own service to be different. What's more, technology
and marketing forces, the great deciders of cyberspace,
might change his mind for him.

Just as he had assumed in the first place, people on
the Net wanted to *talk*—not just to the *N & O* but to each
other about all kinds of topics, including material in the
paper itself. And the more comfortable the readers grew
with the online world, the more spirited, the more Usenet-
like, would be the discussions. No, the meek would not
suddenly turn into flamers. But the thrill of technology

would be less of a distraction, and they would pay more heed to what they had to say and grow more adventurous about it. On the *N & O*'s present BBS, with its often awkward commands, many people were not even leaving messages for each other. Instead they typically used the system at a more primitive level to type out their thoughts with the other person online at the same time. I hated this approach. It brought to mind Dave Barry's crack that the Internet was like CB radio with typing.

Even if Daniels still did not enjoy the political debates on the Net itself, he was living up to the old tradition of sharing material with the rest of the world. In that sense his newspaper was exemplary. The *N & O* didn't just offer news, discussion areas, and games for its subscribers: Sample news and features were free to anyone who wanted to read them. That was how I'd first run across A.C. Snow. I'd seen the *N & O*'s name on a list of newspapers, and A.C. had caught my eye as I was wandering through the Gopher that stored sample news stories and columns from the paper. The World Wide Web, however, was the best way to try out the electronic *N & O*. When I dialed up the main page for NandO.Net, I could see a colorful, bluish logo and enjoy a newsstandish atmosphere, with scads of goodies to explore. The *N & O* differed from many electronic newspapers. It didn't just inflict on readers a digest of generic news, with only the most cursory helping of original material.

I read samples from the regular *N & O* and specialized publications such as the *Insider;* enjoyed brief but regularly updated electronic news intended for the Net itself; wandered through a little bookstore with cover shots from books by Snow and other columnists; wended my way through tens of thousands of words from a journalism seminar at Harvard; soaked up long, multimedia features; dialed up samples of rock music; and ventured into the sports area—the *N & O*'s most popular material on the Web.

The sports area was the baby of a bearded, forty-something editor named Eric Harris who had turned into a Nethead, and who like Schlukbier came with a nickname: "Zonker." A child, seeing the beard and taking in the personality, had compared him to the Doonesbury character. That was a little unfair. Zonker of the comics is a goof-off, while Zonker of the Net is a workaholic whose messages might bear 4 A.M. time stamps. Harris is Webmaster—the man with the daily responsibility for the content of the Web area in general—but his true love was sports. He packed the server with game schedules. During the '94 baseball strike the *N & O* indulged fans with whimsy such as "Cybersox Take the World Series"—reportage of mythical games. "Need something to do while we wait for the owners and players to resolve their differences?" the Web area asked on another electronic page. "Well, the Baseball Server is doing its part. Download the above images, tack them onto the wall, and buy a set of darts. Then, every time you feel a twinge of baseball withdrawal, grab a dart, think a 'warm' thought about one of the participants, and let the fun begin." And sure enough, Netfolks could print out pictures of the villains, each of whom had a superimposed picture of a dartboard and the wonderful caption: "The only losers are the fans."

The *N & O* also shared with the Net a variety of other material, of which my favorite was North Carolina Discoveries. A lively feature writer named Julie Ann Powers sought out offbeat places. In Lake Norman, for example, she found that "houses and hangars ring the airstrip and each lot comes with a grass taxiway to the paved and lighted runway." In Orient, a hamburger-and-hot-dog cook named Red Lee claimed that at twenty-five cents each, his offerings were the cheapest in the country. And in Tryon, the publishers of the *Daily Bulletin* said that at 8 by 11 inches, their newspaper might be the smallest in the world. Powers drove from town to town in a Ford Explorer that she had nicknamed Barlowe after Arthur

Barlowe—one of the first Europeans to behold the state of North Carolina. Barlowe was a gadgeteer's heaven on wheels, full of audio and video equipment. People on the Web didn't just enjoy gloriously descriptive stories from Powers: with Mosaic-style software they could *see* a picture of her wearing a sun hat on a beach or gaze at sand dunes or waterfalls or whatever she happened to be writing about at the time. If they owned a sound card, they could *hear,* too. She walked around carrying a microphone so large that it resembled a folded-up umbrella.

Powers might well be one of the first multimedia reporters to work for a Net-oriented daily newspaper. I asked her to share a few trade secrets. She said she interviewed people twice. The first time she gathered the basics for her regular story; the second time they spoke while tape rolled. Powers said she never knew which sounds would work out and which wouldn't. A recording of a glorious waterfall ended up sounding like a toilet flushing.

I asked about the challenge of balancing her traditional duties as a reporter with those as an audio-oriented interviewer. Some old hands in the *N & O* newsroom saw the gadgetry as a threat. It was all too remindful of the days when computers were replacing typewriters in the newsroom, and many reporters and editors balked at being typesetters. But Powers turned the new technology to her advantage. The microphone and electronic camera—a photographer followed her around—made her more aware of her surroundings and sensitive to new story angles. Once she did a story on Ten Commandment Mountain. It was part of a Biblical theme park, a peak in western North Carolina with God's words spelled out in "concrete letters each measuring five feet high and four feet wide." A roar from a giant lawn mower kept drowning out the voice of the man she was interviewing. "They always ask," he volunteered, "how do you mow that mountain?" Presto, she had the magic quote to use near the lead.

"A special mower with a low center of gravity," she revealed, "tilts and leans up and down the steep planes."

Whether reading about twenty-five-cent hamburgers or godly peaks, I could scoot easily between pictures and words. The *N & O* had a "North Carolina Discoveries" logo at the top of one page, a picture of Powers in the same area, and then a list of the Discoveries stories that she had done. By clicking my mouse on a list of story headlines in blue letters, I could immediately go to the stories. When I chose "Home Sweet Hangar," I sped to the same headline atop a color photo of an aviation buff inspecting "his Cessna 172 after rolling it out of the hangar at his house in Lake Norman Airpark." Yes, the caption was there too. And then I saw the story lead with an apt quote ("It's like being an avid golfer and living on the golf course") followed by a list of other items. I could choose "Audio: Talking about life on the flight line" if I wanted to hear an interview. What's more, if I'd set up my software, I could even have picked "Video" and gone on to a list of short movies. I also saw background items such as a list of "Triangle-area flight schools" and "FAA regulations: How to get your pilot's license." The beauty of this arrangement was that the *N & O* could provide all kinds of wonderful details for the interested without inflicting them on others. Unless they mouse-clicked the appropriate words in blue letters (or whatever the special color), they would never see the material.

The *N & O* used the same approach on news stories. When North Carolina was about to gas a man named David Lawson, readers could click on the item "The Lawson Execution." They could see a schedule of the events ahead—from Lawson's removal from his cell to the EKG examination that would help certify his death. After the Associated Press reported the execution, readers could click on a headline and read the details. They could even summon up "Preparing for the execution" or "How the gas chamber works."

The Lawson story was a just a sample—the *N & O* at the time wasn't constantly doing multimedia on breaking news—but it was easy to envision the future for American newspapers using the Web. Imagine the blessings for journalists who wanted to write on neat little odds and ends without getting in the way of their main articles. They could merely add "links" to offshoot stories. Perhaps the reader could even click and summon up a collateral audio report or even a video. At first it might be hard to do all this on deadline, but links would be a cinch as software improved. What's more, newspaper writers might evolve into true personalities just like their counterparts on television. After all, if a reporter's byline were in blue letters, you could click your mouse to see a photo and maybe even a bio featuring credentials—you could find out, for example, if the legal reporter held a law degree. You could also quickly locate copies of earlier work or a list of his or her favorite books.

Granted, electronic newspapers posed new challenges. Not all stories lent themselves to multimedia, for example. What if newspapers played down those that didn't? "If you tried to do that with a lot of news stories," Julie Powers told me, "you would end up serving the video masters rather than the news functions." Still, in the end, the reader would enjoy far more choices than before.

The Web, as I saw it, held out yet other possibilities for local papers such as the *N & O*. Suppose you lived in Chapel Hill and wanted to see what news had happened there in the past 24 hours; you could click on a map of the Raleigh area and behold a story list from your town. Neighborhood-level submaps could show still more. You could read the most minor tidbits—for example, new requests for zoning changes or items from neighborhood newsletters. Even more helpful, you could find old stories and other background information. Let's say you were shopping for a condo on a certain street. You might think the neighborhood was safe—Chapel Hill is a university town, remember—but learn that many crimes had occurred nearby. Furthermore, you could adjust the *kind* of information that you summoned from the Web. For example, you could see lists of houses for sale in a neighborhood and then retrieve their photos along with audio sales presentations. Moving on to another information category, you could uncover lists of nearby stores or see test scores from the closest elementary school. And you might even see ads from nearby restaurants and click on them to order.

The food-related examples weren't entirely hypothetical; Zonker Harris pointed me toward me some mock ads from Hardee's and a chain called Little Caesar's Pizza. The same business principles I discussed in chapter 2 applied here. Rather than planning to inflict vast quantities of material on the unwilling, the *N & O* made the ads useful and entertaining. Elsewhere in the *N & O* area I saw an ad for a computer dealer, among others, but the real triumph was the area from Mammoth Records—with home pages for bands, promo photos, discographies, tour dates, album covers, and more, including a catalogue and, yes, free samples.

But what about the economics of all this? Via an electronic edition the *N & O* wouldn't collect the fifty cents it charged per hard copy issue, but it wouldn't have to buy newsprint and distribution services. *That* was how George Schlukbier hoped the newspaper would turn a profit eventually. The electronic activities, although not yet profitable as a whole, were coming along. People on the Net, for example, were calling up the pages within the *N & O*'s area several hundred thousand times a week. A page was what you saw when you clicked the mouse to call up an item, and each page could be just a few lines of information, or go on for a number of screens. Zonker Harris expected that by the end of 1994 as many people would be dialing up the *N & O* as called up SunSite UNC, the popular collection of files at the University of North Carolina. Readers retrieved Mammoth Record's pages some 35,000 times a week. That didn't mean 35,000 people—there was plenty of repeat business, and of course the same people looked at more than one page—but the numbers looked good as a start.

Just who, however, was reading the Web areas of the *N & O* and other Internet publications? The *Washington Post* and many other dailies had chosen to avoid the Net for the moment because they thought that the right people weren't there. And some marketers and journalists tried to reinforce such arguments by citing a study of 4,777 Web readers by researchers at the Georgia Institute of Technology. Ninety-four percent were men, and 56 percent were 21–30 years old—almost half were students or faculty members or had other university ties. "These are hardly the type of people to make large consumer or business purchases," a *San Francisco Chronicle* story observed. The experience of JoAnn and Bob Lilienfeld, as recounted in chapter 2, showed that riches would not automatically come to merchants on the Web. And yet the potential was there. The Web readers uncovered by the institute weren't charity cases—just yups. Studying the readers of the Baseball server, the *N & O* found they were a long way from poverty. Twenty percent of these Netfolks, for example, earned $35,000–$50,000 a year, 18 percent earned $50,000–$75,000, and 4 percent earned more than $75,000. And, of course, many of these Netfolks were young people who would carry their Net habit over to their jobs and their personal lives. Not surprisingly, Schlukbier claimed keen interest from representatives of companies such as J.C. Penney and Radio Shack, and, of course, from fast-food chains, which, in so many cases, targeted their ads at the young.

Cleverly the *N & O* built on existing relationships with advertisers. If you were already on the paper and bought *X* number of lines, then you could get the Net as a bonus. North Carolina businesses paid as little as $50 a month in basic fees to be in the *N & O*'s area on the Net, not including add-ons such as design services. Big national firms would pay well into the thousands. Given the newness of the medium, this would scare off many—unless, like the *N & O* itself, they saw the Net as an investment in the future. Then the experiment might work. In my mind, however, there was one other variable: What about *national* publications competing with local papers for the same *national* advertisers? Already Time Warner and the *N & O* were watching each other carefully.

Magazines: Time Warner

Typing away on Macintoshes on the fortieth floor of the Time Life Building in Manhattan, ten floors above *People* magazine, a small team started an area of the Web known as Pathfinder. It offered electronic versions of Time Warner's vast stable of magazines. Zonker Harris at the *N & O* had a slogan, "May the best server win." The Durham newspapers might not be in the game so far, but *Time* and brethren were.

Zonker was justifiably proud of the 300,000 or so accesses a week that the *N & O*'s Web area was enjoying after several months on the Web. But just within a week of start-up in fall 1994, the Time Warner area was drawing more than 80,000 accesses a *day*. That didn't mean that the *N & O*'s efforts were doomed—hardly. But despite all the talk about the Net being nirvana for smaller companies, Fortune 500 corporations arrived with some advantages of their own. Once readers grew comfortable with a certain area of the Web, they might spend less time on other parts of the Net. This wasn't so much a pattern at the time, but as mass audiences descended on the Net, corporate logos might count far more. Beyond that, Time Warner already offered a daily version of *Time*—a *newspaper* in effect. It was just one service among a rackfull of publications. Readers could read up on foreign policy or the latest *Star Trek* film in *Time*, take in reviews from

Entertainment Weekly, keep up with Ice-T and other hip-hop musicians in *Vibe,* or fire off questions to authors of best-sellers from Warner Books.

An even greater threat to the *N & O,* in the long run, was the fact that Time Warner didn't just own magazines and book publishers. It also owned *pipes,* including a cable operation in the Raleigh area. And someday it might use cable TV lines to send the Net into homes there, competing with the *N & O,* which had already been providing Internet services. If no antitrust or other legal boundaries existed, then Time Warner would be remiss in its duties to its stockholder if it did not explore this route. Think what this would mean to users of the World Wide Web. If an article came with fancy photos, they might have to wait several minutes for the whole works to reach them at a speed of 14.4 kilobits per second. But suppose Time Warner used cable TV to bring the Internet to them. Their televisions would still work with cable the usual way. But their computers could share the cable and retrieve Web articles and other material in a fraction of the time. Cable modems sold for hundreds of dollars. But pilot projects were going on with other companies, and the cost could soon drop to a fraction of that amount. More important, big, well-financed corporations might be willing to modify the old cable for these new capabilities.[15] What did this mean for local, *N & O*-sized companies? Just as high tech had blurred the difference between telephones and televisions, the Net itself was blurring the barriers between local and national. It was unclear whether the public would win or lose.

For better or worse, Time Warner's area on the Net was part of an evolution in cyberspace. The process had begun with the small academic magazines and hobbyist publications that turned to the Net as a cheap way to find readers. Many if not most still relied on plain text without graphics; they were little more than archived dispatches to mailing lists—which was fine because the words mattered above all. One of the best of these was Adam Engst's *Tidbits.* Written for Apple owners, it also appeared on the World Wide Web and bulletin board systems, and Engst claimed more than 100,000 readers—no small feat for a kitchen-table-style publisher. Nonconglomerates still provided most of the magazines on the net, and not all were for techies or sci-fi buffs. *International Teletimes* was edited by Ian Wojtowicz, a gifted high school student who lived in Vancouver, British Columbia. *Teletimes* went out over the Web with fetching art, not just text, and some of the prose could have graced *Harper's* or the *Atlantic.* Recounting a winter trip by train, a college student named Paul Gribble wrote: "Every now and then we pass a lake, completely frozen over, flat and white, smooth as a skating rink. I'd love to walk to the center of a big frozen lake like that and just sit there for a while. I'd feel like the first blot of paint on a fresh silk canvas."

Many steps up from *Teletimes,* in business terms, was *Global Net Navigator.* Like the *N & O* in North Carolina, *GNN* was trying to use advertising to support its activities, and you could see ads from companies as large as Digital Equipment Corporation. *GNN* was not just technical. It posted informative, brightly written articles on topics ranging from money to food and travel. *Wired* magazine was on the Net, too, with an offshoot called *HotWired,* which itself wandered far from technical topics and attracted lucrative ads from the likes of Volvo and AT&T. None of these publications, of course, happened to be a Household Name like Time Warner's *Time* or *People.* Many experts felt that as a profitable medium for big-time magazines—and let's not confuse size with quality or lack thereof—the Internet had a long way to go.

Jeffrey Dearth offered at least an interim answer. Teaming up with a small corporation with the grand name of the Internet Company, Dearth offered the Electronic Newsstand. Like the Pathfinder or *N & O's* Net edition, the Newsstand was a godsend to browsers. You could wander through sample articles from *Business Week; Field & Stream; The Economist; The New Yorker; National Review; Maclean's,* Canada's largest newsweekly; or *The New Republic,* of which Dearth himself was publisher. The Time Warner experiment notwithstanding, most of the Names were far behind. Dearth offered them the equivalent of a catch-up course or at least some solid remedial instruction. They could test the waters of the Net to see how much interest their articles drew, before deciding whether to set up their own areas there. Via the Newsstand, magazines could accept subscription orders.

But order taking was a long way from fancier "interactivity"—to use a pet term of media people—and this was where Time Warner's Pathfinder area would shine. The area didn't just recycle magazines on the Net, it also offered powerful tools to find old articles by typing in search words or the names of topics. From the start, the searching capability was among the more popular services. Soon Pathfinder would include hypertext links that let you go from an article on a certain topic to an ongoing discussion. Already Time Warner provided special services such as one for gardeners. They could type in their general wishes about flowers and supply their location and other odds and ends, and then Time would offer tips on what to grow. It also allowed inquirers find out how their congressman or senator had voted on certain key issues. And many more applications like this were on the way. What's more, people could talk back to Time Warner writers and others by way of an advanced bulletin board system designed for the Web. It was *much* easier to use than the *N & O*'s.

Not everyone liked the Web area. One woman hated the "overstuffed" artwork—others said it gobbled up too much downloading time. She also chided *Time* for putting out the online version of *Sunset* magazine "for Northern Californians still living in their '50s ranch houses." I myself, however, enjoyed the kitsch and flashy, busy look of

the Web area as a whole. That was the way the *real* magazines came across; this was pop culture, not the *Kenyon
Review.*

Almost immediately the *Time* board teemed with
lively talk on issues ranging from Clintonian stupidities
to, yes, the future of the electronic medium. I felt much
more comfortable here than in the message area of the
N & O; people on the *Time* board spoke their minds more
freely. Some amusing posts showed up. Amazingly, the
software let people key in their own identities, and the late
Henry Luce, cofounder of *Time,* arose from the grave as
luce@pastmytime.com. One message appeared, truthfully
or not, with the name of a staffer at *U.S. News & World
Report.* He promised that *U.S. News* would set up an outpost on the Net soon, and someone at *Time* twitted him for
not answering e-mail promptly. Despite my fondness for
the reporting in *U.S. News,* I had to agree. Researching a
Net guide for political activists, I'd written *U.S. News* six
months ago and had yet to receive an answer.

Time Warner also showed network savvy by following
the example of *GNN* and similar publications and providing some hypertext pointers to the rest of the Internet,
rather than expecting readers to stay within its own area.
Time Warner even enlisted some of its household names
in the cause. The electronic version of *Entertainment
Weekly,* for example, did not just review Madonna or
Springsteen or the latest Hollywood films; it also directed
people to popular, entertainment-oriented sites on the Net
itself by way of hypertext links. I still wanted to see many,
many more links—a strength of *GNN.* But I suspected that
would come in time.

Planning the Pathfinder service, Time Warner had
even consulted with the publisher of *Wired.* "They're providing real news, not just PR blather or sales areas for
their products," said Chip Bayers, the managing editor of
HotWired, the *Wired* offshoot on the Web. And he was
right.

I myself was no cheerleader for Time Warner in some ways—I worried about media concentrations.[16] But here the Suits deserved their due. *HotWired* offered avant-garde graphics on the Web along with services such as bulletin boards and free archives; I was pleased, yet hardly surprised. *Wired,* after all, was still a bit of an upstart despite heavy investment from a corporate arm of the powerful Newhouse family.[17] But Time Warner was different—the epitome of the journalistic and Hollywood establishments, a company with many benefits from the status quo. I recalled the upbeat stories that *Time* had run about the world of 500-channel television. Such articles betrayed far more tolerance of the "one to many" broadcast model, as opposed to the newer, more anarchistic model of the Net. Many in the Time Life tower, especially on the entertainment side, might still harbor these less adventurous visions. And yet the company was now spreading its bets around. That seemed sensible enough, given the chilliness that some test markets had shown interactive TV.

A *Time* writer named Philip Elmer-DeWitt had grown more and more attuned to the potential of the Net. He was a regular on The WELL, the bulletin board system frequented by many of the elite journalists on the Internet. Again and again Elmer-DeWitt showed up on newsgroups and mailing lists with spunky, opinionated posts on such topics as the media and telecommunications. He lent his name to a successful legal campaign to aid Brock Meeks, a small publisher on the Net who faced a libel suit from a mail-order tycoon in Ohio. What's more, Elmer-DeWitt was sensitive to the threats from the Clipper chip, which Washington might use someday to invade the privacy of millions of Americans. He clearly represented the interests of his employer, but he did so with a good mix of wit and smarts that endeared him to many on the Internet. His electronic signature said, "Read Time on America Online where we are paid to take abuse."

Enlivened by posts from Netfolks and WELLfolks whom Elmer-DeWitt had befriended, *Time*'s message board thrived on America Online. But now, quite correctly, *Time* had run an article pointing out the advantages of the Internet from the perspective of publishers. *Time* raised a big question, the same one Frank Daniels had asked. Did publications really have to fork over such a hefty percentage of their online revenue to commercial services, such as America Online, when the Internet existed? Time Warner's well-stocked area on the Net was itself an answer of sorts. Granted, the company's outpost on America Online wasn't about to vanish. Time Warner was testing both interactive TV and computers as transmission vehicles; similarly the company was not committing itself to any single network in cyberspace. I took it for granted that sooner or later Time Warner might end up on the network that Bill Gates was starting. Just as *Time* reached newsstands everywhere, the electronic equivalent could seek out eyes wherever the phone lines led. *Sports Illustrated, Fortune,* and *People* would soon be on CompuServe. And yet Time Warner's priority in the computer world was clear: the Internet above all else, at least for the moment.

"When we put *Time* on America Online," said Walter Isaacson, editor of new media at Time, "it is done on their server, using their software, and only someone subscribing to America Online and using America Online software can access it. On the Web, anyone using public domain software can get to it." I could just have substituted "*News & Observer*" for "*Time,*" an impression only strengthened by the next sentence: "We have a direct relationship to our readers." Isaacson went on: "There will be massive amounts more content from Time Inc. on the Web than on America Online or CompuServe, which will just feature individual magazines."

Some twenty-two magazines were to go on the Web. Isaacson said around ten editors would participate full or part time. Total investment in the Web site was to reach the "mid six figures," and "with advertising it should be in the black within a year. "There may be a mix of ads and subscription fees," Isaacson said. Mercifully, the advertising would not be the intrusive Prodigy kind that popped up on the bottom of my screen in a garish, Vegas style.

Jim Kinsella, the ex-newspaper editor who presided over the Web area, said he was pushing for a subscription fee of around $8 a month. I would have wanted the price to be a few dollars lower, but it was fine if I got enough for my money. If nothing else, Kinsella wanted readers to be able to stay online without the time charges that made thousands unplug their hookups with America Online and similar services. A product manager with Microsoft would later say as much to the *New York Times* in discussing Bill Gates' new service: "We're trying to reduce the threshold of pain. We think users hate connect fees."[18]

Kinsella's $8 monthly fee—his proposed figure, not Time Warner's—would be for Pathfinder itself, not for the Internet connection. I did some quick math. Pathfinder could indeed be a competitive possibility if Time Warner were able to lower the cost of using the Internet by way of cable television from the $75–$100 a month that people typically paid for such arrangements.

Mass use might enable Time Warner to undercut the $20 that the *N & O* presently charged. Typical readers might want to keep reading a *local* newspaper, and the *N & O* could drop its own prices, but this was still a good example of how national media just might drain at least some readers away from the local media. Understandably, Kinsella was thinking in mass, national terms, as I would have done. He predicted that within five or ten years half the country might be able to reach the Net in one way or another. Others at Time were similarly optimistic.

Not everyone in late 1994 was so sanguine. Mark Stahlman, for example, a media expert in New York, shrugged off Net publications as "just the latest in a series of fads." Richard M. Smith, *Newsweek*'s editor in chief who was running the new-media committee of the Magazine Publishers of America, was skeptical about online services in general: "The people who are making money are the people who are running conferences about it." [19]

Smith was oversimplifying somewhat, but formidable barriers did exist, of which one of the biggest happened to be the limits of the technology. Reading electronic text for hours on end could be murder on both the back and the eyes. All day long I sat in front of a computer screen; the last thing I wanted was to have to do it while I wandered through magazines or books. Television wouldn't do: I hated the idea of reading a magazine or novel from ten feet away. Besides, didn't magazines and books exist to be enjoyed in bed, on the hammock, or at the beach?

Mightn't Silicon Valley, however, come out with small, tablet-style computers designed for reading? "TeleReaders" could feature optional keyboards for people who wanted to use them as general purpose computers. Screens, needless to say, must be much sharper than today, and without so much flicker. Batteries should last longer. And, ideally, you should be able to dart from place to place in a newspaper or magazine by merely touching a "pen" to the appropriate part of your screen. *That* was what the magazine, newspaper, and book industries needed, rather than just more conferences. Washington could even encourage this by way of a focused procurement program for schools and libraries; the same machines could even be used for electronic forms for government and commerce.

Roger Fidler of Knight-Ridder had already been experimenting with mockups of tablet-style machines. He was more interested in a newspaper-oriented approach and less in a general one than I was. But the basic idea was the same—words needn't be captives of the printed page. The real question was this: How soon until the right technology appeared? Electronic magazines such as Time

Warner's would still make money without a TeleRead-
style approach, but the full potential would not be
reached, especially if more children abandoned words for
TV and computer images. That was even truer for the
world of books. Even more than magazines and newspapers, e-books suffered from the limits of technology. It
wasn't just a question of the right machine for viewing; at
issue were other matters such as copy protection and
billing. But at least some partial solutions were on the
way, and even with the present difficulties of the medium,
online bookstores were sprouting up on the Internet. One
of the best was run by Laura Fillmore, an editor in
Massachusetts who had once worked for Little, Brown.

Books: Laura Fillmore and
the Online Bookstore

An elderly man owned a charming old store in a
southern town with the standard magnolias, wrought iron
staircases, and hot, moist summers, and he loved to brag
about his shiny new safe. Most customers did not know
about it or care. Rather than worrying so much about the
protection of his wealth, he might have been better off to
imitate his rivals and invest his money in air-conditioning
instead of the safe.

The man reminded me of myopic publishers and authors. Not quite grasping the full potential of the Internet,
they fretted too much about copyright protection, and not
enough about making their wares friendly to shoppers. A
pay-per-read company in Virginia was typical here. You
could download its books off the Internet, but you did not
enjoy such niceties as links to other titles online. Nor
could you print more than a page or so at once. Beyond
that, you had to clutter up your computer system with a
$25 gadget hooked up to the printer port. If you were

working on tight deadlines and were rich and desperate enough, you might stomach this copy protection system. But I dreaded the possibility of its adoption by the book industry as a whole; established publishers and writers just might see the world pass them by if they cared too much about cybersafes and not enough about customer amenities. Many megabytes of good, free reading awaited the public on the Web, and not everyone understood the value that professional editors and writers could add.

Nowadays, however, more publishers and hangers-on were catching on to the nuances of the Net. Among them was Laura Fillmore, a publishing consultant who owned the Online BookStore in Rockport, Massachusetts. She must have driven some traditionalists crazy. Fillmore actually had the notion that ASCII—text in a popular format, without italics and the other trimmings—should be free to everyone. She loved Project Gutenberg, which an Illinois academic had started to put classics and other works on the Net at no charge. Fillmore was the antithesis of a techno-geek, the kind of woman who just might read Dickens to her two children on snowy days, and who was a regular on the speaker circuit within her industry. She had majored in English at Barnard College and worked for a publishing company that dated back to the nineteenth century. Fillmore helped bridge the past and the electronic era. Her vision wasn't quite the same as mine, but it was worlds apart from that of piracy-fixated publishers who saw electronic readers as a criminal class.

The move to the Net was, in her opinion, part of a long evolution toward a new form of decentralized publishing. She recalled when the great houses didn't farm out editing and other tasks as often as they do today, and when almost every book took nine months to reach the stores. "Back in the late '70s when I was at Little, Brown," she said, "we needed to get special permission to use Fed Ex. When an author wanted his sales figures, I'd walk up the street to the top floor of a separate building where Rose, the lady with the P & L cards, had been keeping tabs for twenty years, and I'd sign out the neatly penciled card and carefully carry it to my boss, wrapping it in plastic against the weather if necessary. I passed the copyediting department with their well-stocked reference library, a bastion against inaccuracies, and the design department, smelling of wax, hung with rulers, sizing wheels, and X-acto knives."[20]

The industry, though, had changed; now freelancers throughout the country, not just in New York or Boston, were often editing and even publishing books. Fillmore herself had gone into freelance editorial work years before, and she still remembered "the shrinking feeling in my stomach the first time I bought a computer setup back in 1984: $10,000 of the bank's money for an XT and an HP LaserJet. The salesman left, I was back at the C prompt, and the room grew dark. No matter which buttons I pushed, 'Abort, Retry, Ignore' glared back persistently. Finally, I chose none of the above and unplugged the whole thing."[21] Fillmore overcame her technophobia, but the chaos of change still made her uncomfortable. "Increasing speed and volume have led to high job turnover, a blurring of disciplines. Our computerized tools allow the editor to become a typist, a designer, and a typesetter, the designer becomes a software junkie, a graphic artist, a prepress house. No time for galleys! Straight to pages! No time for pages; straight to film. The drop dead date is bottom line. Sales are needed this quarter."[22]

Years ago, competition had reached the point where many typesetting jobs left the United States. "We even hired freelancers thirdhand in Singapore and Haiti," Fillmore recalled in a speech. "The publisher hired me; I hired someone stateside to hire someone in-country to hire the keyboarder and, still, the publisher ended paying maybe half what the job would have cost him at $15 per hour. Our topic today is slavery."[23]

But in Fillmore's opinion, this distributed form of publishing, where tasks went every which way, would take a

newer and more humane form. In the 1980s books had
appeared on computer networking, a kinder technology
than the brutal, production-oriented variety of the past.
And now Fillmore saw in networks a chance to "elicit life
from people" who used computers to communicate. Her
own "epiphany" came when a Net-oriented writer, John
Quarterman, author of *The Matrix,* introduced her to "the
then alien concept of electronic mail. My assistant would
pick up mail from my lone correspondent, the author,
print it out, put it in my in box, and I would handwrite responses which she would input and send back in due
time. It sounds quaint, but it seemed to make sense to me
at the time—in the same way computerized typesetting
distributed though unconnected PCs made sense." On the
Net, everyone could publish, not just giant publishing
houses. And so Quarterman could forward to her some
public messages from students who were defying the
Chinese Army in Tiananmen Square. They could speak
for themselves; no one edited them. They weren't like the
freelance typists in Haiti: They were not "hidden and
voiceless behind four middlemen" and "with no hope of a
phone, much less an Internet connection." [24]

The overlap in Fillmore's mind, between publishing
and communicating via the Net, was entirely natural.
When the Haitians typed, they created a digitized version
of the book they were working on. They were not just
transferring words to paper. Bits and bytes, once created,
could go anywhere.

Fillmore, of course, was hardly the first to think of con-
solidating knowledge. As early as 1945 a scientist had published a preternaturally farsighted *Atlantic Monthly* article
that was to electronic publishing what Leonardo da Vinci's
notebooks were to inventions in general. Vannevar Bush
had proposed a memex, a microfilm-based device that
could bring together knowledge from many disciplines—
along with the thoughts of the user. It would be, in other
words, a cross between a personal file cabinet and a giant

library. In a speech, Fillmore quoted a key passage: "The human mind . . . operates by association. With one item in its grasp, it snaps instantly to the next that is suggested by the association of thoughts, in accordance with some intricate web of trails covered by the brain."[25] Bush might as well have been describing the World Wide Web and its links that allow you to click on "Boeing" and see "Airplanes" or click on "Clinton" and see "Presidents." Ted Nelson, a dreamer–writer–programmer, was thinking of the memex when he invented hypertext links. That concept, in turn, excited Tim Berners-Lee, a staffer at a physics institute in Berne, Switzerland, who was the father of the Web—the vast network of computers through which I could retrieve the Raleigh *News and Observer, Time,* and Fillmore's offerings.

Back in 1992, however, the World Wide Web was a fraction of its present size, and programmers had yet to release easy, graphically oriented browsers such as Mosaic that would help tame the Web. Even more than today, people needed books to fathom the Net. And yet no popular-level guide was in print. So it was entirely fitting that when Fillmore decided to create a book from scratch—rather than just produce it for a publisher—the Internet was the subject. This how-to guide was *The Internet Companion,* the author was Tracy LaQuey, and the paper publisher was Addison-Wesley. Fillmore kept the network rights and looked forward to distributing the book through her new Online BookStore. Barry Shein of Software Tool & Die, the first commercial service to hook ordinary mortals into the Internet, had offered her space on his bank of hard disks. "He described his operation," she said, "as basically an electronic store with empty shelves and a cash register at the door. I decided that I'd find electronic properties to fill these shelves."[26] But the Internet at the time had Acceptable Use Policies that prevented her from making a profit. What to do?

Fillmore hit on a solution that actually rewarded her for an idealistic approach to publishing. She gave away—

with great luck in the end—ASCII files from the book in hopes of drumming up interest in the paper version. "Who wants to read hundreds of pages in ASCII anyway?" Fillmore would later ask. Unadorned ASCII by itself wasn't always that pleasant to read, and many people liked the Net version well enough to shell out money for a paper book. "Even our publisher was supportive of our effort," Fillmore said, "and happy with the resulting sales figures."[27] Orders poured in from as far off as Finland and Korea. Netfolks all over the world could learn of Fillmore's offering immediately rather than waiting for reviews to show up in local magazines and newspapers.

Within two years, *Companion* had sold hundreds of thousands of copies. Al Gore had written the foreword just before his election as vice president, but the freebies on the Net certainly hadn't hurt. Other publishers also found that free copies could be a boon, not a bane. *Zen and the Art of the Internet* (Prentice Hall) and *The Hacker's Dictionary* (MIT Press) similarly flew off the racks. "Giving something valuable away for free," Fillmore said, "can make money."[28]

Of course some would say she hadn't actually published online. Rather she had used the medium to promote a paper book. Still, the prospect of purely electronic publishing beckoned. "I was seduced by the prospect of the then 10 million people on the Internet—10 million literate people with disposable incomes—attached to the Net. Why not acquire lots of Internet rights to lots of books and put them online at the Online BookStore. Surely some percentage of those people would buy files of a popular author's books for a reasonable price."[29] Fillmore was sensible enough to price her offerings for consumers who were spending their own money, not their bosses'. Some commercial databases were charging as much as $200 per hour or more, while Fillmore was thinking more in terms of $5, say, for a short story downloaded from the Net.

The test story was "Umney's Last Case," a fifty-page Stephen King story from a collection called *Nightmares and Dreamscapes.* King was among the best-selling writers on the planet. Fillmore dreamed of tens of thousands of dialups even if "Umney" intrigued only 1 percent of the 10 million people on the Net at the time. Fillmore had picked out just the right King story, one where a time traveler gave a Toshiba T-1000 laptop computer to a tough detective around 1939—someone who in turn used his "plastic Buck Rogers steno machine" to write a story within King's own tale.

Fillmore's "Umney" project was a sensation at the biggest book fair in the world, the one at Frankfurt; upbeat stories appeared in places ranging from European news programs to the *Wall Street Journal.* She witnessed "a vast amount of smoke, a tremendous marketing boost for the printed book again, lots of noise—and by extension, lots of profit for the publisher and for the author—but handfuls of per-copy sales." [30] They didn't even pay for all the phone calls used to set up the deal.

I was hardly surprised. Enjoying access to many megs of free material on the Net, the typical denizen didn't want to shell out even $5 for the story even if she or he could simply fax in a credit card number. It wasn't that King's work was worthless—quite the opposite. Rather, on the Internet and with this business model, "Umney" at most any realistic price could not compete with free material such as Usenet postings.

Yes, the Net teemed with sci-fi and fantasy fans. But as I saw it, they were too busy talking to each other, and, while they would have been delighted to download "Umney" for free, they balked at spending the $5. You might say that "Umney" was like a typical TV program. The appeal was potentially broad but not deep. Pay-per-view wasn't that much of a hit on cable TV, and the same principle applied here. "Umney" could enhance a collection of material for subscribers—we go back to the flat-fee example of the *News & Observer* and Jim Kinsella's vision for Time Warner—but even a Stephen King story wasn't strong enough on its own for online use. Part of the problem, I believed, was the medium. The right technology for reading fifty-page short stories just wasn't out there yet. With the proper equipment, the value would increase.

Besides, even now, Fillmore could use a license or sponsorship model. She sold "Umney" to two computer networks, one of them CompuServe, which gained the right to post the story for a week during a conference on paperless publishing. "Hundreds of people have accessed it," Fillmore said. The future possibilities were evident now. Corporations someday might sponsor books on computer networks the way they sponsored programs on CBS or NBC. In fact, whole sites on the Net—with the names of companies—could serve as homes for innovative projects. Sun Microsystems was oriented toward UNIX, relied heavily on sales to Net users, and benefited from the goodwill and publicity that its SunSite libraries enjoyed. Fare ranged from presidential speeches to the Internet Underground Music Archive; there could be a place for commercial e-books as well in these high-tech sandboxes, as Fillmore jokingly called such areas.

The sponsorship model wasn't perfect, of course. Fillmore herself was the first to wonder which corporations would have sponsored writings about the uprising in Tiananmen Square. Big companies often favored upbeat material. As I saw it, fiction and nonfiction books alike might suffer if this model alone prevailed. They differed from newspapers and magazines; book publishers thought more in terms of individual properties, and beyond that, publications such as the *N & O* and *Time* already enjoyed strong identities from their paper incarnations. The new media were less a challenge to their editorial integrity. But many sponsored books might degenerate into the Net equivalent of the wretched infomercials on TV, the ones

where over-the-hill actors "interviewed" astrologers or
memory experts, and where the audiences clapped thun-
derously on cue.

Wisely, Fillmore did not give up on "Umney" entirely—
it was still online when I was writing this chapter—nor
did she quit using the Net to promote writings on paper.
Even more important, she tried out writings that took advantage of links to other material on the Web.

Bless This Food: Amazing Grace in Praise of Food was
an example of prime material for hypertext. The paper
book bought together food-related prayers from many
times and places. But everything was contained. You could-
n't wander outside the printed pages. Thanks to Fillmore,
however, you could click on Buddhist-related material and
see a Buddha's image piped in from the Smithsonian. You
could even e-mail the author of *Bless*, Adrian Butash.
Fillmore wasn't just selling the book itself—she was offering it as a "dashboard" that could take you to related material on the Net. Certainly the Smithsonian hadn't had *Bless* in
mind when it posted the picture of Buddha. However,
through the pointers in the electronic edition, you could
learn of this image and view it in just the right context; that,
after all, was the splendor of the Web. Quite honestly, then,
Fillmore could charge $25 for a book that sold in hardback
from Delacorte for $18.95. She was giving you *more* for
your money. Besides, if you proposed new links and·she
liked them, you would receive some royalties. You, the
reader, could be part of the book and the author's life. We
could all be editors.

As a writer, I had somewhat mixed feelings about this.
I loved e-mail from readers. But I was already spending too
many hours a day on electronic correspondence of one
kind or another. I hated the idea of suffering a constant
stream of e-mail from Project X when I wanted to move on
to Project Y. If this model won out, writers would have to be
much choosier about the projects they took on—knowing
that publishers expected more commitment.

Given the deluge of 50,000 titles a year that readers face just from U.S. publishers, more than a few people would enjoy such a prospect. But they shouldn't grow too complacent. With electronic publishing much cheaper than the paper variety, we might eventually see 100,000 commercially published titles a year. I, for one, wouldn't mind as long as quality and royalties don't suffer. The problem is not too many books, but rather the need for better software to sort through them—or for more hyper-text editors to issue good pointers. That is one reason why I loved the idea of publishers selling pointers as well as actual material.

Not every writer would be open-minded, of course; even Fillmore at first had feared hypertext. When O'Reilly and Associates put one of her papers on the Web through *GNN*—spreading around her observations on electronic publishing—she saw all kinds of links. By clicking on blue letters, for example, readers would call up material about a founder of Internet. Fillmore felt as if a Philistine had taken her beautiful bowl, her self-contained piece of writ-ing, and turned it into a colander. Some writers might see a parallel in another way: Suppose the colander leaked readers, who, seeing the links, dove off into another area of the Net, and *never* returned. Fillmore had adjusted to this possibility, and I could, too. Just like Zonker Harris I was of the "May the best server win!" mentality, except that I refused to confuse popularity with merit. Books weren't like sports servers.

From society's viewpoint, another issue presented it-self here. Both Fillmore and I wondered about the dam-age that television and computers might be doing to people's attention spans. "Attention deficit disorder seems to have arisen at the same time that computers have spread to the home and office," she said, "and I don't think that's an accident. How many people age twelve and younger are capable of reading 300 pages of sus-tained argument about anything?" Another worry arose, too, in my mind. Like Frank Daniels, I realized that an entire generation of children was spending more time gazing at computer and TV screens than they devoted to books and traditional newspapers.

I felt that technology was destiny, that Washington and other governments should promote computers that encouraged the receptive to read e-books hour after hour. Too much of the new-style education, as envisioned by many, would be task oriented—would be *training* as much as *education* per se. That was fine for technical matters where, for example, a future factory worker might want to learn the basics of engine design. Hypertext was superb. The student could study a diagram of a diesel engine, click on an individual part, and read and hear a detailed explanation of its function. But I wanted technology that also encouraged people to read and absorb whole books.

If book readers were too small a minority, then countries such as the United States would be less democratic and more oligarchic, with the elite all too able to manipulate the other citizens. Some social critics such as Neil Postman demonized technology as a source of mindless distractions for the masses. I, however, saw opportunity if we acted soon enough before we lost more children to TV. That meant sharp screens, smaller, lighter machines, and other advances—which would come sooner or later, but which could be hastened by the coming of a focused procurement program. Washington should assure the Valley a market for the right hardware. It should also try harder to help schools absorb it, so the machines wouldn't just sit idle in closets.

A national digital library, not just a digital store leading to commercial collections, was just as essential as better hardware. Today a college student researching the effect of Shakespeare on popular culture is able to find the Bard's work at the school library. But what about tracking down newer books that the library couldn't afford to buy?

Also, only one student could read a paper copy at a time; suppose a professor wanted many students to compare impressions of a novel, especially one that was out of print and long gone from the bookstores? People on the technical side could benefit even more than those in the humanities. The best and most recent guides to Microsoft Word or Windows, for example, didn't come from educators; rather they came from the private sector. The faster this knowledge could reach average citizens, the easier it would be to upgrade the labor force.

A national digital library, moreover, would help many businesses market their goods. A food company trying to sell a new line of rice, for example, could instantly call up cookbooks of many ethnic groups and find out the relationship between food and the cultures. In an era of customized products, companies needed to learn quickly about niche markets. That would be especially true as business globalized; corporate planners had to keep on top of conditions in many countries.

So TeleRead-style libraries—which let people look through many kinds of information, everything from books to UN reports—could make real contributions in the United States and elsewhere. If nothing else, governments needed to understand the possible efficiencies. Yes, public and academic librarians would choose books. But innovative, private firms would own the computer banks (well backed up) storing the books and other material; many different contractors, always trying to outdo each other's technologies, could compete. Other efficiencies would accrue. Pooling the public libraries of rich and poor citizens would help everyone by increasing the variety of books available to all.

Big Brother needn't run a national digital library. Subject-oriented librarians in many cities might acquire material; in effect they would be putting a public library system online, one that reflected the tastes of, say, Lyons as well as Paris. How much more supple than the overcentralized approach that the French now favored for their national library! The elite librarians could still identify the books *they* had blessed, but the provincials could have their say as well; and, given the variability of literary tastes over the ages, the latter in some cases might prevail anyway.

What's more, by gambling money up front to qualify for royalties from TeleRead, writers and commercial publishers could bypass the librarians. Book people such as Laura Fillmore could thrive under this approach. A national library could offer e-books not only to citizens directly but also to independent-minded entrepreneurs such as Fillmore, who could charge for their custom links. I loved the idealism she showed in suggesting that ASCII be free. It was a good model in many cases for today. But I feared that as computers grew better for book reading—and it would happen eventually, with or without a TeleRead program—free ASCII would take away too many paying customers. And if ASCII books weren't free? Then, more than ever, piracy would occur regardless of various legal and technological precautions. So the answer should be free national digital libraries—well stocked and with fair pay for writers and publishers—to reduce the temptation to bypass copy protection. Use tracking to report dialup counts and pay originators of material, but not for billing. *That* was the way to take full advantage of the technology and keep market incentives while promoting literacy.

Rich countries would be the first to start libraries of this kind. They could safeguard their intellectual property by helping poorer countries get books online if the latter agreed to honor copyright laws. The time would come for national and international Electronic Peace Corps to make this possible. EPCs could help upgrade Third World phone systems on site and share knowledge via e-books, e-mail, two-way video, and otherwise. To enforce global copyright law, we needed carrots as well as sticks.

What's more, governments could protect books with technology far less cumbersome than the $25 gadgets that the pay-per-read bookstore in Virginia used. *Then* e-text stood a chance. I thought of the old merchant down South: Safes were useful, but only if the customers could enjoy an air-conditioner—an easy-to-use digital library for all of a country's citizens.

National digital libraries, of course, could link up with each other and form an official world library someday. But, given the many cultural differences, that was impossible now. National libraries, then, were the way to go—with opportunities for citizens in different countries to read each other's books when governments allowed this. I pitied the censors. In an era of international computer networks, national libraries would end up anyway as one big global library for citizens of open societies and for the more resourceful people of countries such as Iran. Simply put, national digital libraries would make it so much easier to market or shop for books internationally. When a Swedish anarchist heard about TeleRead, his big question wasn't, "Isn't this an opportunity for cultural imperialism?" Instead it was, "Will I be able to read American best-sellers as quickly as people there can?" Whatever the kind of book—a Tom Clancy thriller or an anarchistic tract—TeleRead libraries would allow easy global distribution.

In rich countries such as the United States and Sweden, the need for national digital libraries would only grow with the introduction of better televisions and video games, not to mention the distractions of the Net itself—including virtual reality, at some point. Even in wealthy nations, people had only so much disposable income. How much of it would be left for online books? Mightn't we use e-forms and digital libraries to transfer resources from paperwork to knowledge? As much as I applauded the good work that Frank Daniels was doing with the third graders in Raleigh, I was a little put off by the online questionnaire for adults and children using his BBS. It asked about favorite TV programs, physical appearance, sports, and other activities, but a simple question

was missing—one that I felt certain would have been on
the list twenty years ago: "What are your favorite books?"

Spring 1995: An (Interim) Afterword

Whatever the medium—newspapers, books, or magazines—many Netfolks saw the Internet as a path to diversity. That was partly why I liked seeing *The News &
Observer* online with A. C. Snow et al. Maybe the Internet
could rescue locally owned newspapers before they all
tumbled down the maws of conglomerates. On May 17,
1995, however, *The NandO Times,* the Webbed newspaper
of the *N & O,* ran a story that I'd never wanted to read. A
chain was buying up the company. For perhaps the first
time, a Net daily reported on the sale of it and its pulped-
wood siblings.

A color photo showed Frank Daniels III briefing his
staff. What really caught my eye, however, was a revelation that I saw later in the *New York Times:* "Frank Daniels
III said he was convinced that the paper needed to find a
larger parent in part to give the paper the resources necessary to nurture those new electronic efforts." More than
a few of us newspaper junkies had hoped that the new
technology would help keep the *N & O* local. I recalled one
reason why Daniels had not dumped his *N & O* stock in
the 1980s in favor of an investment in an online service.
"The relationship between a newspaper and a community," he had said, "has such a richness and history that
communities shouldn't lose that." Now, however, after 101
years in the Daniels family, the *N & O* and trimmings were
going to a California chain for $373 million. The buyer
was McClatchy Newspapers Inc., the former employer of
George Schlukbier, the Daniels's new-media guru.

No wicked corporate conspiracies existed here. The
Danielses simply felt comfortable with McClatchy, which
not only shared the *N & O*'s still basically liberal politics

but also enjoyed a good reputation in the newspaper business.

Run out of Sacramento, McClatchy Newspapers was a family-owned chain with just twelve dailies. It allowed much more leeway to local editors than many others did, and I might well have reacted just as the Daniels family did when the McClatchy people came calling. The *N & O* mustn't end up in the hands of some skinflint chain; McClatchy Newspapers could be an excellent alternative.

Still, the sale did not delight me. The Net, after all, was supposed to be good for small guys, including, presumably, family-owned enterprises. Josephus Daniels had bought the *N & O* at that bankruptcy auction in 1894, seen it through the Roaring Twenties, the stockmarket crash, and the heyday of his friend FDR. He must have died thinking that the Daniels name would forever grace the masthead. From a portrait in the boardroom, he looked out at his progeny announcing the transaction. Just why couldn't all the computers and cables and videocams have helped strengthen the family business, not force its sale?

I could see how the latter may have happened. The Daniels had had to invest in both the printing press and the new med*ia*, with an emphasis on the plural. A story on newsprint, an Internet audio, and a video would cost more than just an old-fashioned version. Network-related expenses of the *N & O* may have been smaller than the investment in new press, but they would only grow in the future. No-frills Web areas cost next to nothing to set up. But net.papers with the very flashiest graphics and full-motion video would need programmers and designers and other specialists, not all of them cheap. At the same time the Daniels wanted to cover their circulation area well, and that meant a big, expensive staff of reporters, too.

Just as important, however, the *N & O* faced strong competition for advertisers and readers. Yes, the Net

shrank distances and gave smaller companies some new
marketing opportunities. But as shown by Time Warner's
giant electronic newsstand, it could also create some good
synergies for media conglomerates offering package deals
to national advertisers. In certain respects—hardly all—
readers also benefited. I could key in "Carly Simon," for
example, and see any stories that might have appeared
about her, not only in *Time* but also in *Entertainment
Weekly* or *People.* Frank Daniels could bring together wire
service news and offbeat items from technical publications and others. But in the future he couldn't match the
brand appeal of corporations such as Time Warner.

Daniels had a right to be proud of his technological
accomplishments, of course. But from now on, assuming
that he stayed, as he apparently would for the moment, he
would be an employee rather than a member of the own-
ing family. Forget the Third Wave talk of Net saving us all
from conglomerates. We could all have our own home
pages on the World Wide Web, of course, and maybe put
out little magazines; and IUMA-style startups could always use the new technology to startle the Goliaths—and
in the end, exceptions notwithstanding, the Internet did
foster diversity. Clearly, though, it was far from an all-
purpose savior for the *N & O*s of the world. However powerful in North Carolina, the Raleigh newspaper was
hardly on an equal footing when it competed against the
very largest media organizations.

As if to underscore that point, eight huge newspaper
publishers had banded together earlier that spring to form
New Century Network, a club for the big boys on the Net.
Some people wondered if the giants might lose out in the
end—readers wanted to tour the Web themselves, not just
confine themselves to material favored by newspaper
coalitions. And maybe New Century wouldn't end up so
exclusive after all. Also, advertisers might prefer to sprin-
kle their cash around the Web rather than focus it on

newspaper chains—they could pay for links to their pages
from many sites without much ado. The natural economies
of the Net might yet win out over the business plans of the
giants. Still, for the moment, publishers such as Gannett
and the Washington Post Company were apparently setting
the tone of New Century itself. The 185 New Century papers claimed more than 23 million paying readers.

"New Century might raise antitrust questions," wrote
Rory O'Connor, a reporter for the *San Jose Mercury News,*
part of Knight-Ridder, a chain in New Century. Peter
Winter, interim chief executive of New Century, said the
publishers were "comfortable with our conformance to
antitrust statutes."[31]

Antitrust was the talk of the newspaper and online industries. In early June the U.S. Justice Department said it
was studying the network that Microsoft aimed to launch
in August. Just by clicking on the proper icon available
through the Windows 95 operating system, people could
join the Microsoft Network. And some newspapers and
other online services feared that Microsoft could stifle the
competition. In a year Windows might sell 20–40 million
copies; what if several million users clicked?

Newspapers worried increasingly about the Microsoft
Network and other online services. American Opinion
Research of Princeton, N.J., found that almost a fifth of the
surveyed editors and publishers thought they might lose
more advertising to online services than to television.
Nearly three-quarters said the business was in good shape
now. Just a half felt the same would be true by the year
2005.[32]

The newspaper chains tried to fight back. Large papers
now owned 11 percent of the shares in Netscape
Communications, the wizards behind the fastest and best
browser on the Web. For the moment things seemed fine
for the public. Netscape came up with new wrinkles that
other companies didn't offer, such as the ability for Web

pages to sprout color backgrounds without much fuss. But so far it was working with standards-setting bodies rather than saying, "Hey, you guys, these features will be *mine* alone." I just hoped that in the future Netscape wouldn't fashion its software to bind people to specific sources of news from conglomerates such as Knight-Ridder. Perhaps half the people cruising the Web were now using Netscape.

In a buying spree of its own, America Online purchased Internet fixtures such as WAIS Inc., the software company. WAIS had made some of the best publishing tools on the Net. America Online also bought the WebCrawler, a first-rate index to the Web. The company acquired Global Net Navigator, too, the wonderfully Netcentric magazine from O'Reilly and Associates, a guardian of Net culture. Just like Frank Daniels III, Tim O'Reilly alluded to the cost of online services. Explaining the sale, he told a GNN mailing list that "in order to really do justice to the information problem GNN was created to solve, GNN would have to be scaled up beyond our ability to fund it on our own. With many large players entering the Internet information services market, the best way to keep our lead was to team up with one of them."

The most dramatic—and, some critics might say, ominous—alliance may have happened when MCI teamed up with Rupert Murdoch to form a new partnership that could offer many kinds of material on the Net. It committed as much as $2 billion toward his News Corporation.

MCI wasn't just eager to be a pipeline for publishers and others—it wanted to Originate Content. The phone company was already publishing readers' short stories electronically by way of Gramercy Press. Soon it would release a trade paperback—yes, a book on pulped wood— from a novelist writing under the name of a fictitious Gramercy author. But the Murdoch alliance meant so much more. This global entrepreneur controlled Harper-Collins through News Corps. Would his electronic books enjoy global distribution advantages via MCI's pipelines, compared to offerings from smaller, less connected publishers?

Within the book business itself, the movement toward the Net was accelerating as summer 1995 neared. More and more authors were online, getting feedback from fans—just as the fledging rockers of IUMA did. It was a great morale booster, but only to a point. The novelist Nicholson Baker, author of the *New Yorker* article on electronic library catalogues, complained that e-mail had "the problem of promptitude. You have to answer within four days or you're being rude. I like the stateliness of paper, where you can take six months. You're still being unforgivably rude, but somehow it's okay because other people have been rude in this way before."[33] Obscure writers, however, found the fan mail from the Internet to be more helpful. In that way the Net was a *friend* of diversity.

Smaller publishers were also growing more comfortable with the Internet. Bookport, a California-based service, let them post their books on the World Wide Web for Netfolks to read page by page. Alas, a customer could not obtain a whole e-book at once. The idea, of course, was to discourage piracy. I disliked the idea of pay-per-read prevailing; the library model would make books much more popular among the young and actually *help* good publishers. But the Bookport was well done with oodles of great links to book-related sites on the Web. One of the first titles was *Netiquette,* a guide to manners on the Internet; that was in the community-minded spirit of the traditional Net.

Larger publishers, too, pushed ahead on the Web. Time Warner was selling "Quick Reads." It was a series of reference books, self-help guides, and others that you could download in full and search for, say, the right quote from a famous business executive (*Bartlett's Book of Business Quotations*) or the appropriate recipe (the *Cooking Library*). I could understand Time Warner's fondness here for reference books. Most readers didn't want to gawk at electronic novels hour after hour. The big question, in cases of tech-savvy conglomerates like Time Warner, was not whether the publishers were ready. It was whether the *public* was; whether enough people would end up soon enough with the proper hardware for reading books in bed or on the sofa.

That, of course, was where TeleRead came in. Whatever their sizes, publishers needed to hook the nonelite in this videocentric era before they gave up on the written word.

• • •

The above is not to suggest that text is the only way to communicate knowledge over the Net. The right graphics certainly can as well. One of the most intriguing examples of the potential here is a remarkable endeavor—the Visible Human Project—in which, so to speak, a murder lives on forever in cyberspace to the benefit of medical education and cancer research. I'll discuss this in the next chapter.

FIVE

Wired Knowledge: When They Let a Murderer Loose on the Internet

Paul Jernigan was a tattooed ex-mechanic just under six feet tall and weighing 200 pounds. He had been a drug addict and a chronic drunk, but nearly all his organs still looked in textbook shape by the standards of gross anatomy—a stroke of luck that would later help him win him a macabre competition. Jernigan had fatally stabbed and shot a seventy-five-year-old watchman after stealing a radio and a microwave oven. More than decade had passed. So had his hopes for a successful appeal to the courts.

Lying on a gurney in a Texas deathhouse—his arms outstretched, as if in a crucifixion—Paul Jernigan just gawked upward as his brother watched. No last words came before the poison flowed into Jernigan's veins.

Jernigan gave himself to science. A not-so-loquacious sister told me this was to spare the family the cost of burial. "It was like, matter of fact," his last attorney said of the donation. "It was a gift. He wasn't going to laud himself, pat himself on the back. We didn't send an embossed announcement that 'Paul Jernigan has donated his body to science and this is his ticket to redemption.'" [1] A former cellmate offered his own twist. Supposedly, Jernigan wanted his family to be able to sell his life story for a true-crime book. The donation just might make the planet care more about him in death than in life.

Within a year of the execution, in fact, I was reading clips about Paul Jernigan from the *London Times, Jerusalem Post, New York Times, Washington Post, Los Angeles Times,* and the *Boston Globe.* My favorite lead came out in a British paper called *The Independent:* "A killer was yesterday let loose on the Internet computer network." I wondered how he'd respond to flaming. The new Jernigan lived on as a digital atlas of the human body, a few steaklike cross sections of which I could dial up on the World Wide Web.

The Visible Human Project had come out of the National Library of Medicine in a Maryland suburb near Washington, D.C. It was one of the most spectacular examples of the Net's potential for spreading knowledge, the topic of this chapter.

Researchers had cut Jernigan into four blocks, frozen him in a blue gel, ground him down millimeter by millimeter, digitally photographed the 1,878 cross sections that emerged, scanned these slices [2] into a computer, put them on magnetic tape, and then on the Internet. Now the cadaver would be grist for medical educators and cancer researchers and perhaps even the designers of a "Fantastic Voyage"–style game. Players might explore the human body from the inside, just as Isaac Asimov's characters did in his novel. The government itself was spending $1.4 million on the project; expected commercial payoffs could reach the tens of millions and maybe more. Research and education, however, would be paramount here.

The Visible Human Project is but one of thousands of uses that academics and researchers have found for the

Internet. The Net is why many scientific luminaries were quick to slap the "fraud" label on efforts to create energy through cold fusion. Skeptics throughout the world could compare notes. If Paris couldn't replicate an experiment, then Boston would know within hours. Working in the other direction, fusion stalwarts have used the Internet to swap data and maintain the faith. Cyberspace is to knowledge what beehives are to honey.

Already the Net teems with thousands of mailing lists devoted to the most arcane disciplines, not just to the mainstream ones. Many scientists and other researchers envision the Net as a substitute for paper-style academic journals, subscriptions to some of which can cost as much as a Ford Escort. Stevan Harnad has caught the imaginations of many academics with "A Subversive Proposal" for scholars to publish their finished works formally on the Net without offering them to academic publishers. He puts out a vigilantly edited, psychology-related magazine with a circulation of tens of thousand on the Internet; he sees no reason for the Net just to be a repository for pre-publication papers. In his opinion, academics could use such opportunities to enjoy greater bargaining power with existing publishers.

Yet another glory of the Internet is that it serves as a bridge between experts and nonexperts, as well as one between authorities in many academic disciplines. A dean of a law school, for example, can sign up for mailing lists on electronic serials to learn more about the technology that is fueling the drive for copyright reform.

From Day One, the Internet was a creature of the elite research establishment, but knowledge-related uses have steadily grown more egalitarian—starting with the brightest students in elementary and high schools, then moving on to average children, and even to problem kids.

To dispose of a major issue, No, the Net shouldn't replace teachers. I couldn't agree more with Cliff Stoll when he rants against lax standards and mindless technocratic schemes. Well-trained teachers can provide inspiration and guidance to help children explore networks on their own. The last thing we need is to turn the educational reaches of the Net into one big flash card. What the Net can do is prepare children to deal with source material, with actual papers written by researchers, as opposed to pabulum in textbooks.

Correctly, Stoll criticizes some educators for teaching astronomy without children studying the actual sky; computer programs should only supplement such activities, not replace them. But shouldn't he apply the same "real thing" logic to Web-distributed source material and applaud students' easier access to it? Only the brightest children will benefit from a complicated mathematical treatise. But surely even an average student could take advantage of a historian's paper on a nearby Civil War battle. If anything, teachers could use the Web and other areas of the Net to demand *more* research from students. Just why must Stoll compare the Net to a fun but dumb educational film? Is a Web version of the *Odyssey* to be confused with some educational Looney Tunes?

Intriguingly, Web technology makes it possible for students to produce information, not just soak it up. In Fairfax County, Virginia, students at Thomas Jefferson, a high school for the gifted, are posting their "pages" on the World Wide Web. I can remember when college applicants submitted tape recordings of their music. Now they can also give M.I.T. or Caltech the addresses of their Web pages and demonstrate, in the most direct way, their familiarity with networking. They can post their papers and point to other people's pages that interest them.

Also, at Jefferson and countless other schools, students can electronically send their classmates to knowledge-rich sites on the Web. Clicking on "NASA" in blue letters within Bob's area, Jill can see what the space program is doing. Then she can return, click on other blue letters, and check out his tip to visit a history-related site discussing the Sputnik and Vanguard days. Via a project called MendelWeb, Ellen can read the famous treatise of Gregor Mendel, the geneticist, and retrieve other scientists' opinions; then she might write her own paper and post it on the Web for classmates and even for students elsewhere.

Clearly the value of the Net, for students and researchers alike, isn't just in the information per se—it's also in the ease of sharing it. Teachers can point to common Web resources (such as MendelWeb) from Web pages where they add their own comment, or even their own study guides. They can also link to other guides.

Some Web sites even offer electronic forms with questions to which students can respond—in either a multiple choice or an essay format. Andy Carvin, a specialist in educational technology with the Corporation for Public Broadcasting, praises the World Wide Web as "an excellent tool in which to design online curricula." Understandably, even elementary schools are getting on the Web with their own areas.

Other good things are happening. By way of a project called Big Sky Telegraph, Native Americans in Montana have been pen pals with children in the former Soviet Union. What better way to stir up an interest in writing, politics, and geography at the same time? Significantly, in Montana and other places, many schools are not on the Net directly. Instead, schools use affordable bulletin board systems—their own or perhaps those operated by hobbyists—which can relay Net-originated material. If need be, such systems can run on ancient computers of the kind found at garage sales; some messages may be delayed for days, but that's better than no connection at all. Within the BBS world, moreover, nets even exist especially for education. Consider K12Net, which includes at least "three dozen conferences specifically related to K-12 curriculum" and reaches some sixty school-associated systems in New Zealand alone. More and more, however, lucky schools are hooking into the Internet directly or at least arranging for teachers and students to get accounts elsewhere.

As a ninth grader at Poolesville Middle Senior High School, in Poolesville, Maryland, Chris Gazunis used the Net to study catastrophes such as earthquakes, hurricanes, and oil spills. "We didn't just look at a textbook diagram of what caused an earthquake and the casualty number associated with it," he recalled. "We used the networks to learn what happened to the people's lives and homes. Instead of just being given a set of directions and material that would result in an earthquake resistant building, we designed and tested them ourselves."[3]

Randy Hammer, a high schooler at Timberline High School in Lacey, Washington, who is blind "with two glass eyes," once had to have sighted people read the newspaper to him. No longer. Via network connections, he can enjoy the *Washington Post*, the *Moscow News*, and science-oriented publications—thanks to a gadget that reads aloud to him the words on his screen. "It's hard now," he wrote, "to remember how I lived without this wealth of materials and information at my fingertips."[4] That's what happens when the hardware is around.

Even in a wealthy place like the United States, however, society so far has been stingy toward high tech in public schools. The ratio between students and computers is something like 16 to 1. Some 75 percent of American schools have computers capable of getting on the Net, but the children can't all use them at once. What's more, just 35 percent of public schools have Internet hookups in classrooms, media centers, or computer labs. Only 3 percent of the classrooms themselves are wired in, according to a survey from the U.S. Department of Education.

We're talking almost Third World here. "It's amazing to me how people outside of education have no idea how teachers still have to line up outside the teachers' lounge to use the telephone," says a senior analyst at the Congressional Office of Technology Assessment.[5]

In the end, as I see it, the real solution is a TeleRead-style program of the kind described in the previous chapter. It would connect the students to the nets from home, reduce the future communications costs of the schools somewhat, and allow students to explore computer networks at leisure rather than just during the school day. A few small steps are already being taken in this general direction. The state of Maryland has granted limited—but free—Internet privileges to school children and other residents. Without leaving home, they can dial up material ranging from weather reports, to academic papers, to Shakespearean poetry. Joseph Peightel, a cable splicer with Bell Atlantic, says that the Sailor program is just the ticket for his ten-year-old daughter, whose hunger for books outstrips the family budget. While the Peightels can't retrieve the latest best-sellers, they at least can enjoy Project Gutenberg–style material in the public domain. The Maryland program helping the Peightels is not TeleRead, and it comes with problems and inefficiencies, but it may be as close as any state effort to the nirvana envisioned by Al Gore, in which all children could dial up the Library of Congress.

Needless to say, I bristle when Cliff Stoll glosses over the reasons why the Net can't provide easy answers to questions such as "What political compromises caused Bismarck to become the capital of North Dakota?" or "Why isn't Kyoto the capital of today's Japan?" or "What's the history of the Ruhr Valley, and what are the implications of its new Eastern European competition?" Of course. Worried about piracy, publishers have understandably kept their textbooks off the Net. The last laugh, however, just may be on the more zealous of the copyright interests. Right now Stoll couldn't be more correct about the need for more and better books on the Net; but as shown by, say, MendelWeb, the academic community is doing plenty on its own. And if this keeps up, the demand for copyrighted, commercial books, the kind that feed me, my editors, and yes, my publishers, too, could suffer. Far better to have a national digital library with privately originated books available from the very start.

Ahead I'll examine more closely some scientific and educational uses of the Net. Selections—yes, the print kind, not the Jernigan variety—will appear on:

- The "hows," the positives, and the negatives of the Visible Human Project—it stands out for reasons beyond the drama. The Clinton administration has encouraged high-bandwidth, scientific users of the Net. The original Visible Man requires sixteen gigabytes of storage—enough space to hold fifty *Encyclopaedia Britannica*s. Some say this isn't the best use of Net resources. I disagree, however, and I'll tell why. Along the way I'll pass on information about the Internet's Visible Man before he became so visible.

- High school use of the Internet. The United States is hardly the only nation with thousands of children in cyberspace—countries ranging from Canada to Singapore are putting students online, directly or indirectly. Significantly, computers and networks can help students outside the elite. Some proof of this comes from Nova Scotia, where, for several years, a high school has been using the Internet to benefit some "at-risk" students. I'll tell you about the Internet success that a Canadian teacher named Jeff Doran has enjoyed with leatherjacketed teenagers. Many are racing into the computer lab and, let's hope, away from fates such as Paul Jernigan's. The Internet project at Park View Education Centre is far from an unqualified triumph—many Park View teachers still fear the technology—but patterns there suggest a vast potential for educational uses of the Net if schools will modernize their curricula.

The Visible Man

The doctor, a Scottish-accented man in his fifties or sixties, had collected a wall full of diplomas and plaques. Perhaps that's why he felt entitled to give only the sketchiest of explanations when he told a Midwestern friend of mine that she might need heart surgery to avoid a possible stroke. Karen* would be in the hospital just a day or so. But during this time a surgeon would insert a catheter up her groin and go on to kill off selected heart cells. With luck, the operation would end her atrial fibrillation. It had made her heart throb as quickly as 200 beats a minute on occasion and had sent her to the emergency room.

Karen pressed for details about the recommended operation. "Ma'am," Dr. S. said in a peremptory burr, "this is too technical."

It was Valentine's Day and Karen and her husband would rather have been thinking about hearts in that way alone. But she wanted to know all. "Ma'am, I'll draw you a picture," Dr. S. said a bit grudgingly. The doctor sketched a crude heart that might as well have been on a greeting card. Hastily drawn lines showed how electric impulses were traveling through Karen's heart with an extra path. The operation would cut off the surplus wiring, so to speak.

Well, this was a start. But Karen still felt ignorant, and it was *her* body into which the catheter would go. And so it is with many patients, not all, but many. Even good doctors don't always tell enough.

The Visible Human Project, however, would make it easier for Karen to learn more. Dr. S. could have shown Karen a computer image of an actual human heart and have pointed to the exact areas that the surgeon would kill off. Karen would have picked up a better appreciation of the complexities of the proposed operation. At the same time, Dr. S. could also have juggled around computer images to show the increased risk of clotting that would result if she *failed* to have the operation. Karen would have emerged better informed and more confident—or less, whatever the facts justified. Someday she might even be able to dial up on the Internet an animated, perfectly detailed series of pictures of the operation.

That was what the Visible Human Project would mean. What's more, patient education was just one of many uses; the right technology could revolutionize the training of doctors and advance medical research.

As far back as the 1980s, such ideas intrigued Michael Ackerman, a Ph.D. in biomedical engineering who worked for the National Library of Medicine, part of the National Institutes of Health. He heard of a project at the University of Washington that was digitizing the human brain, although not the entire body. Researchers at other schools hoped to do the same with other organs. But they were less keen on collecting images and other data than on using the them, so why duplicate each other? Like the Internet itself, then, just one digitized corpse could help many researchers at once.

In North Carolina a marketing executive with a drug company was dreaming of a human atlas on a computer screen. Why should medical students have to make do with fold-out drawings in anatomy guides? Michael Du Toit, Vice President of marketing for Glaxo Inc., passed the idea on to a small company called Butler Communications, which checked out the technology. Glaxo had three goals. First, it wanted to create the basic images. Second, it wanted viewers to be able to wander through the body; ideally they could move the body for the best view, spin it, travel through it. And third, it wanted researchers to be able to give the lungs cancer, clog the arteries to the heart, and demonstrate the effects of drugs. But computers weren't ready. "The hype versus the deliverable," Robert Butler told me, "was miles and miles apart." To meet Glaxo's specs—to show the body by way of artistic recreations and virtual reality—might cost as much as $100 million.

Imagine the excitement that Du Toit and Butler must have felt on learning that academic and government researchers were finally coming up with the means for this to happen at a fraction of the expense. The Feds put out a request for proposals for the dissection job, and the crew at the University of Colorado made the final cut. Still unanswered was the question of whose corpse would end up on the Internet. The contest judges allowed a bit more leeway than did the people choosing Miss America and Mr. Universe.

The ideal candidate for Visibility could be anywhere from maybe thirty to sixty years of age and be a bit thin or pudgy, albeit not exceedingly so. Height mustn't go too far beyond the norms for male and female. Above all, the innards of the body had to be photogenic from an anatomical perspective. That weeded out anyone worn down by cancer or similar disease, not to mention any victims of automobile accidents or knifings.

A little unfairly, this contest had geographical limits. Texas, Maryland, and Colorado were the states with subcontracts to provide the body. I could understand Maryland and Colorado, but Texas? I wondered if the reason would be the fondness of the people down there for capital punishment. No longer did bodies have to roast in electric chairs. Texas helpfully killed its murderers with lethal injections. So, in this competition, Paul Jernigan was a strong contender from the beginning.

Murder is an act of the will no matter how poor or Hitlerian our parents are, or what genes shape us and our brains. But if Fate sent anyone to the deathhouse gurney and to Visible Manhood, it was Paul Jernigan. He lived out an updated Dreiser novel.

His full legal name was Joseph Paul Jernigan, and he was born in Geneva, Illinois, on January 31, 1954, the youngest of Earl Jernigan's six children. The boy suffered from asthma and almost died of it. He and his brothers and sisters typically owned just one pair of jeans each. Their mother eked it out in a chicken-processing plant, as a clerk at Montgomery Wards, and at other low-paying jobs, and they lived in public housing. She married a truck driver who, like Earl, was a strict disciplinarian toward the children. Later she suffered a stroke. Afflicted with a learning disorder, Paul flunked a grade at school and dropped out two years before graduating. He was a drunk and eventually was doing a pharmacy's worth of drugs, from Quaaludes to horse tranquilizers.

The Army trained Paul Jernigan as a mechanic, sent him to Germany, then tossed him out as unsalvageable. Perhaps recognizing the cruel matrix that shaped Jernigan, it gave him a general discharge (a "no comment" in effect) rather than a dishonorable one. A shrink later found Jernigan to be a passive-aggressive man who was sometimes TNT-volatile. In the years after the military Jernigan kept a cooler of ice and beer in his automobile; a typical paycheck went for pot, cheeseburgers, and enough octane for himself and the car.

Paradoxically, though, friends trusted Paul Jernigan with their children. Jernigan was the perfect baby-sitter who enjoyed romping around with his charges. He married for a stretch and loved his stepchildren.

But he failed at marriage just as he had failed in school and in the Army.

Jernigan bungled at burglary, too. He was already a two-time loser in 1981 when he and a pal named Roy Lamb were driving down the road in Corsicana, Texas, a small, howdy-neighbor kind of town south of Dallas on Interstate 45. Emboldened by a night of booze and pot, the two decided to rob Edward Hale's house. They began stuffing their loot into a pillow case when Hale surprised them. Lamb ran out. Jernigan beat Hale over the head with an ashtray, hoping to kill off the witness. Hale stubbornly survived. Then Jernigan stabbed him with a rusty, dull-bladed meat knife, which just bent on Hale's chest. And so he took a shotgun and fired until the watchman was dead. Edward Hale did not die painlessly.

After the murder, Jernigan went to Houston to try to straighten out his life. He was in a halfway house when arrested.

Some would say Jernigan needn't have wound up on the gurney; the law prevented the courts from accepting an accomplice's testimony. Mark Ticer, his last attorney, believes that Jernigan may have felt so contrite that he wanted to die. Ticer grew truly fond of his client. In character, Jernigan would constantly inquire about the lawyer's two-year-old and remember birthdays.

Jernigan gave Ticer's wife, Cecily, some earrings made from gold bought with his military pension, and he crafted a wishing-well bucket for Ticer. Ticer was as trusting of the murderer as Jernigan's friends had been; he would have trusted him with his own young daughter. Even on death row Jernigan would write to the stepchildren from his failed marriage.

Smoking a hand-rolled cigarette and sipping a Pepsi, he would discuss legal strategy with Ticer until finally there wasn't quite so much to be strategic about.

"Paul," Ticer more or less said, "things are not going well. I guess I have to talk about your burial arrangements if they're going to execute you. I know your family doesn't have a lot of money." And it was there in the Ellis prison in Huntsville that Ticer learned of The Gift. Neither knew Jernigan would eventually become the Visible Man.

Mark Ticer tried for a stay of execution up to the last minute. Aware of Ticer's devotion to him, Jernigan asked his lawyer not to witness his last minutes. Death was almost instant. Paul Jernigan died much more smoothly than he had lived.

The state anatomical board, a subcontractor of the University of Colorado, took it from there. Jernigan got one and a half gallons of 1 percent formalin. That was a light touch. Often cadavers are embalmed with ten gallons of a stronger preservative, and they sit and pickle for a year, so that when medical students cut them up all the tissues are gray. But the idea here, in case Jernigan won the Visible Man honors, was to keep his tissue looking nice and bright like prime meat; the students would be able to enjoy a better, more realistic view.

Writing this chapter, I pondered the use of the state anatomical board as a cadaver procurer. Thank God the board was separate from the court system. Given the rage for businesslike government, I could just imagine some of the wilder politicians setting up an execution quota to work toward a balanced state budget. But the real reason for the use of Jernigan's corpse was more prosaic. Texas had one of the best cadaver-donation programs in the country, and of some 2,000 bodies that year, his just happened to show up at the right time and in the right condition.

A Learjet flew Jernigan from Texas to Colorado. Awaiting him were the masterminds of the dissection effort at the University of Colorado Health Sciences Center in Denver. Victor Spitzer specialized in radiology and cellular and structural biology; David Whitlock was a professor of cellular and structural biology. The people working most on Jernigan would be the research assistants in the dissection room, which, day to day, was overseen by Tim Butzer, thirty, and his wife, Martha Pelster, a bright, curly-haired woman of twenty-five who would later apply for medical school. Helen Pelster, another assistant, was the sister of Martha Pelster.[6] The whole scenario—the family connection—begged for embellishment from Stephen King or Robin Cook.

I asked Martha Pelster if her work haunted her at night. "I kind of keep it on a pretty even level," she said. "I don't have too much trouble with it."[7] She said Butzer felt the same.

Had Jernigan inspired much after-hours talk with her husband?

"If there was a problem that needed to be worked out."

But did Pelster and Butzer reflect on the Visible Man's past in relation to what was happening now?

"Not too much. Getting emotionally involved with something like that—you don't want to discuss it. It isn't relevant to what we're doing."

Inquiring about the university's most famous cadaver, I learned that Jernigan had come with at least two tattoos on his chest area; they looked vaguely like dragons. His build and muscles were impressive. The lab had to modify some of the machinery to handle Jernigan. He showed up with just one testicle, which, I learned elsewhere, was the aftermath of painful surgery from his military days. I also heard that another operation had left him without an appendix. Students and researchers seeking to unravel the mysteries of appendixdom would just have to turn elsewhere. As a taxpayer, however, I didn't feel cheated. This was the States, not Bangladesh; did that many Americans die without any remnants of surgery? Jernigan's cadaver stood head and shoulders above a rival, a woman who was a chronic alcoholic with visible damage to her liver. In the hierarchy of the dissection room livers must have counted more than appendixes.

Before the millimeter-by-millimeter grinding, the scientists treated Jernigan to magnetic resonance imaging (MRI, mixing radio waves and magnetic fields) and computer-aided tomography (CAT or CT, which is like topography except that it's on the innards of the human body). MRI picks up soft tissue. CAT scans are good for hard tissue, and for the differences between it and soft tissue. The researchers CT'ed Jernigan both before and after he was frozen, and these scans had to correspond with the alignment of the digitized photographs. Imagine the precision required here.

Preparing to slice the icy cadaver into four blocks for convenient grinding, the lab crew sharpened up on a less exalted cadaver. Vertebrae were a problem. "This saw would curve," Pelster said, "so you wouldn't have a perfect perpendicular flat cut. It would have a curve to it. So we took the cadaver back to the CT scanner and found the level where we could make a cut." In the end there were three cuts and four sections of Jernigan—head and torso, abdomen and pelvis just down to the thighs, the rest of the thighs and the knees, and just below the knees to the feet. The frozen pieces went into an aluminum mold, one at a time. And then the researchers poured a blue gel around them (the same blue you'll see on the edges of the cross sections if you dial them up on the World Wide Web). The result was four chunks of ice, each approximately 20 by 20 by 15 inches.

The grinding area was the next stop. Plexiglass enclosed it. That was a must. Pieces of cadaver would fly everywhere as science turned Paul Jernigan into dust with a spinning, carbide-tipped blade. "You'd think we'd have trouble sectioning bone," Pelster said, "but that's not been the case. Bone always cuts very clean. But sometimes we have a lot of trouble with the tendons. The tendons are such that they don't want to shear off cleanly, and so a lot of time we did hand scalpel work on each slice. So the slices might take ten minutes each instead of four minutes each." Actually the time varied. "Ninety slices were the most we cut on any one day, and we averaged sixty. Sometimes it was ten a day. It was about four months of sectioning."

"Were you worried about damaging the goods?" I asked.

"Definitely. We just did the best we could."

"Any near misses?"

"There were definitely a few. We never were to the point where we torpedoed the whole project. It would be more a possibility of losing a slice. We never came close to botching the whole thing. You look back and you see a little dot of ice here or there, things like that. You do the best you can. But I think it turned out well."

All along, of course, cameras and lights were clicking and flashing away. The slices went into a black-walled, reflection-proof chamber for photographing by one digital camera and two with film. A table held the cameras. It turned to give each a view of the cross sections from the same angle. The results went into a Macintosh Quadra 840AV with 128 megabytes of random access memory and 2 gigabytes of hard disk space. It was, in other words, many times more powerful and could store at least several times more than the average personal computer. As with the grinding, problems sometimes arose. "You think computers are so precise," Martha Pelster said, "but they're not. Things are always going wrong." Typically working with her and Tim were such people as the man who kept the grinding machine running, a camera expert, and a computer expert (Helen Pelster, Martha's sister), who would transfer the digitized Jernigan to tape and CD-ROM. Come the end of a hard day of photography, the lab crew collected everything and put it back in the freezer. "And then when we were finished doing this," Pelster said, "we had many bags of things that needed to go be cremated." The dust went to a contractor for incineration.

Digitized photos and CAT and MRI images from Jernigan went to National Library of Medicine in Maryland and to the Scientific Computing Division at the National Center for Atmospheric Research in Boulder, Colorado. The latter worked with a Cray Y-MP/8 supercomputer and Silicon Graphics workstations to study the results. A headline on the World Wide Web summed up the magnitude of the computational task: "The Visible Human Project: Can It Bring a Supercomputer to Its Knees?" A machine with the power of the Cray could take the 1,878 cross sections, stack them like slices of an upright bread loaf, and create electronic bones or hearts or brains that looked as if they had never been taken apart in the first place.

By fall 1994, Michael Ackerman at the National Library of Medicine was ready to tell the world about the electronic Jernigan and to have his images posted on the Net by way of the weather forecaster's facilities. "We hold this out as an example of the future of health care," Ackerman said. He predicted that the study of medicine would become increasingly visual. No one talked then of a murderer, and so the first stories on the wire services blandly mentioned an anonymous thirty-nine-year-old donor from Texas who had died of a drug overdose.

Learning that a digitized corpse would go on the Internet, not everyone greeted the news with unalloyed praise. Some reviled this as a waste of Net resources. Why not use CD-ROMs to distribute the information? To an extent I could see their arguments. The Library was releasing sixteen gigabytes of images at the start, and even someone with a deluxe Net connection could spend a week or so downloading it. Critics believed that this squandered bandwidth, that it was a bit like cruising down a narrow country road with an overgrown tour bus and fifty cars honking at it from behind. The strain on the Internet was far from that bad. But even by Net standards this was indeed a behemoth, and much more importantly, the bandwidth defenders worried about the precedent being set here. Sixteen gigabytes of images was equivalent to 8 billion pages of double-spaced typing. Individual e-mail messages commonly took up only a page or two.

Even so, the Visible Man had his friends out there in cyberspace. Anxious to beat rivals to the data, one company kept its modems pumping away for a week until it had received all of Jernigan. It didn't want to wait weeks or months for tapes. Thanks to the Net, many people throughout the world could receive Jernigan at the same time. In the first few months of the release, more than 900 companies, schools, and people wrote Ackerman about licenses giving them permission to use the data in experiments and products. Some 100 actually followed through—everyone from pharmaceutical firms to a young artist who, according to Ackerman, assured him that she would make tasteful use of the images.

Luckily from a bandwidth perspective, you didn't have to download all of Jernigan. Each slice was a mere seven megabytes in a spatial resolution of 2,048 by 1,216 pixels (several times sharper than that of a typical personal computer). A maker of software for ophthalmologists could pull down only the images dealing with the eye and related brain areas. Those aiming for the podiatry market could focus on the feet and ankles. What's more, even without a license, ordinary Net users could dial up Jernigan Lite, so to speak, from the World Wide Web.

Coming over the Net eventually would be more than just the raw, unprocessed images. Refined versions—for example, animated Jernigans, rotating in 3-D, or even virtual reality versions—could go anywhere in the world. And when they did, researchers and students would be wanting their own pet views. CD-ROMs just didn't store enough data to anticipate all the possibilities. Typically they could hold maybe 650 megabytes of data. Even extended, the storage would offer a fraction of what could be available via high-speed connections to sites from Paris to Melbourne.

Jernigan, you might say, was more than just the material for a medical experiment. He was also a focus of a research project to develop special formats for libraries of visual information on the Net. Eventually people would be able to download not just images but also the "objects" that made up the images.

"These objects will have knowledge in them," Michael Ackerman said, "so they know how they relate to each other and the rest of the scheme. Say you ask for the heart. What you get of course is the not a picture of the heart but the objects that made up the heart that your software has now rendered as the heart. If you point to something on the heart, it can open up because it's made up of these objects. And if you point to something on the margin of the heart and say 'What is attached here?' that object on the margin knows what its nearest neighbor is even though it's not in the picture. And it knows to go back to the database and bring up what's attached to it."

Such an approach might even take advantage of Web-style technology to link together libraries at a number of locations. So you might smoothly travel from, say, a processed image of a blood vessel done up at School X to an animated image of a heart as tweaked by Company Y.

Those uses would increase the load on the Internet, of course. But ultimately the principle of the expanding pipeline might work to the benefit of all. That is, the heavier the traffic on the Net, the heftier the connections would be built. So in the end, everything would be cheaper—from image transmissions to sending one-page notes by electronic mail. The challenge, of course, was for this to happen without the costs of ordinary Net users being driven up by the workload that the image libraries and similar endeavors would bring about. That's where TeleRead might come in. It could systematically promote the mass use of electronic forms for tax documents, business transactions, and other purposes. And indirectly the money saved on paperwork could go not only toward a national library but also to help upgrade the present Internet for researchers and the world at large.

Right now people tended to see the applications of the Net in terms of one use versus another—in terms of money for low-cost networks for consumer education versus high-bandwidth connections of the kind that Ackerman wanted. With a TeleRead-style approach and enough imagination, however, we could take full advantage of the economies of the technology. And so although we would not end the clashes between Net users with different priorities, we could at least reduce them.

Several other cost-related questions arose beyond those of the expense of the network connections. I wondered how much patients would be charged to see a picture of the innards of Jernigan or a Visible Woman. Robert Butler doubted that his client, Glaxo, was ready to say. However, he left me with the impression that this probably would not be pay per view. Glaxo had its own reasons for going ahead—for example, showing doctors the effects of its pharmaceuticals on the body. So, no, he said, this was not a plot to gouge the public with peep shows.

A related issue, arising from the involvement of drug companies, was the question of proprietary information.

While the images were on the Internet for all to see, this project was not entirely in the spirit of the Net's openness. Butler, for example, might have feared that I was working for a rival corporation, and he waited several weeks to return my calls. I could understand his reasons. Still, I was startled to learn that Ackerman at the National Institutes of Health would not even release to me a list of the companies that had licensed the use of the images. Nor had NIH organized a newsgroup or a mailing list. Surely all the hundreds of licensees would have common problems, common opportunities, that they could discuss without imperiling each other's projects.

Yet another question went back to one of the main reasons given for the project. Could medical students really learn by hooking into the Net and dialing up the images from the Visible Man? David Dean should have been a complete booster of this endeavor. He was, after all, a Ph.D. who worked in medical imaging and taught anatomy at Case Western Reserve University. And yet he told me, "I feel you can't replicate the experience in the anatomy lab. Students will have no time for this stuff. They're totally overwhelmed. They can see the same structures again and again in different bodies."

At the University of North Carolina in Chapel Hill, Gerry Oxford, professor of physiology, said that seeing organs in three dimensions wasn't the same as *feeling* them. "Physicians in training need a visceral appreciation of the fact that they will have responsibility for the human body." Even a believer in the project, Marc Nelson, assistant dean of medical education at the Stanford University School of Medicine in Palo Alto, worried that electronic anatomy could lessen contacts between students and teachers.[8]

Real bodies, however, cost universities $600 each— assuming they could get them in the first place. And students would not have eyeballs, hearts, hands, and livers to themselves.

Of all the boosters of the project, Martha Pelster may have been the most persuasive. She worked as a lab assistant, had cut up dozens of bodies, and now was headed to medical school. "When you look at this cadaver," Pelster said of the digitized Jernigan, "everything is still in its orientation. When you go in and dissect, you take a lot of stuff out. If you cut something wrong or cut through something and toss the object into the reject bin, you've lost it. But with this visible male, you can go back in again. You can see what happened before your lab partner went in there and messed up your cadaver. This cross-sectional anatomy is going to be the be-all and end-all. A book can't have this many cross sections, this good."

Just as important, no one in the project, from Ackerman to Pelster, was touting electronic cadavers as a complete substitute for the real ones that the medical students studied. The digitized versions would simply augment the real cadavers, the ones that you couldn't reboot if you cut them the wrong way. In the new era, medical schools could even require students to put the human body together, not just take it apart.

Cadavers in cyberspace would offer yet another advantage: even schoolchildren could study them. People for the Ethical Treatment of Animals and some rock-n-roll musicians such as Pearl Jam were asking schools to "cut out dissection" and use computer imaging or model frogs. Thanks to the Visible Human Project, however, students someday would do better than just viewing pixels flashing across the screen. They would be able to tour the body of an actual human. Potential medical students, moreover, could get a head start. Long before they reached the slicing rooms, they would be familiar with electronic cadavers and be able to make better use of the real ones. What's more, the digitized Jernigan could revolutionize training in laparoscopic surgery, where doctors inserted tubes in patients and operated with tiny instruments and TV-like monitors and cameras. The view on the video screen of a training computer could be true to life.

All this was not even to mention other applications—for example, computer-simulated crash tests to improve auto safety, efforts to study the range of wrist motion and reduce carpal tunnel syndrome in typists, or investigations of ways to protect athletes against injuries.

I asked Mark Ticer if Jernigan's family had ever thought of suing for any of the wealth that the project might create from medical products and the rest.

The answer pleased me in this litigious era. Ticer said that if anything the family would be offended that anyone raised the issue. That was the way Jernigan and his kin were. "There wasn't a condition attached to his gift," Ticer said.

Sharon Kuster, Jernigan's sister, said her brother would "probably be happy about it. I am."

"Now he can be remembered for all the good he did rather than all the evil," Ticer said. "I think he'd be quietly delighted." I picked up on the "quietly." Jernigan's invisibility, prior to his crimes, was not just because of his station or lack of station in life. That was his way. Many other inmates on death row gravitated toward microphones. Jernigan spurned them. The true crime book, if one ever resulted, would never have come out while he was walking and breathing.

Shortly after I talked to Mark Ticer and Sharon Kuster, my friend Karen got the results of an intensive examination by a second doctor. It seemed that Karen would not be undergoing the heart surgery. But even now she couldn't tell for sure. What's more, if Karen received drugs instead, the medical benefits of the Visible Man might still help her someday; a major pharmaceutical company, after all, was hoping to use the digitized cadaver as a tool to explore and demonstrate the effects of its products.

My thoughts shifted back to Jernigan the human. Lying on the death gurney, awaiting the poison, would he

have wanted to make The Gift if someone had rushed in
and asked at the last minute, "Do you realize you'll be all
over the Internet? That you'll suffer the ultimate invasion
of privacy? That strangers from here to Oslo will see your
guts?" I'd like to think that Jernigan would have nodded
and the Learjet would still have flown the body up to
Denver. For the sake of Karen, of other sick people, of
those who just might live longer and better if their sur-
geons were slightly more skilled, or if they themselves
could make the right decisions about their medical care—
for the sake of them all, I was not-so-quietly delighted that
the invisible man was now visible.

Schools: Park View Educational Centre

The big motto out of the United States, in the 1990s,
seemed to be, "Build jail cells, not classrooms." Again and
again, politicians would promise to shrink the bloat in
school budgets while Fighting Crime; I shared some of
their skepticism toward the edutocracy. Washington, D.C.,
was Exhibit A here. In one recent year the city had shelled
out half a billion on public schools but paid just $2 million
for books.

Suppose, however, that U.S. schools had been spending their money in a way that helped keep children out of
jail *and* helped them learn. Americans might do well to
study Park View Education Centre. It is a high school up
in the Canadian province of Nova Scotia, and something
weird and wonderful had been happening there over the
past few years. At Park View the Internet was not reserved
just for the usual suspects—the would-be Bill Gateses, the
local Steve Jobses, the prodigies who already owned PCs
and Macs and were dialing up Christie Brinkley photos on
electronic bulletin boards. Many of the children on the
Net were the at-risk students, those in danger of leaving
Park View because of academic or disciplinary problems.

They were in the "general-stream" track. And just as in the States, the college-bound children looked down on them. That was unfair. Many of the general students were bright and simply didn't want to go to college. Some of the general boys, not all, wore black leather jackets, tight jeans, and black boots. And they used razor blades to tattoo the logos of Ford and Chevy onto their skins. The at-risk girls were less colorful. But some had disciplinary problems of their own, along with the same lack of interest in academics. What's more, certain teenagers in the area were doing marijuana and hashish and boozing it up; teachers at Park View worried constantly that the wilder of the students would turn up on the police blotters.

Fighting against pot smoking and other behavior of the Jernigan variety, some teachers at Park View systematically used the Net to bolster the egos of the general students while also improving their scholastic skills. Yes, alarms went off in my head when I heard the word "self-esteem." Too often, at least in the States, this quality came at the cost of academics. Saying, "You're good!" was not enough. Gold stars—if dishonestly earned—would just teach the children that the educators were liars.

Some teachers at Park View Education Centre, however, were mixing self-esteem with reading and writing in a way that true Net nerds would love. And it was happening in a cash-strapped place a continent removed from Silicon Valley in both distance and technical expertise.

This was not borderline Canada. Park View Education Centre was a good two days' drive from the state of Maine. The school served Lunenburg County, a mostly rural area settled by German-speaking people whose descendants still reverted to dialect. Bridgewater (pop. 9,000 or so) was the nearest town. Named for the modest bridge across the La Havre River, it was in many respects All Canadian— with streets with names like "King" and "Queen" and "Prince." Businesses such as Gow's Hardware and Rofihe's Men's Wear had been in the same families for generations.

The Bridgewater area boasted a Michelin tire plant, too, and a mall and twin cinemas. And it was growing. But many inhabitants were displaced farmers, lumberjacks, and cod fishermen; tensions from work or the lack of it could show up in some homes, to the disadvantage of the children. When I was researching this chapter, Canada's unemployment rate was 10 percent, while Lunnenburg County's was 12–13 percent.

In at least one way, Park View Education Centre may have reflected both the business climate and the Canadian winters, or perhaps just some of the educational crazes of yesteryear. Park View was built in the late '70s with narrow little windows that more or less cheated the classrooms of a river view. Those slots were somewhat emblematic; many children hadn't been outside Nova Scotia. Even among the academic-track students, fewer than 40 percent were making it to college. Park View, then, was not quite the stereotypical place for educational high tech.

Still, the provincial government, colleges, and the business community had been quietly working with Park View and other schools to upgrade the workforce. In this spirit an education professor at Mount Saint Vincent University, in Halifax, organized a project called Learning Connections. Pitching in was the Nova Scotia Technology Network. One idea was to use computers to hook students in with employers by way of the Internet to give them a taste of the workplace. It would happen. But something would overshadow it—student-to-student communication over the Net.

Jeff Doran, a technophobic English teacher at Park View, wasn't sure what to think when he first heard of the grand plans. His tenth grade class of general students did not exactly teem with computer nerds. Many of the children had flunked a grade. "Some of them had reading levels down around grade three or four. One or two maybe would have been considered at a grade ten level. I didn't have any goal except to try to keep them in school and keep them in class." He also had his share of questions about the project itself. "All we were told was that we would get some computers, and then we'd get this connection through the phone lines, and the students would be able to write to people around the world, and then when the project was over at the end of the year, we could keep the hardware. I had no idea what we were then going to do with it, and I certainly had never used it before." Doran didn't even own a television or answering machine. "I still had a phonograph. But I didn't even have a tape player, and I had been writing on the typewriter all my life."

But Doran had something else going for him, something even more helpful than technological expertise. And that was an abundance of good, teacherish skills and empathy for his students, even the ones with the tattoos. He himself had rebelled. A Harvard graduate, he had fled the United States during the Vietnam War to avoid the draft. Doran's exact political beliefs weren't the point here, though; a dare-devil Green Beret might have shown the same ability to brook the foibles of the general students. What mattered was that Doran cared more about results than about whether the children followed every little rule. Above all he cultivated rather than feared the students' ability to think on their own.

The Nova Scotia Technology Network provided some technical help, but would not instantly answer every question. "So," Doran recalled, "we did a lot of muddling through ourselves and a lot of teaching of each other. And that was one of the best things. Some of the students became teachers because they learned by experimenting, and then they showed each other. And invariably they showed me, and so I learned from them. The first thing I discovered was that there could be no front of the room. It had twelve computers in it that circled around the walls. And there was no way that I could stand at any point and demand everybody's attention. I learned that in about three minutes of the first period."

Significantly, Jeff Doran's English class for general students had a one-to-one ratio between students and computers, a stark contrast to those in just about all other public schools in Canada and elsewhere. Students could use the machines not only for networking but also for word processing. In fact, they started using the machines so often that in those early days, Doran was holding classes in the computer lab regularly rather than in the scheduled rooms.

I asked Doran which students he remembered most vividly from those first days on the Net, and two came to his mind: Betty* and Mac*. Betty was the only girl of the twelve students on the first day of school. "She was, uhm, kind of an old-fashioned, sweet-faced girl," Doran said, "with one of the foulest mouths that I ever encountered. Yeah. But she had to be to hold her own against these boys. She was surly and sullen and stubborn with me, and I don't think she ever actually came to blows with any of the boys, but she came pretty darned close." Betty was brighter than most in the class. And yet, feisty or not, she lacked self-confidence. Many would have written her off. More than a few teachers regarded the general classes as a dumping ground. "She was pretty unimpressed by what she could do in the computer room," Doran said. "She at first was doing most of her assignments by handwriting."

Meanwhile Mac was hardly off to the most promising of starts. His head was shaved into a Mohawk. A reform school alum, he was short and stocky and looked a bit like a small World Wrestling Federation champ, according to Doran. Mac's face bore scars from the fights he got into. He would regularly pound the bejeezus out of other teenagers. "I'm not sure why Mac was in school," Doran said. "It may have had something to do with the law—either school or jail. He was not happy to be here. And his skills were very, very low. He was about the lowest I had ever seen in a student."

Okay, so this was the raw material. I didn't expect Doran to turn either Betty or Mac into Oxford dons—everything was relative—but I wondered how far he had gotten with the computers and the Internet.

"Well," Doran said, "once she finally started on the computer, she started writing more than she had ever written before. And I believe that's how you learn to write, by writing." She organized her sentences and paragraphs better, her vocabulary expanded, and fewer spelling errors popped up in her work—not just because she could spell-check but because she cared more. Her scrawlings in a loose-leaf notebook hadn't looked so impressive. But now she could use a computer printer and see the same, beautiful results as an honors student doing a ten-page thesis.

"The second big difference," said Doran, "was that she was writing e-mail to other students. Suddenly she had an immediate audience. This wasn't some make-believe English project where we would pretend to have a pen pal somewhere and pretend to write to them. This was a real person who was going to read that message and respond right away, and that kind of feedback made her, and made all of the students, suddenly aware of the importance of an audience. And an audience in writing is something that they had never experienced before, because the audience was the teacher and who cares what the teacher thinks? Except that the teacher gives you the mark, so you just write what you think the teacher wants you to say.

"But now Betty and the others had people who would write back and forth about their weekends, and their boyfriends, and their dates, and their sports, and their hobbies, and their cats, and so on. And I think it opened up a sensitivity to what was acceptable in print, and how your words can affect people, and the differences between people—especially over great distances, because a large number of the students that we were writing to in Vancouver were Asian. In fact they were fairly recent immigrants to Canada, so their English wasn't that great. So actually Betty's writing skills were better." And that, in turn, helped her think better of herself.

Meanwhile Mac, too, was progressing. At the start Doran gave Mac and others a list of twenty words; they were then to look up the definitions and use the words in sentences. The time limit was four weeks. Mac needed the month. He couldn't even cheat well; copying others' work, he blundered because he did not know what he was cribbing. "The last thing that he could ever see himself doing," Doran said, "would be sitting in front of a computer, you know, at a keyboard. With these beefy fingers of his, he was gonna tap away? I mean, that was out of the question."

Doran, however, managed to stretch out Mac's attention span to put up with the limits of the machines—to give them the detailed instructions they needed. In computerdom, people use the term "boot up" to mean turning on their machines or loading programs into them. And, Doran recalled, "There were times I half expected he was gonna literally boot this thing across the room."

"Yes," Mac snapped back at Doran, "I'll boot the friggin' thing up!"

"And yet," Doran recalled, "within that one year he was writing messages to pals in other schools and to me as well."

By then Betty wasn't just sassing back the boys when they teased her. She was actually teaching them how to use the equipment. Her marks shot up to the 90s. Not content just to write a few short paragraphs, she was turning out well-organized letters several hundred words long in a professional-looking business format. That was unimpressive by the standards of academic students, but a true triumph for Betty; she even zapped off a paper letter to a suspense novelist she admired. The writing skills she developed on the Net had helped make this possible.

Simultaneously her opinion of herself rose to the point where she was one of the chattier participants in a video that Park View students helped make, and that was later shown on a Halifax television station. Students shot scenes to send across Canada to counterparts at a school in Vancouver, British Columbia. And Betty showed up again and again on camera. It would have been nice to write that she went on to college, but she did not. She ended up a waitress. Partly due to the Net, however, she surely was a better waitress—more at ease with her customers, and better material someday for management if that was what she wanted.

And Mac? "One of the last things I got from him," Doran said, "was a message about how he felt he had been changing that year, and how he had been improving. And I agreed—I thought he had, too. And then just about that time, he pulled this stupid move and got drunk while he was on a class trip and got kicked out of the school." But the story didn't end then. "Mac moved to British Columbia and is gainfully employed. In the boys' cases, the measure of success is that they are not in jail. In 1990, probably ten boys were at risk of failing and dropping out of school. Two were at risk of ending up behind bars or dead."

Reflecting on past and present students at Park View, Doran noted the little triumphs which led to the big ones. The Net helped whet the children's interest in school—to the point where, often, just about all the students in his first period showed up. It was a virtual miracle, given the sleep hunger of adolescents.

Clearly the Net could be a truant officer's best friend. "I use computers a lot," one enthusiastic student e-mailed me from Bridgewater. "I come in on any free time that I have, I even give up my lunch hour to play with the computer, but I would really like to have more class time in the computer room." She said that computers "hold so

much wonder to a person. Like me. Writing on a computer does help out with reading and writing skills."
Another student, a tenth grader who lacked a computer at
home, told how much he'd enjoyed corresponding with
an aunt and uncle in Winnipeg. At the time he e-mailed
me, his relatives had just had a son, and his e-mail was
going into their baby book. Textbooks alone would never,
never have encouraged him to look forward to school the
way the Net did.

I asked Doran if there were any test scores for the children to document the Internet's benefits to the children at
Park View. He said that scores by themselves would mis-
lead since he had improved as a teacher in other ways.
And yet he believed the Net had helped; since he couldn't
supervise the class constantly, he had learned to foster curiosity among the students as they explored the Net on
their own. He and some other teachers in the experiment
understood that they and the children would be learning
from each other, that the old authority models were gone.
The same trend was gradually happening in industry in
Canada and the world at large. So if Doran wasn't turning
out Ph.D.s, he at least was creating better workers.

Other reasons existed for his success. The videotape
reinforced the Net experiences. The Park View students
looked forward to seeing their counterparts. Much more
importantly, Doran let children use the Internet in ways
that meant the most to them. The Net was like the videotape. Doran had expected his students to shoot pictures of
quaint homes, of beaches, of the usual, touristy sites,
when they were showing off the Bridgewater area. Instead
the students photographed the places where they worked
and shopped. And that told all. The e-mail was the same
way; students would most benefit from the technology if it
was on their own terms. At Park View, some virtual romances even developed between the students and those
elsewhere. One boy wrote to a Florida school asking to be
put in touch with a cheerleader.

Yet another explanation for Doran's success was that students could spend hour after hour on their computer. So they had plenty of time for school compositions and for writing letters to friends in Vancouver and elsewhere. (That wasn't true of all the students in latter years. Although Doran felt they did well, they might have done still better with more time.)

Perhaps most important of all, the machines didn't put down the general students the way so many humans did. "It's been my experience that the technology benefits the struggling student much more than it does any other student—in literacy growth, self-esteem, tech skills," said Lorri Neilsen, the education professor at Mount Saint Vincent University who had started the Learning Connections project at Park View and elsewhere.

The positives aside, the Bridgewater experiment was not a complete triumph. "It's very important to know the spirit of this project was carried by a handful of teachers," Neilsen said. In fact, just eight of forty teachers in the school participated in the project. Skeptics were worried about it taking time away from the usual curriculum. Yet another problem was the authority question; some teachers had to know everything and were nervous about students learning behind their backs. A third complication was gender: Many female teachers were uncomfortable around technology.

Answers and solutions existed to all those challenges. In the case of academic students, I could appreciate the need to cover a vast range of subjects that colleges demanded. But with a TeleRead-style arrangement, just about all the major resources would be online anyway. Old material over a period of time could be scanned into the national database—a highly economical way to distribute it, and even better by archival criteria alone since unread paper material might well disintegrate anyway without anyone caring about it.

Even with the Net as it existed then, students of all kinds learned many shortcuts that enabled them to turn out better papers. The knowledge on the Net was far, far shallower on the whole than at, say, the Library of Congress in the States. But it may well have exceeded what the students could find in some small-town libraries. If nothing else, by logging onto the Net, they could learn how to stay up with the most current knowledge—no small edge in an era when new products replaced old ones in months rather than in years, and when academic journals proliferated.

What about the authority question? That could diminish in time if schools of education shifted gears and encouraged teachers to foster curiosity rather than have students focus just on textbooks and teacher-certified facts. Would it happen in the United States without a concerted, TeleRead-style effort? Maybe. But I doubted this.

If nothing else, public schools needed to give their teachers more time to master the hardware and the Internet so they would not feel so lost when their students roamed the Net; the equipment alone wasn't enough. "Basic technology training is one of the most neglected aspects of educational reform," said Andy Carvin, the Net-oriented educational expert at the Corporation for Public Broadcasting. "More often than not, when a school or a school district implements a major technology overhaul, teachers are introduced to the Internet and all of its tools in a day or two of 'training.' " Carvin told me, and he was right, that teachers should enjoy regular use of the technology at home and at school so the knowledge wouldn't fade away. Too, they needed to know how to "combine that knowledge with traditional teaching and curricula. . . . It's like learning to use a telephone—you can be taught to pick up the receiver and press a few numbers, but if you don't have anyone else's number or don't know how to give out your own number it's useless."

I asked Lorri Neilsen about Canada, and she said that schools of education up there were making good progress toward correcting deficiencies. They had better. In the new era of giant databases there should be more emphasis on finding *and* evaluating information from many

sources, and less on parroting textbooks. Teachers should
encourage children to look for malarkey in all media, but
especially on the Net, given all the self-publishing there.
Perhaps with more women growing up with computers,
female teachers in the future wouldn't suffer so much
from the old bugaboos about networks and smart, curious, uppity students.

That still left another issue—the possibility that students might send offensive messages over the Net and
perhaps fixate on its wilder areas such as the alt.sex series
of newsgroups.

"We did have a couple of cases of students in the school
sending threatening and hateful messages," Doran said,
"but these were not my students. These were what I would
call hackers, computer nerds." Later Park View forced students to sign agreements under which they would lose
their privileges if they abused the Net. This was not a hypothetical issue to me. As I was researching this chapter, I
found "Fuck you all" in the subject line of a public message
of a list devoted to educational uses of the Internet. A student at an American school had taken over someone else's
account. Making students sign agreements wasn't a total
solution, but it was a good one. If a student misbehaved
and lost Net privileges, then he or she would be at a con-
siderable disadvantage in competing with peers.

Addressing the newsgroup question, Park View fil-
tered out the groups it deemed objectionable. I suspected
that a smart student could circumvent these precautions,
but if that happened, he might well have been intelligent
enough to cope with the virtual temptations.

Off the Net, at any rate, students could just as well find
questionable reading material. I remembered the pictures
of Marilyn Monroe that my classmates passed around in
elementary school back in the 1950s. Did anything
change? Should we really deprive children of the glories
of the Net under the assumption that the kids were all potential pervs? The best approach was the Park View one—

making children sign agreements that they would be responsible for their own actions, and suspending or ending their much-cherished Internet privileges if they abused them.

Risks aside, the Internet was a natural place for students of all kinds. Only a fool would dwell on the hazards of the net to the exclusion of the possibilities there.

• • •

Would that all activities of government be as benign (well, for the most part) as those of the schools. In the next chapter we'll learn about Phil Zimmermann and his brushes with the darker, almost Big Brotherish side of government.

CHAPTER

SIX

Governments and the Net: Making Sure Orwell Was Wrong

f a programmer named Phil Zimmermann had his druthers, he would be leading a pretty sedate life on the whole. He drives a Saturn, lives in a small house in a middle-class suburb in Colorado with his wife and children, and dons a suit and does a pretty good yuppie act when he consults for East Coast companies. In California he fits in with his blue jeans. Short and paunchy, he is bearded yet harmless.

Some American bureaucrats, however, would lump Zimmermann in with CIA turncoats and peddlers of illegal plutonium. In November 1994 customs agents detained him at a Washington-area airport when he was reentering the States from Eastern Europe. Twice they combed through his bags then warned him that in the future he might be in for more of the same.

Why this Kafkaesque treatment? Because many in the U.S. national security establishment hate Phil Zimmermann's guts. He came up with Pretty Good Pri-

208

vacy, or PGP for short—a snoop-resistant way of transmitting e-mail over the Internet and other networks.

Zimmermann loathes snoops and jackboots. Clearly he was not in the former communist Europe to subvert democracies; in fact, he was telling people how encryption[1] could help preserve their freedom. "I don't have to explain to Eastern Europe," he said, "why it is important for their governments not to get too powerful."[2]

This dictator-proofing helped win Phil Zimmermann a "Pioneer Award" from the Electronic Frontier Foundation, the civil liberties group, which praised him for creating "a worldwide standard for e-mail encryption."

Zimmermann, however, as the Net's many libertarians are quick to note, may end up in jail for allegedly having violated an American export law that carries penalties as high as a decade in prison and a million-dollar fine. The Feds treat PGP-style software as a weapon just like Stealth bombers, ballistic missiles, and nuclear warheads. And some Washington bureaucrats hate the idea of such a privacy protector in the hands of too many civilians who are not, well, Washington bureaucrats.

Even if the Feds don't indict and convict Zimmermann, the U.S. government has already done its share of bullying here.

The U.S. Constitution forbids prosecutors from dragging Zimmermann into an overlit room and interrogating him without a lawyer present. Tell that to Washington, however. Although the law bans the export rather than the import of powerful encryption software, customs agents at Dulles Airport, eager for any excuse they could find, quizzed Zimmermann when he *returned* from Eastern Europe. An oft-zealous enemy of privacy, the Clinton Administration has even promoted the manufacture of encryption devices that would let Feds listen in on supposedly confidential phone calls. Washington is also spending billions of tax dollars to make telephone lines more susceptible to tapping.

Zimmermann, meanwhile, has been working on a phone-style piece of software. Used on the right computer with a $50 sound card and a $7 microphone, it would let people speak securely over the Internet or ordinary phone lines.

Bill Clinton's snoops must love Zimmermann about as much as they enjoy static during wiretaps. Here's a man who they fear could break the connection altogether. Many in Washington, especially FBI Director Louis Freeh, would love to see unauthorized encryption banned entirely, the real issue here. And Republican Senator Charles Grassley of Iowa has proposed to make it a crime to distribute scrambling programs by way of international nets if the Feds lacked the electronic keys to defeat them. The Grassley measure would even ban some software now classified as exportable.

Like it or not, however, Washington no longer can control the fate of industrial-strength encryption.

Far too many Americans—and Russians, Germans, Czechs, Iranians, Singaporeans, Malaysians, Japanese, Chinese, you name it—know about the technology. The Feds instead should focus on different law enforcement techniques, and on powerful computers to unravel the bad guys' codes. But the Clinton people and their allies won't budge. They keep dreaming of the mass use of D.C.-blessed hardware and software to let law enforcement people listen in on supposedly confidential phone calls. Just like the old Soviet KGB, the Feds think that bureaucracy can prevail over technology, and that government has a God-given right to force citizens to be snoop-friendly.

The saga of Phil Zimmermann is hardly the only indication that *some* Big Brotherism is alive and well in the United States—especially when one considers other outrages, such as the recent net.censorship jihad or the elitist copyright proposals that would crimp public debate.

In all fairness, the United States is less backwards on encryption matters than are countries such as France, which bans powerful cryptography for private use.³ And certainly Bill Clinton isn't a dictator. In fact, the trouble with him, at least at the personal level, is the opposite: He is too much of a wimp to resist civil liberties threats from the FBI, the National Security Agency, other bureaucracies, and the more maniacal of the "law-and-order" crowd on the Hill.

Whatever Clinton's problem, though, his encryption policy is making him reviled among many skeptical young people in Generation Net, not to mention the baby boomers, who suffered lie after lie from LBJ and Robert McNamara during the Vietnam War. A lifelong Democrat, I voted for Clinton. I might not again. His constitutional lapses, or at least those of his bureaucrats, just might help pave the way for true Orwellian scenarios in the United States and elsewhere.

So might the shameful war that a powerful Clinton appointee has waged against public libraries, one of society's best defenses against Orwellian Ministries of Truth.

"Making Sure Orwell Was Wrong," then, is an apt subtitle for this chapter. You'll remember the basics of the novel *1984*—bureaucrats tinkered with back issues of the *London Times* to suit the policies of the moment, brainwashed the proles of Oceania, and spied on most everyone with TV cameras. All had to obey the mythical Big Brother. The most vivid image from *1984* was a boot smashing again and again into a man's face. In the era of mainframe computers bigger than overgrown Cadillacs, many critics of the Vietnam War invoked Orwell and similar pessimists. Wouldn't pasty-faced drones in windowless rooms use the technology to keep dossiers on us?

Then microcomputers popped up. Suddenly good people could use bits and bytes to fight back against Big Brother. Amnesty International, for example, could keep databases documenting murder, torture, and other crimes by dictators. And then, via the Internet and other networks, Amnesty could spread the news around and marshal world opinion against the thugs. Other human rights groups and environmental organizations benefited, too, and soon most everyone agreed about high tech: George Orwell had been wrong. Progressives with unpopular ideas celebrated the new tools available to them. And conservatives didn't disagree that Big Brother was dead; if microcomputers could nurture freedom and diversity, why worry so much about antitrust laws and other regulations? A New York think-tanker would eventually write a reverse *1984* in which hackers won over Big Brother.[4]

Meanwhile, an open government movement was growing on the Internet, along with efforts to use networks as an efficient conduit for services. Far from being Big Brotherish in all ways, Clinton's people commendably put a wealth of official documents on the Net, everything from White House speeches to reports from the Agriculture Department. The states, too, acted. Californians could track down a complete set of laws and proposed laws on the Internet. North Carolinians could hook into an electronic job bank, indicate their desired kind of work, click on a map to designate a favored location, and watch jobs pop up. Oregonians could get fishing- and hunting-license information online.

Bureaucrats in Canada, the United Kingdom, Australia, New Zealand, Argentina, Finland, Austria, Poland, Japan, and a host of other countries went on the Net to one extent or another.

Even Singapore, hardly famous for civil liberties and freedom of information, took a few steps to open up. I was surprised and pleased to find on a government server a 1993 *Wired* article with the not-so-flattering title of "The Intelligent Island?" Like many countries, Singapore faced a dilemma. Would the country's strict culture suffer if the masses were allowed access to the Net? Singapore had flogged an American teenager merely for vandalizing automobiles; imagine if authorities instead had caught him in a sex act with a local. The whip was in character; it was a source of local pride, not shame. And yet if Singapore didn't truly open itself on the Internet, if it couldn't provide a hospitable electronic environment to megaconglomerates, the country would fall behind nations with a freer flow of information.

"Most Singaporeans are little rule followers," a local hacker told *Wired*. "They are used to being spoon-fed what they are supposed to know by the government." He predicted that Singapore would turn into a "controlled information center. The government will try to suppress hackers." [5] And yet the very distribution of the article—for all to see on a Web server, amid official government documents—told me that the Orwellian scenario was not a full certainty. If *Singapore* could ease up a little, there might yet be a little hope for the rest of the cosmos.

However, the need for some healthy paranoia remains, even if, yes, Orwell overstated his case. An Internet Central doesn't exist for bureaucrats to shut down, of course; messages can arrive by way of many paths, and electronic mail if need be can travel over normal voice lines. But martinets of all ilks can't resist the urge to censor or unplug. A government computer in Canada is rumored to be programmed to reject Anglo-Saxonisms as passwords, and I don't doubt it. Would that all outrages were so funny.

Claiming software piracy, cops shut down the electronic bulletin boards of scores of Italian progressives. "In some places," the activist Bernardo Parrella reported, "sleeping people were abruptly woken up facing machine guns." The boards were part of FidoNet, a worldwide BBS system with electronic mail connections to the Internet. Significantly the police didn't undertake similar harassment against the high-tech admirers of Hitler and Mussolini. The victims were liberal or left wing. Within a year, the Italian cops were back at it again, seizing computers, disks, books, diaries, and other materials from citizens suspected of anarchistic sympathies. This time the police made no pretense; the raids were clearly political.

Politicians and bureaucrats can be just as prickly about sex as about politics. In Singapore, prudes searched the hard disk of computer systems to see if the good citizens were enjoying the alt.sex newsgroups. And back in the States, Senator J. James Exon of Nebraska concocted a nutty scheme to ban "indecent" material from the public areas of the Net. *1984* once more came to mind. Big Brother loathed sex, as Winston Smith, Orwell's hero, knew all too well in carrying on an illicit affair with a female bureaucrat.

Jim Exon also hated sex—at least on the Net. I could appreciate his worries; did nine-year-olds really need to gawk at alt.sex.bestiality, or kiddie porn, or the next Brandy's Babes? Exon, though, again and again, scrambled his facts. He relied partly on a breathless article that the *Washington Post* had run under the headline "Molesting Children by Computer." Among other things, writer Sandy Rovner had advised parents to check their kids' computers for files ending in ".BMP". None other than the Microsoft Windows software, however, left .BMP files on hard drives—as a way to display images such as the corporate logo. Might Microsoft be a new Sodom?

"Obviously I had not researched the story enough," Rovner admitted to her great credit. "I am new to the world of cyberspace. . . . I have a computer coach, but even he is behind on the Internet. Yes, I violated a cardinal rule of journalism—I didn't know enough about what I was writing about. And I certainly wasn't thinking censorship. Mea culpa. I am a staunch supporter of the First Amendment, as all journalists are or should be." And yet Exon cited "Molesting" on the Senate floor to justify his repressive, cyberspace-oriented change in the existing Communications Decency Act. "Argghh," went Rovner.

Even more significantly, Exon, as noted earlier, failed to grasp the difference between the Internet and television. Children wouldn't just flick on a computer and see a Madonna look-alike climaxing with a German shepherd.

They would have to *look* for pornography. And the industry was ready to work on software, such as SurfWatch, to help parents keep their kids out of pre-designated areas of the Net.

Nothing would be foolproof or teen-proof, of course. Brilliant technologists had designed the Internet to survive 100-megaton H-bombs. "The Net," said the hacker John Gilmore in an oft-repeated quote, "interprets censorship as damage and routes around it."

Parents' best response would be at home. Mothers and fathers shouldn't expect Uncle Sam to play nanny. As Steve Case, president of America Online, noted in connection with his company, parents should never turn their children loose in a city of millions of people. And I believed that the same held true of the Internet. Why should parents count on *everything* being constantly under control. Put the Net on a leash short enough to suit Exon, and the pornography would still persist—encrypted and on non-Net bulletin boards if nothing else—but legitimate users would suffer. Some Internet providers might even shut down to avoid legal liabilities. Moreover, in an era of global commerce, Washington shouldn't put America at such a disadvantage. The losses in trade and jobs eventually would reach the billions, given the estimated hundreds of billions of Net-generated business.

"The only thing that censorship will do is drive the best and brightest members of the U.S. Internet community to countries where they can express themselves without risk of reprisal—and drain the United States of its valuable intellectual capital," *Interactive Publishing Alert*'s Rosalind Resnick would later write.[6] "Personally I'd rather see a few four-letter words flicker across my computer screen every now and then than risk losing talented writers, artists and programmers to our economic competitors." A mother of two, she counseled parents: "Keep the computer in a public area of the house, such as the den or living room, not in your kid's bedroom. Warn your kids about the dangers of pedophiles and urge them never to give out their phone number or address to anyone they meet online." *That* was a far better approach than Washington-mandated net.censorship, one that could work with the smartest hacker-child. Even the hyper *Post* article had played up similar solutions. But Jim Exon couldn't keep his hands off the Net.

In a superb illustration of the dark side of electronic democracy, Exon held up a blue binder full of net.smut and, on the C-SPAN television network, argued for censorship of cyberspace. The vote in the Senate was 84 to 16—how could U.S. senators oppose "decency?" Given all the sex scandals on the Hill, it was scene worthy of *Elmer Gantry*, the Sinclair Lewis novel about a moralizing preacher who nonetheless indulges in sex and booze. The book, of course, ends with the Rev. Gantry promising, "We shall yet make these United States a moral nation."

Around the same time the Senate was hoping to Disneyize the Internet, Bob Dole, the Republican majority leader, was protecting Bob Packwood by opposing a move to open the Ethics Committee hearings into the personal behavior of the oversexed senator from Oregon. As reported by the *Washington Post*, Packwood allegedly had grabbed and kissed scads of women—from campaign workers to female staff members, lobbyists, a hotel clerk, and a baby-sitter—"sometimes forcing his tongue into their mouth or fondling them." Packwood, while not owing up to every particular, had apologized for being "terribly offensive to women." And now he and Bob Dole had voted for Draconian net.morality? Dole had even teamed up with several other senators, including Charles Grassley, the champion of snoop-friendly software, to offer a cyber-censor bill worse even than Exon's.

The ironies wouldn't stop. None other than Donna Rice, whose escapades with ex-Senator Gary Hart had helped kill off his political career, was now praying and crusading against cyber smut—as a spokeswoman for an antiporn group.

Another irony hit me. Tobacco and liquor advertisements, which promote products far deadlier to children than any obscenities, were reaching the Net. The Internet Sleuth, for example, one of my favorite collections of Net indexes, had advertised Smokin' Joe's tobacco products over a period of at least several weeks. And yet the Exonians could not stop fixating on words and pictures, as opposed to a massive, proven threat that had killed millions of Americans. I didn't want the government to ban even cancer-weed ads from cyberspace, lest the regulators go wild and try to make the Net TV-bland; but if Exon and allies had to crusade, they might as well be consistent about it. Perhaps as a true children's advocate, Exon could even give back the more than $27,000 that his campaign had collected between January 1989 and December 1994 from the tobacco and liquor industries. That was just a fraction of his total take, but a statement just the same. Maybe the operators of "adult" bulletin board systems—who used the Net to post samples, the real source of the problem—could befriend Exon-style pols with a well-funded political-action committee. "PornoPAC"?

I wondered what would happen next if the net.censors won in the House of Representatives. Earlier, in chapter 4, I had quoted Peter Lewis of the *New York Times* as alluding to the "pencil-dicked geeks" who flamed him. Would Washington let *NetWorld!* go out over an Exonized Internet? This was the only time I had ever seen such language in e-mail from Lewis, a gifted professional. Society didn't prevent a woodcarver from using a certain kind of wood just because hoodlums might buy some baseball clubs made from it and split each other's skulls open. Why, then, draft legislation that so despicably intruded on writers' work? And what about teachers and students of literature, including bright, stable teenagers under eighteen? Or readers who just loved good, expressive writing? Knowingly or not, the savages in the Senate could be banning even *Ulysses* from the public area of the Internet. Never mind the forthcoming age of electronic books; might Washington someday go on to suppress the paper editions from stores and libraries?

Quite correctly the Electronic Frontier Foundation warned of the folly of turning the public regions of the Internet into "the equivalent of the Children's Room at the public library," and forcing Netfolks to seek out "adult" areas. Get carried away on an Exonized Net, use the wrong word, and the Feds could fine you up to $100,000 and jail you for up to two years. Even in private e-mail you'd need to behave yourself: You could not harass anyone with an "obscene" remark or image, lest he or she report you. What if an ex-lover took innocent comments and put them in the wrong context? Tough luck. Sooner or later the courts would probably clean up after the politicians and toss out the censorship, but that would hardly matter to the many who suffered in the meantime.

In July 1995 the censorship debate was still at full blast. Just as Jim Exon had relied on the misleading *Post* story, so did his side brandish a sensationalistic *Time* magazine cover. A shocked, wide-eyed child gaped at "CYBERPORN," as the headline described it. "EXCLUSIVE: A new study shows how pervasive and wild it really is. Can we protect our kids—and free speech?" Out of character, Philip Elmer-DeWitt, one of the most Net-aware of all the reporters in the mass media, had relied on a flawed paper out of Carnegie Mellon University. The student perpetrator of the study, one Martin Rimm, had overgeneralized, and two professors at Vanderbilt disemboweled him with a 9,000-word rebuttal on the World Wide Web. If nothing else, the Rimm study had blurred the distinction between bulletin board systems and the Internet itself and also confused Usenet with the Net as a whole.

Carnegie Mellon investigated whether Rimm had violated people's privacy. Most deliciously of all, however, from a Net perspective, he had written something else—a self-published novel with such picturesque terms as "rectum rocket." Would that Sinclair Lewis and H. L. Mencken had been around to chronicle the circus.

Over on the House side, Speaker Newt Gingrich sensibly let his libertarian side prevail and opposed Exon. I wasn't surprised. How could Gingrich play nanny while railing in general against regulation and bureaucracy, especially when he himself had set up shop as a novelist? My fellow liberals, though, were amazed. It was as if they were watching the T-Rex in *Jurassic Park* gobble up a velociraptor that was about to enjoy a human snack.

Maybe the Exon-style proposals by now will have suffered the fate of the smaller dinosaur, but similar lunacy is bound to break out anew.[7] Among some on Capitol Hill, the urge to censor is as powerful as the passion for reserved parking places.[8]

If the censors do win, their narrow-mindedness may backfire in ways beyond the ones I've already described— and these risks will only grow in the future, as the Net becomes still more international. Puritanical countries such as Singapore might arbitrarily jail visiting Americans who, from the States, had made Internet postings deemed offensive by the standards of local dictators.[9] The possibilities are endless. A U.S. novelist passing through a Mideastern country could become the next Rushdie if the local ayatollahs deemed his online work offensive.

Clinton's Feds hardly helped when they went jurisdiction shopping and prosecuted the owners of a California BBS for sex-related material that violated community standards in *Tennessee*. Applied internationally, the local-standards principle could send an American to a sword-wielding executioner someday. The Bill of Rights, alas, is just a U.S. phenomenon.

However, a borderless Internet can also hinder the censorship crowd. If American bluenoses such as Exon tried to restrict an electronic *Tropic of Cancer,* for example, a U.S.

Exon You!

When the U.S. Senate passed Jim Exon's net.censorship bill, the journalist Brock Meeks wrote a lead for the ages: "U.S. Capitol, Senate Gallery—It's all over. Fuck it." But what happens if net.censors prevail someday on the House side, too (if they haven't already), and you can't use the F word? Netfolks have a solution:

Just substitute the last name of the senior senator from Nebraska. Enemies and lovers can then say, "Exon," to each other.

That's obvious. But the gifted trolls at Bianca's Smut Shack, spreading a post from the mythical "Ezra Pound Is Innocent Committee," have actually promoted a whole new lexicon in honor of Exon and allies. For example:

Byrd: (noun) The posterior or hinderparts, specifically the anus.

Coats: (noun) Excrement, or as a verb to excrete.

Exon: (verb) To copulate with, the act of copulation.

Gorton: (noun) The female genitals, or specifically the vagina.

Gramm: (verb) To orgasm. Also colloquially used as a noun.

Heflin: (noun) The female secondary sexual characteristics.

Helms: (noun) The male phallus.

Specter: (noun) The clitoris.

publisher just might set up shop in countries with less infantile politicians. People in the States could then dial up the computer overseas.

Already the Net has made fools of martinets in the Canadian government. Ottawa tried to squelch newspaper accounts of a murder, claiming that the coverage would preclude a fair trial. So people in the States sent electronic care packages to their Canadian friends—articles from U.S. papers. Canadian officials banned a pulped-wood issue of *Wired* for attacking their stupidity; that was one of the biggest debacles of all, given the ease of dialing up electronic versions of the magazine, one of the planet's most plugged-in publications.

Consider, too, the ramifications of anonymous servers, which strip names and other identifiers from messages, allowing Netfolks to circumvent legal bullying by governments and others. In 1995, the Church of Scientology in Los Angeles got Finnish police to raid a server in Helsinki that was posting anonymous exposés of this rather litigious organization. The server survived. But the cops forced Johan Helsingius, operator of the server, to reveal the name of a Church enemy who originated the messages. "Now users fear their secrets are at risk," *Time* said of people using his computer service. Case closed on anonymous servers? Hardly.

Within weeks after the incident I read a note from a hacker telling how encrypted messages could wend their ways through chains of anonymous e-mailers in several countries, with the names of the senders remaining hidden unless most or all of the e-mailers broke under pressure. Yes, abuses are possible, such as the release of trade secrets, outright libels, forgeries, or the most vile and violent of pornography. But how much better to live out this future than one of the Orwellian variety. Tyrant-bashers in the Thirteen Colonies used the wizardry of their day, the printing press, to agitate against the Tories; now let's hope that if Exonian politicians try to stifle the Net, enough hackers will have their most dangerous presses ready to go, the servers I've just described. Obsolete or not, the censors aren't going to stop.

Other Big Brotherish urges have surfaced. While some Power People hope to be able to learn more about us by

fighting PGP-style programs, they are stymieing our efforts to learn more about *them*. At the same time the Feds
put online thousands of public documents and even the
visage of Bill Clinton's cat, some politicians on the Hill
sought to *weaken* the Freedom of Information Act, which
makes it easier to dig up dirt on public officials. Just as
important, Clinton people in early 1995 were proposing
new copyright laws that in effect would discourage the intelligent discussion of public issues on the Internet. It
would be harder to share electronic newspaper clips.
Even more disturbingly, Clinton's copyright policy could
menace our public library system in the future. Bruce
Lehman, his czar of intellectual property, was coming
across as Andrew Carnegie in reverse.

Carnegie is remembered as a Scot who grew rich off
steel in the States and who encouraged people throughout
the world to start libraries for all. He gave millions toward
library buildings, with the understanding that the local
taxpayers would finance their support. Carnegie wanted
public libraries to be universities for the common man,
and the metaphor holds up. Today, without paying for college or even for books, American can educate themselves
on subjects ranging from microcomputer chips to medieval history, to Alexis de Tocqueville's writings on
democracy, to the case for or against feminism or abor-
tion or public broadcasting or capital punishment. That is
life in the era of paper books.

If Lehman had his wishes, however, Americans would
not be able to dial up copyrighted electronic library books
from home by way of the Internet. Instead they would
have to tote around CD-ROMs and floppy disks.

William F. Buckley Jr. wrote that, in the era of the
Internet, the Lehman vision would be "the equivalent of
requiring everyone who listens to music to buy 78 rpm
shellac records. What will the children dial in to read?
The collected speeches of Vice President Al Gore? And believe it or not, there's also talk of the Postal Service getting
involved in local public libraries through information

kiosks."[10] In effect the White House approach would jack up the price of independent, privately originated information, while making it easier to obtain Washington-blessed information.

The information kiosks led some librarians to think of noses and camel's tents. For the Postal Service at one point said it would let local librarians and citizens use the kiosks to retrieve only designated categories of information, as opposed to, say, everything on the World Wide Web. On a 1 to 10 scale of Big Brotherism, the kiosk idea as originally proposed was an 8.5 or worse.[11] If the postal bureaucrats weren't trying to be Big Brother in the strictest sense—and no, they weren't—then they at least were unwittingly paving the way for him.

Worse, the Postal Service has talked of issuing tens of millions of "U.S. Cards" that would "mediate all government services and controls over citizens," while at the same time an Internal Revenue Service official has proposed a system that would file our tax returns for us.[12] I hate both ideas. Rather than compiling Orwellian dossiers on citizens, governments should help us computerize via TeleRead-style programs so we can more easily do the "paperwork" ourselves by way of electronic forms. Investigators could audit the forms, but only under appropriate circumstances. How much better this would be—not just e-books, but electronic empowerment against bureaucracy—than the vision that Washington and other governments have in mind for us.

Perhaps the Lehman idea and the Postal and IRS plans will have been beaten back or rendered harmless by now. Whatever happens, though, it is clear that new technology may harm both privacy and democracy if our vigilance lapses.

The threat of electronic oligarchy, stanching the free flow of facts that intelligent nonmillionaires demand, is hardly unique to the States. In the United Kingdom, for example, *The Times Higher Education Supplement* has warned against a copyright regime that would be a paradise for read-o-meter companies but a nightmare to people valuing free libraries. Just like Lehman's proposal in the U.S., the wrong laws in the U.K. could lead to a Copyright Gestapo; let's hope that neither country will criminalize one of the prerequisites for democracy: curiosity.

Given the global nature of both encryption technology and copyright law, the whole world should be watching Washington's policies. The Clinton Administration, after all, hopes to internationalize the same mindset that could send Phil Zimmermann to jail; in fact, many of the American export controls *are* in effect in other countries, raising the possibility that an Australian or a British hacker could end up someday in the same predicament. In the pages that follow I'll tell about the battles that Zimmermann and his allies have fought with Washington.

You'll read, too, of my fight for an alternative to the Lehmanesque copyright law. My little case history suggests that the White House is not so eager to listen to ordinary mortals who speak up on the Net. Clinton's people would rather pander to the usual campaign contributors. So far at least, pious rhetoric notwithstanding, they have basically neglected the need to put the public library system online with free or low-cost books from the private sector. Video just might end up reigning even more supreme than it does today—at the expense of abstract thought and democracy. Winston Smith would not be happy.

PGP and the Fight for Privacy— and Against Clipper—on the Internet

Father Bill Morton, an Anglican priest in Woodstock, New Brunswick, could take confessions via e-mail without violating his vows. Encryption software guarded the privacy of his communications. In Florida a bright teenager without any vices—but with a nosy mother—could protect her diaries. And in New York, an employee of a leading investment house could routinely guard his credit card number. The same software made it possible for thousands to use the Net for confidential business transactions. At the same time, democratic activists in the former Soviet Union would be able protect their messages if tyranny returns.

The name for this encryption package was PGP and by 1995 it was as much a cause as a program. Thousands had downloaded it off the Internet and other networks. Named in tribute to Ralph's Pretty Good Grocery on Garrison Keillor's radio show, PGP stood for Pretty Good Privacy. PGP lived up to its name—people needed it. Part of the reason was the nature of the Net itself. A skilled hacker could intercept unencrypted e-mail more easily than on the regular commercial networks. Mail often passed through computers at a number of universities and companies before reaching its destination. Without question the best way to protect the contents of your outgoing mail was to scramble its message before you sent it into cyberspace.

PGP was also popular because its use showed that the Net would never accept Clipper chip encryption schemes—designed to make it easier for the government to snoop on citizens.

Not surprisingly, then, at the time I was writing this book, Phil Zimmermann was a hero to many on the Internet. His program meant dignity. It meant safer commerce on the Net. Other privacy protection programs existed, but his was most popular, making it all the more useful. So when the Feds threatened Zimmermann, many people correctly felt as if Washington were attacking them along the way. The irony was that the federal government's policies against safe encryption could actually threaten world security and had already set back efforts on behalf of computer security.

In a sense the PGP story was part of a continuum, and not just because the Egyptians had scrambled messages four thousand years ago or because encryption had been a staple of Cold Warriors.

Even while growing up in Miami and Fort Lauderdale, Phil Zimmermann had tinkered with secret codes. At around age ten he had learned Morse code, Braille, and, via lemon juice, invisible ink. By his teens he was building code wheels; at Florida Atlantic University, he kept up his passion for puzzles and secrets. He started out there in physics; switched to computer science; married; packed up for Boulder, Colorado, where he became a computer consultant; and thought of a move to New Zealand. Phil Zimmermann believed it would be safer, in the event of nuclear war, than Ground Zero countries.

Instead of leaving the States, however, Zimmermann decided to stay and help throttle back the military. Along with the astronomer Carl Sagan and Daniel Ellsberg of Pentagon Papers fame—and hundreds of others—Zimmermann was arrested at testing grounds in Nevada. Soon his love of computers would be converging with his distrust of people in uniforms.

Zimmermann in the early '80s was selling a gadget that plugged into an Apple II computer but used an 8088 chip just like the then-new IBM personal computer. This gadget was designed to allow people to keep their old Apple hardware and software while running new programs for the fast new chip. Zimmermann called his company Metamorphic Systems. A programmer from Arkansas saw a Metamorphic ad and called Zimmermann to pitch to him an encryption system that was too long to run on most machines. Would Zimmermann care to adapt the system to run on an 8088 chip? He would.[13]

RSA was the encryption method here. Named after its three originators—Ronald Rivert, Adi Shamir, and Len Adleman—RSA was a virtually uncrackable form of public key encryption. So what did *public key* mean? Well, you didn't have to worry about the wrong set of eyes seeing the jumble of letters and other characters that made up keys for messages transmitted to you. You could freely spread it around. Then someone who wanted to send something confidential to you didn't have to contact you for a secret key known only to you. He could use your public key by way of his RSA software.

Simply put, the public key approach did away with a major problem: how to send descrambling tools over networks if the information itself wasn't secured. People who didn't know each other could trade public keys, then share secrets from the start. They could even use the same software to verify their identities with the help of trusted third parties, who "signed" the keys with sequences of their own. Imagine the many possibilities for allowing safe business transactions on networks between strangers. A lucrative business just might await Zimmermann if he added his own wrinkles.

With RSA, however, came a series of legal nightmares for Zimmermann. Starting work on his own software using RSA, he hadn't any idea at the start that Rivert, Shamir, and Adleman would be claiming a patent on it.

The trio farmed their rights out to RSA Data Security and, eventually, Public Key Partners. Jim Bidzos, negotiating for RSA, in many ways stood out as a political and philosophical opposite of Zimmermann. Bidzos carried a Greek passport for business reasons but at the same time felt patriotic enough to have volunteered for the U.S. Marines. The way Bidzos tells the story (to Simson Garfinkel, author of *PGP: Pretty Good Privacy*), Zimmermann asked for a "free license" for use of RSA. "When I told him 'No,'" Bidzos said, "he was really upset. He told me that he was behind on his mortgage payments and that he had invested years in writing this piece of software." Bidzos said he suggested that Zimmermann try licensing the patent from a larger company.[14]

Zimmermann's own side of the story differed starkly—in 1991 he wrote Jim Bidzos a letter saying that Bidzos and Ron Rivert had told him that "you would grant me a free license to make and sell products with your algorithm."[15] A few years later he would note to the *Wall Street Journal* that he hadn't sold PGP before his contract with ViaCrypt, one of RSA's licensees.[16] He steadfastly maintained he had not broken any laws. Many on the Internet would have agreed, if for no other reason than that they considered software patents to be abominations. Without patents to limit them, many programmers felt they could be more creative. Their ethos was quite in line with the traditional Net ethos. The predecessor of the Internet, after all, hadn't just been started to allow the Pentagon to survive nukes. It also existed to share knowledge.

By 1991 the patent issue wasn't the only one dogging Zimmermann. The U.S. Senate was considering a law that would in effect ban Fedproof encryption here in the United States and potentially prevent him from selling the software on which he had been toiling for years now. Washington already forbade export of encryption abroad. The Cold War was winding down, but export controls were still draconian. Hadn't we won World War II because our technology was better, because we had had nukes, because we could even snoop on secret code transmissions from the enemy? The export laws and the Pentagon put strong encryption equipment in the same category as munitions.

But what about at home? Not surprisingly, the FBI didn't want the wrong technology to fall into the hands of dope rings, Mafiosi, and others planning or coordinating crimes. In 1991, then, perhaps at the Bureau's request, Senator Joseph Biden of Delaware inserted the following language into an omnibus crime bill: "It is the sense of Congress that providers of electronic communications services and manufacturers of electronic communications service equipment shall ensure that communications systems permit the government to obtain the plain text contents of voice, data, and other communications when appropriately authorized by law."

A Senate staffer assured civil libertarians that the measure would not ban strong encryption. Many disagreed. Computer Professionals for Social Responsibility, library groups, academics, and industry managed to get Washington to drop the offending language.

By then PGP was all over the Net. Smart lobbying, not the software, killed the Biden plan. But Zimmermann's work was still a good, sound precaution against a relapse. Via bulletin boards and the Internet, a free version was circulating from one end of Planet Earth to the other, having gone overseas within a day of its release. In Zimmermann's words, it spread "like thousands of dandelion seeds blowing in the wind." PGP reached Russia and scores of other countries. It wasn't like nuclear weapons or minicomputers; you couldn't stop a ship from loading or search the luggage of the suspicious. No, PGP just moved silently over the wires as hackers throughout the world shared Zimmermann's craft. The way Zimmermann told it, however, he had not broken any of the export laws. And others supported him.

Jim Warren, founder of *InfoWorld* and a software man respected for his civic activism on the Net, would later recall that Zimmermann gave PGP to an acquaintance named Kelly Goen, who "studiously" limited the uploads to electronic bulletin boards and Internet sites within the United States. Warren was aware of the uploading process while it happened. "The whole idea was to provide it to *Americans*," he would remember, "so *Americans* could have personal privacy and security" in case the U.S. Senate tried to bottle up decent encryption.[17]

The National Security Agency—the secret agency that dealt with many of the best cryptographers and dominated the encryption scene in the United States—did not complain formally when PGP first hit the Net. And Zimmermann fretted. Had his baby failed to safeguard privacy enough to worry the National Security Agency?[18]

Back at RSA Data Security, Jim Bidzos wasn't thrilled when PGP appeared with RSA technology. He maintained that PGP violated both patent and export law, and at his urging, some commercial services and universities banished PGP from their servers.[19] Legally, Bidzos may or may not have been justified. But once again the hacker ethic prevailed on the Net. Not everyone online took Zimmermann's side, but by now he was a serious hero to a group of encryption boosters known as "Cypherpunks," the name that a magazine writer had once given them as a joke.

Many of the Cypherpunks were libertarians, or variants thereof, and they believed in perfect privacy. The punks were to encryption laws what the Nation Rifle Association was to restrictions on firearms

Along with scores of corporations, not just people whom the White House might dismiss as fringe, the Cypherpunks wanted to use encryption to protect digital money. They envisioned a society in which bits and bytes—representing cash—could pass from person to person without Party A knowing Party B's identity. The Cypherpunks were smart, and often very right. Frustrating for others, but rewarding for them, they tested the tolerance of the most ardent Voltaireans.

Tim May was among the punk leaders. He had once worked for Intel, the chip maker. As Steven Levy put it in an article for *Wired,* May had " 'retired' at 34 with stock options sufficient to assure that he would never flip a burger for Wendy's." He in some ways came across as the Internet's Abbie Hoffman, say, or Jerry Rubin. Baby boomers will forever recall these bearded crazies of the 1960s who ran a pig for president and protested materialism by going to Wall Street and scattering money around.

May did not mind getting rich. But he had something of his own to scatter in cyberspace. It was a series of taunts that appeared at the bottom of the many messages he posted to the Net: "Crypto Anarchy: encryption, digital money, anonymous networks, digital pseudonyms, zero knowledge, reputations, information markets, black markets, collapse of governments." If Washington had rigged up a machine to scan the Net and measure people by levels of subversion, May would have blown out all the lights and needles. And one of his programs of choice, as advertised amid the other subversion? PGP, what else?

Timothy May and other Cypherpunks over the next few years would tap out thousands of messages, exchanging technical tips, dreaming up new forms of crypto madness, rallying support for encryption and for Phil Zimmermann. This was a whole subculture with a language and an ethics code of its own. Sometimes the Cypherpunks fought among themselves. Later a punk in Colorado "spoofed" Timothy May and, using May's Internet address, posted malarkey all over the Net. But true to his anarchistic leanings, May did not press for the dissident's expulsion from the punk mailing list.

Back in November 1992 the punks may have breathed a little easier. George Bush lost the election. No longer would the president be a Republican, a World War II veteran, and a former director of the Central Intelligence Agency. Bill Clinton was a baby boomer. He had spoken out against Vietnam, he had avoided the draft, he liked Fleetwood Mac, he played a saxophone, and his vice presidential candidate had made a name as a loyal supporter of advanced computer networks. So perhaps the Feds would back off on Zimmermann. At the very least maybe the security bureaucracy would face a long delay while the Clinton people puzzled out what to do.

Clinton's sax and the rest did not count, however; in encryption matters he might as well have been a ninety-nine-year-old fan of Lawrence Welk. Within just a few weeks of the inauguration, two men from the U.S. Customs Department were quizzing Phil Zimmermann. According to the book *PGP: Pretty Good Privacy,* they said Jim Bidzos had described PGP as a rip-off of the RSA approach.

Following the Zimmermann interview, Customs pressed ahead both on the patent front and on export law issues. Zimmermann, however, denied having swiped PGP from anyone, and he said patent matters should be between him and Bidzos, not between him and Customs. At the time the Feds told him he was not the target of an investigation.[20]

Soon, however, two subpoenas suggested that Washington was still quite eager to justify any and all of the Cypherpunk's paranoia.

One subpoena went to Austin Code Works, which sold public-domain software that contained some of Zimmermann's work. Washington struck out. It had been seeking evidence of overseas sales, and Austin lacked any in this case. Zimmermann hadn't even sold Austin his work directly.[21]

Washington was more lucky at ViaCrypt, a company in Arizona, where the subpoena stuck. Zimmermann had just given ViaCrypt a PGP license. Now he indeed would be under investigation. In *PGP: Pretty Good Privacy,* Simson Garfinkel observed that RSA Data did not win similar honors even though it had placed encryption-related software on the Internet. Nor did Internet providers such as Netcom, which stored PGP on computers that people overseas could reach.[22] Bill Clinton's people were letting foreigners dial up this export-controlled software again and again. Needless to say, the bullying of Zimmermann still made the industry nervous—who was next?

As if the Clinton White House hadn't sinned enough, it was about to embarrass itself in a high-tech version of the Bay of Pigs. That's how critics regarded a nitwit scheme to control encryption and discourage the public from using good software such as PGP. The Bay of Pigs, a cuckoo plan for the invasion for Cuba, was a legacy that had come to John F. Kennedy from the Eisenhower Administration. The odds would have delighted no one but a masochistic squad of kamikaze pilots. Castro crushed a small band of Cuban exiles who showed up on Washington's behalf at the Bay of Pigs. Like the debacle on the Cuban beaches, the Clipper chip was really another Republican leftover. The national security apparatus hadn't been able to con the Bush Administration into implementing Clipper before the election. But Bill Clinton himself lacked the guts to resist the NSA.

"No Such Agency," as Washington wags called it, operated out of Fort Meade, Maryland, near the Chesapeake Bay, perhaps explaining its fondness for assigning nautical names to encryption plans. Many billions of tax money had gone into the NSA over the years. Thousands worked for it. And they weren't just interested in the survival of the United States. They wanted job security. Clipper was going to be a meal ticket. Just as some wishful planners had deluded themselves into thinking that a small band of men could tame Cuba, now the NSA was telling Bill Clinton's people that it could use Clipper to control the world of encryption.

All those irksome constitutional details aside, the NSA's plan might actually have made sense once. The people at Fort Meade had done the United States a service by staying ahead of Soviet encryption in the era of tail fins and air raid drills. But today such an approach was about as appropriate as a backyard bomb shelter. As far back as the 1970s, two men outside NSA's control had invented public key encryption, which, as noted before, was a good way for strangers to exchange secure messages and authenticate their identifies from the start. Whitfield Diffie was a mathematician, computer scientist, and encryption expert. Martin Hellman was an electronic engineer. Both were grouchy about a computer system whose users had

to entrust their passwords to the systems managers. So
they came up with public key encryption—the same principle that was behind the RSA approach used in PGP, and
now available from Boston to Brisbane.

Even Bill Clinton couldn't repeal the past. Just as
the Kennedy Administration had justified Castro's paranoia, so the Clinton Administration worked hard to do
the same with that of the Cypherpunks. This time
Washington wouldn't deploy humans. Instead it wanted
to rely on a little computer chip that Steven Levy described as "just another tiny square of plastic covering a
silicon thicket."

"Tumor-sized" might have been more apropos. Clipper,
in fact, was a tumor of sorts.

In a human body a tumor serves itself, not its host.
And that's what Clipper was supposed to do. The Clinton
Administration wanted to license Clipper to the private
sector, where it would show up in millions of telephones
and dominate the market—displacing future encryption
schemes based on technologies such as PGP. Washington
hoped to make Clipper too cheap to resist and to provide a
federal market for Clipper products. AT&T and the rest
could put Clipper in telephones, and then, supposedly,
dope peddlers couldn't peddle and terrorists couldn't ter-
rorize without the Feds having a chance to intercept their
conversations. The government would also work to make
computers snoop friendly.

That was the scenario. Like tumors these govern-
ment-issue chips were to spread—not only in the States
but also overseas. Eventually the Feds would also an-
nounce plans to make Clipper available through software,
rather than just through the chip. Whatever the incarnation of Clipper, though, Washington would play down the
fact that it would corrode the country's constitutional right
to privacy. America's Winston Smiths would have to trust
a government that had covered up an unhealthy number

of deaths from nuclear fallout, given us Watergate, and illegally spied on thousands of Americans.

An old friend of mine, Margaret "Peggy" Engel, a former *Washington Post* reporter who ran and still runs a respected journalism foundation, was among the snoops' victims. Bureaucrats got the phone company to turn over a list of Peggy's calls even though she had not committed a crime. It seems a freelance writer had managed to dig up some inside information on the failure of the IRS to collect several billion dollars in back taxes from corporations that had profited from currency hedging. This same writer later applied for a grant from Engel's organization, the Alicia Patterson Foundation. Vindictively, the Feds snooped on Engel, too, simply because the writer had made a call to Engel's office for an application for a fellowship.

So it went. Because Peggy and I talked from time to time, the Feds had also tracked her telephone and computer calls to me. They acted against her under a casually issued court order signed not by a judge but by an assistant deputy clerk—one of more than 20,000 such actions issued in the Washington area in 1992. "It's like getting your parking ticket stamped," she told me. "That's the level of scrutiny that these things get. And the number keeps growing. I think it's because of the increase in fax machines. I think agencies are using it on their employees to find out who talked to the press or Congress." And now the Feds wanted to license the manufacture of a chip that would spill our secrets on demand.

Granted, the Feds claimed that in the Clipper's case, one bureaucrat could not spy alone. The official line was that people from both the Treasury Department and the National Institute for Standards and Technology would have to agree before an interception could take place. If they did, the electronic keys would go over the wires to local police or others needing the tap. All this would require a court order. Some Clipper boosters might well have argued, "We're talking about strict controls." But Peggy's experience still showed the potential the Feds had for promiscuous Big Brothering, especially since both the Treasury and the Institute were within the Executive Branch.

Later the front pages would sprout articles about bureaucrats reading the supposedly confidential tax information of their neighbors or of movie stars. Yes, the tax people tightened up their operations to avoid repeats. But supposedly the IRS had been secure in the first place.

The NSA might itself prove capable of some nasty twists. What if it could call up escrow keys from a database despite all talk to the contrary? Or suppose it had a database of its own to unlock all the keys? Would it really want to go to court for authority to snoop? In *PGP: Pretty Good Privacy,* Garfinkel wisely noted that Washington would let Clipper chips be exported. And the NSA was allowed to spy on nondomestic conversations. So he logically wrote: "If Clipper-equipped radios were being used by Iraqi fighter pilots, the NSA would want to listen in. Although the NSA hasn't said so publicly, it is doubtful that the agency would jeopardize national security in order to play along with the escrow system." The NSA might even work out secret deals with the company making the chips, to assure that the results didn't frustrate the snoops.

Adding to the quite-justified paranoia was the fact that only the dumbest of criminals would rely on Clipper to protect privacy. So what was the point of using technology meant to turn the bad guys into jail bait? Why bother to create it in the first place?

Washington countered that criminals would want Clipper phones to talk securely to the world at large. And I suspected that, yes, they indeed would buy some equipment with Clipper. But for plotting a $10 million dope shipment or a terrorist attack, the black hats would quickly learn to use other scrambling systems; in fact, they could run them on top of Clipper so the Feds *still* got only gibberish. Even if the Feds banned PGP-style protection, criminals would spread the right hardware and software among themselves. Like drugs or sex, this would be a fine opportunity for entrepreneurial lawbreakers.

The underworld might even sell Clipper-crackers that could make criminals just as good at snooping on America's Winston Smiths as the Feds would be. High-tech hoods could call their new business Credit Card Numbers Unlimited. Small wonder that Clipper appalled many security specialists.

At the same time, experts for the software industry raised questions about whether the Clipper chip could penetrate the market and, if so, to what extent? Any way you looked at it, the plan was crazy. If Clipper couldn't catch criminals (and did *everyone* in the White House really swallow this bilge?), then who was left? People like Peggy Engel, her muckraking grantee, and me. At least part of the time, we would need Clipperish encryption if somehow it surprised the experts and did catch on; our banks might not let us use anything else. How much better if a PGP-style alternative were the standard instead.

Technically, Clipper was just as scary as it was politically and in law-enforcement terms. Scientists and mathematicians loved to dissect encryption schemes in academic papers, and keep checking and rechecking them over the years for flaws. But Clipper's designers withheld the information that outside experts could use to poke holes in the concept. Unknowns indeed existed. A well-connected scientist at AT&T would later find a significant weakness in the network version of Clipper, a way to cripple the snoop-on-me-please feature.

All in all, Clipper actually emerged as a world security threat. Washington was harming electronic commerce by promoting a crippled and questionable program for encryption. The Administration in effect was delaying the adoption of truly comprehensive security standards for the international community, especially business people outside the States. The standards were on the way, but not as fast as if Clinton's people hadn't wreaked havoc on the private sector by way of moronic expert controls.

"We need strong cryptography for mainstream society on the Net," Zimmermann told me. "It's like making locks. It's as if I were in the business of selling very, very strong locks." He reminded me of the case of Kevin Mitnick, who was arrested for breaking into scads of computers and stealing oceans of valuable information. The FBI chased him for a couple of years. "Isn't it ironic that this guy was able to inflict such damage because our systems are so insecure?" Zimmermann asked. "Our own government suppressed the availability of strong encryption technology. They brought it on themselves, or, I should say more accurately, they brought it down on us."

At the same time, through Clipper and through efforts against PGP and other effective software, Washington in effect was lending moral support to dictatorships. Clipper used a technique called *key escrow*. That was a nice way of saying you had to trust Uncle with your secrets since he had a copy of your key. But what if Uncle weren't Uncle Sam? What if he instead were Uncle Saddam?

"You may have the Saddam Husseins of the world, the North Koreans, being able to hang on to power," Zimmermann said, "by using this technology to oppress their own political opposition."

Clipper could do harm even in countries friendly to the United States. Washington wanted them to adopt Clipper-style standards. And at the very least the Clinton Administration was encouraging these governments to demand the keys to whatever encryption schemes their citizens used. That could boomerang mightily against American companies doing business outside the States. Phil Zimmermann recounted to me a rumor he'd heard about a giant entertainment conglomerate that had negotiated a huge deal in France; its executives found the

French to be uncannily prescient about the Americans' tactics. The espionage rumor might or might not be accurate. But fear of French spying against Yanks was common enough for many people from U.S. firms to be very careful about what they said on the telephone, or where they left their suitcases. The French had prohibited strong cryptography. And the Clipper plan, while not a ban on decent encryption, certainly deprived American companies of the moral foundations they needed to protest the French law. In the long run a Clipper arrangement might indeed pave the way for a ban in the United States itself against PGP-strength products, and already it could prop up such moves abroad, to the great disadvantage of American companies with secrets to protect.

In another way, too, Clipperish approaches would make U.S. companies less competitive. American software firms wanted to build encryption into spreadsheets, databases, word processors, and other major applications. If the Feds bullied them into using Clipper, then their products would be less attractive than those of rivals. Consider the market for software to store sensitive material such as medical records; would a European hospital favor a crippled American program over a German program with robust encryption?

That wasn't so abstract a question. An engineer from the giant Siemens conglomerate in Germany told me later that he was working on medical software, and he expected his employer to clobber U.S. rivals if their products used a questionable, Clipperish encryption scheme. What's more, crypto mavens were common enough overseas for even American companies to think about hiring them in the former Soviet Union to bypass the export controls. If it happened, it would be the ultimate statement on the absurdity of both the controls and Clipper.

Not surprisingly, a great hue and cry against Clipper came from the American software industry, and meanwhile the hackers themselves were waging full-scale warfare against it on the Net. Thousands of Netfolks participated in the anti-Clipper activities of groups such as the Computer Professionals for Social Responsibility, the first group to sound the tocsin.

In 1994, however, as clueless as ever, the White House officially endorsed Clipper—no ifs ands or buts—and made arrangements for the production of the chips. "Encryption is a law-and-order issue since it can be used by criminals to thwart wiretaps and avoid detection and prosecution," Al Gore said in justifying Clipper. "It also has huge strategic value. Encryption technology and cryptoanalysis turned the tide in the Pacific and elsewhere during World War II." But exactly. People on the Net thought that Clipper was just plain brain-dead as a way to protect security, a triumph of bureaucrats over techies.

You even didn't have to be on the Net to hate the tumor chip. At the request of *Time* and CNN, Yankelovich Partners polled 1,000 Americans; did they think that private phone calls mattered more than wiretap powers for police? Four-fifths opposed Clipper. Newspapers churned out editorial after editorial, and with good cause: Imagine the joys of trying to expose government corruption if the biggest crooks on the public payroll might someday be able to monitor your conversations whenever they wanted.

Quite properly, then, most citizens did not trust Washington. Hackers wore sweatshirts that played on a slogan that Intel used to promote computers using its chips. Alluding to Clipper, the sweatshirts read, "Big Brother Inside." Tens of thousands of people on the Net lent their names to an anti-Clipper petition originated by Computer Professionals for Social Responsibility. John Perry Barlow, the Grateful Dead lyricist who cofounded the Electronic Frontier Foundation, told how snoopy Feds would have to kill him and pry his private PGP key from his "cold, dead fingers." Through it all, meg after meg of messages went out over the Net—everything from sophomoric diatribes to carefully reasoned pleas for anti-Clipper letters to local members of Congress.

After questioning some arguments against Clipper, one man found himself vilified all over the Net, complete with a lie that he had made a homosexual advance against a hacker. The privacy movement was supposed to defend Americans' right to dissent, not enforce its own form of alternative orthodoxy. I felt grumpy, then, about the smear. But that was a relatively rare incident; typical opposition to Clipper was passionate but high minded.

Except for the smear described above, the meanest statements came not from Clipper foes but from Stewart A. Baker, a PGP critic who was about to return to private practice after serving as chief counsel for the National Security Agency. *Wired* commendably let Baker give his side. The magazine did so "with all the enthusiasm," Baker wrote, "of Baptist ministers turning their Sunday pulpits over to the Devil."

Understandably Baker began by denying that Clipper would "create a brave new world of government intrusion into the privacy of Americans." Baker said that key escrow would merely maintain Washington's rights to do wiretaps as presently authorized. That was a wrong; the government actually was going out of its way to make us all tap ready, as if we were back in the old Soviet Union in the KGB era. But at least in this case Baker wasn't maligning the Net. The nastiness oozed out later when his article took on "Myth Number Two: Unreadable encryption is the key to our future liberty." Baker shrugged off such reasoning as "the long-delayed revenge of people who couldn't go to Woodstock because they had too much trig homework. It reflects a wide—and kind of endearing—streak of romantic high-tech anarchism that crops up throughout the computer world." Then he let loose against PGP-style programs itself. "Some argue that widespread availability of this encryption will help Latvian freedom fighters today and American freedom fighters tomorrow." Presumably thousands of PGP boosters were hunkered down making bombs in Manhattan basements.

Having tried to ignore the legitimate uses of PGP by thousands of peaceful, law-abiding citizens, Baker then told how "a high-tech pedophile in Santa Clara, California, had a PGP-encrypted diary of his contacts with suscepti- ble young boys using computer bulletin boards all over the country." Oh. So between overthrowing the govern- ment, PGP users would be seducing eight-year-olds. Baker huffed that "if unescrowed encryption becomes ubiquitous, there will be many more stories like this."

Poor Baker. If he'd really wanted to do his attacks right, he could have quoted with full grimness the writ- ings that Timothy May, the Cypherpunk, had posted on the Net in the spirit of Jerry Rubin and Abbie Hoffman.

May was the author of a long, detailed, sometimes even Talmudic list of frequently asked questions and an- swers on cryptography and the fight for privacy, which might or might not have been on the Net at the time Baker was writing his *Wired* piece. But if not, he could have found equivalent thoughts among May's many postings to the Cyperpunks' rather public list. Laying out the case against strong encryption programs in the PGP vein, May conjectured that they could make killing for hire much more practical. People using encryption could rely on trusted agents who dispensed anonymous digital cash. "There are some ways to reduce the popularity of this Murder Incorporated system," May said, and kindly as- sured readers that he had been thinking about them.

For good measure May noted that racists such as the Aryan Nation were using encryption, and "other kinds of terrorists" might be relying on it as well. "Expect more uses in the future, as things like PGP continue to spread." As if that weren't enough to pull bureaucrats' chains, May said: "Many of us are explicitly anti-democratic and hope to use encryption to undermine the so-called democratic governments of the world."

May, ever the idea juggler, also weighed in with some powerful arguments *for* PGP that appealed strongly to a stodgy old Democrat (small "d" as well) like me. Even the Feds should have grasped them. "Could strong crypto be used for sick and disgusting and dangerous purposes?" May asked. And then he answered himself: "So can locked doors, but we don't insist on an 'open door policy' (outside of certain quaint sorority and rooming houses!). So do many forms of privacy allow plotters, molesters, racists, etc., to meet and plot." Whatever May was, anarchist, libertarian, objectivist, or nothing, he was making more sense in those three sentences than Baker could have in a 1,000 essays.

After May signed up for Cyberia, a legally oriented list, he was one of the favorite nonlawyers there, winning friends even among those who disagreed with his politics. In one limited way he may have been more threatening to Washington than Hoffman or Rubin, for, rather than just ranting and raving and putting on a good show, he could communicate all too cogently with members of the establishment. At the same time the Feds were fixating on Zimmermann, May casually told the lawyers how he moved in and out of the country without letting Washington veto his speeches on encryption. In effect his gleeful confession made mockery of the laws. If D.C. couldn't even control a traveler—there in flesh and blood—how could it monitor electrons speeding over the phone wires?

"I myself just presented a paper on 'Crypto Anarchy and Virtual Communities' in Monte Carlo," May told the cyberlawyers, at least one of whom was an attorney from the Justice Department. "I described algorithms, methods, etc., and was never asked or instructed to submit to the Men in Black in D.C." He was even carrying around "several gigabytes of code, essays, programs." But never was he "ever stopped, questioned, or searched. Only upon landing in San

Francisco was I asked to state my business overseas. I said I was meeting with cryptographers from around the world! This was met with confusion by the twenty-two-year-old Customs officer; but after asking if any of them were from Russia or Iraq, and I told him I had no idea if there were or not, he waved me through." May said most U.S. cryptographers "just shrug and ignore the *possibility* that our papers may be illegal to present outside the U.S."

His observations came as the Electronic Frontier Foundation was trying to resolve matters in a more tidy way. It was sponsoring a lawsuit to prevent Washington from restricting the spread of encryption-related writing and software. Quite correctly the EFF argued that the encryption laws were an "impermissible prior restraint on speech, in violation of the First Amendment." An EFF victory, needless to say, could nuke the government's case against Zimmermann.

With Hooverian tenacity, as if Phil Zimmermann were Dillinger or a godfather, Washington kept up its harassment and even escalated it in some ways. Jim Warren saw this happen firsthand. He had asked to testify several years ago in Zimmermann's defense, but the authorities ignored his request. Then in 1995 he had published op-ed pieces in San Jose and San Francisco papers, in which he throttled the FBI and NSA for getting in the way of the best possible security on the Net. In the wake of the Mitnick break-ins, he had accused the Feds of "endangering millions of innocent citizens and law-aiding businesses that use the Net or cell phones, in order to protect their ability to monitor the few who might be guilty of something." Almost immediately two U.S. Customs agents favored Warren with a surprise visit to his house and quizzed him about Zimmermann and PGP. "When they began the interview," he said, "they handed me a subpoena that said I was 'COMMANDED to appear and testify before the Grand Jury of the United States District Court' in San Jose."[23]

"Who says government isn't responsive," Warren quipped.

He said this in a folksy newsletter sent to hundreds of people on the Net. Its well-earned name was *Government Access;* he had been the main organizer of a successful campaign to get California to put legislative information on the Internet for free. As much as anyone he was trying to work within The System. Yet he was ever skeptical toward "Congress Critters." Again and again Warren's newsletter in effect depicted a Washington that could be Torylike in its contempt toward Netfolk.

Warren didn't just write of the well-publicized threats like the Exon bill, or the Clinton Administration's prosecution of a couple in California because their sex-oriented BBS did not come up to Bible Belt community standards in Tennessee, or the Zimmermann case itself. Warren also wrote of obscure people such as a Berkeley-area hacker who, enraged by restrictions on encryption and by other actions in the vein of King George's Stamp Act, had fled to Sweden.

"Sweden is no paradise," the expatriate told Warren via e-mail, "but I don't ever worry that the government is going to break into my home. I know that I'll be able to run my BBS, maintain all the contacts I've developed over the years, and continue to use the various nets without fear of Uncle Sam attacking me. So now I'm trading in my U.S. passport for one that is a lot less threatening to me and my PC." Warren added: "This is the second former American I have known who has done this for exactly these reasons!" I remembered a hacker libertarian who had been hoping to construct an island in the Caribbean, beyond the reach of technophobic politicians.

Warren was disappointed enough with Washington to tell the Net: "I'm beginning to feel like a German Jew in 1935." He didn't just hate Clipper and the harassment of Zimmermann. On top of everything else, Washington had recently passed a digital telephone bill that "would make Lyndon Johnson, Nixon's Watergate team, and J. Edgar Hoover drool on their bibs." The project would cost the taxpayers billions of dollars over the years—all this to make the phone system more tappable, out of fear that crooks might otherwise forward phone calls to bugfree locations. Washington was actually setting aside more money for snooping than for electronic libraries. And now Warren feared that the Feds someday would ban encryption outright.

Beyond D.C.'s computer-related stupidities, he loathed the way the Feds played fast and easy with the Constitution on matters such as drug law enforcement. Agencies, for example, could keep money and equipment taken from suspects and use them for their own purposes, thus giving police "a profit motive" to abuse Americans' rights.

"No doubt," Warren said, "many in Germany told that nation's Jews, 'It's not that serious' and 'It's just a phase—it'll pass' as they disarmed the citizens in the name of law and order only a few years before filling the camps and ovens that somehow good, law-abiding Germans just never knew about until after the war. If we don't watch out, our government's cure for 'crime' will become even more dangerous than the illness. And this time, I don't think Sweden will be a safe haven."

Clearly Warren was a long, long way from the optimism of *Orwell's Revenge*, the book in which Big Brother lost to the hackers.

I doubted that the United States was quite as Oceania-like as Jim Warren obviously believed, and his own German parallel might be stretching it. Stamp Act parallels did, however, fit. An old, ignorant, Torylike order wanted to pass laws to contain the new, and I could envision an increasing number of ugly confrontations between bureaucrats and Netfolk. Baker, the ex-NSA man, hadn't hesitated in the least to come up with his wacky characterizations of Clipper foes. To the D.C. policy elite, we on the Net were fair pickings.

All the hype about the Information Superhighway notwithstanding, most of the Feds didn't feel quite as at home on computer networks as billed. Most Congress members in mid-1995 still lacked public e-mail addresses.

Meanwhile, the Net was catching on among millions of younger American who surfed freely, while their elders could barely master commercial networks such as CompuServe. By way of Clipper and blatantly anti-network copyright proposals, the White House was kissing off all too many within Generation Net.[24]

A further embarrassment was the contrasting enlightenment of some Republican conservatives, who many Democrats on the Net might have dismissed entirely in the past. Rush Limbaugh, the right-wing talk show host, didn't just show up on CompuServe as a visitor. He personally logged on again and again and even met his wife there. He might not be on the Net itself, but he was much more at ease with the technology than were the majority of the liberals on the Hill. Meanwhile, the most powerful conservative of all, House Speaker Newt Gingrich, spoke out against the Exon amendment. William Buckley, the noted conservative journalist, was a major backer of my proposal for a decentralized national library system online. And the conservative writer George Gilder, while all too zealous at times about free markets, had made some of the most prescient predictions on the direction in which the technology was headed.

Too many Democrats were TV-centric, while Gilder believed that computers would be the new entertainment medium, prevailing over television. Sales figures proved him right. More Americans bought desktops computers in 1994 than purchased color televisions, and it was only a matter of time until they logged onto computer networks and worried about their privacy there. And here were

Clinton and Gore pushing Clipper with more ardor than they could summon up for well-stocked electronic libraries for all.

Of course, not everybody on the Democratic side was hopeless, and many Republican law-and-order types loved Clipper, the Bush leftover. Also, these same politicians might well applaud the Clinton Administration's anti-Net copyright proposals, not understanding all the undertows that could ultimately drag property rights under. But at least they hadn't enlisted civil libertarians and populists in their campaigns to the extent that Bill Clinton had. I'd never have voted for the man if I'd known in advance about Clipper, the harassment of Zimmermann, and the antediluvian copyright policies. Bush in some ways might have been preferable. Not knowing the difference between a potato chip and a silicon chip, he would have done much less damage. A smarter, more principled Democrat than Clinton could pick up the pieces in '96.

Clinton's Justice Department showed a brazen and bizarre lack of fairness toward Zimmermann. Until the statute of limitations expired—and that was fuzzy, even to lawyers—the Feds might just let him dangle. Without finding Zimmermann guilty of anything, or even charging him, Washington in a sense was already leveling penalties. He had to spend hours and hours away from his regular consulting business to work on his case.

Total costs might reach $300,000 if the prosecutors decided to act. Even if lawyers donated their time—and Zimmermann might enjoy the services of some noted attorneys outraged by the threat to civil liberties—there would be the burden of telephone costs, travel, and hotels. Appeals for donations went up in such areas of the Usenet as talk.crypto.politics, comp.org.eff.talk, and, of course, alt.security.pgp. People could pay by credit card, encoding their numbers via PGP.[25]

In the end, no matter what happened to Zimmermann, the real victory might be in the marketplace. And there Clipper was losing. AT&T and a chip maker named VLSI Technology came out with a chip that would challenge even the NSA's supercomputer. Given a choice between that and Clipper, who'd want the latter? Even before then, in fact, few customers were going for Clipper-based equipment.[26] In the end it looked as if Washington would resort not to a chip but to continued pressure on U.S. corporations to make available the key schemes of more secure plans. And even then, I hoped, the industry would balk. The more such foolishness became a habit here, the less protected would be American companies abroad, as people outside the States followed Washington's example.

Some of the biggest Clipper haters, meanwhile, were overlooking their differences to unite against the tumor chip. Jim Bidzos' company had already granted a license for the basic technology to ViaCrypt, which, at least in the latter's opinion, left it free to sell a commercial version of PGP. And this past action may have been a door opener in a way for Phil Zimmermann. PGP was no longer so much of an outlaw program in the eyes of many, and businesses felt they could use it and get technical support. Beyond that, professors at the Massachusetts Institute of Technology, whence much of the RSA technology had come, were sick of all the patent wars. They just wanted to see solid encryption in use. And Bidzos, however much he quarreled with Zimmermann, was himself determined that the Feds not control encryption. The compromise could go a long way toward enshrining RSA as at least an informal world standard, and thwarting RSA's biggest competitor, the NSA.

And so Bizdos and colleagues let PGP be used for noncommercial purposes as long as the newer versions were incompatible with the older ones that lacked the blessing of RSA and Public Key Partners. Of course that still didn't solve the hassles of securing international commerce with a truly strong encryption standard with which the U.S. government felt comfortable. But even if PGP-style products weren't official, they were murdering Clipperish schemes before snoop-ready chips and programs could take root. The world's governments might well have to join countries like France and try to ban strong encryption.

But could they? Too many people in too many countries were already using software such as PGP. Hackers proudly included their public PGP keys—those weird combinations of letters and numbers—at the ends of their messages or told how people could obtain them. PGP keys were becoming status symbols. PGP wasn't yet built into popular e-mail programs such as Eudora for easy use, so, if nothing else, the keys indicated a certain level of technical expertise. They were the new vanity plates of the dataways. PGP was even becoming a small industry; for example, you could shell out $20 and officially register your key with a company in Palo Alto, California, called SLED. And then people receiving messages from you would know they were really from you.

SLED required a mailed or faxed driver's license or passport, or a preprinted personal check. This wasn't the best proof of identity, but it would at least let Netfolks spot obvious forgeries immediately. If nothing else, you could "register" your key with friends who were well known and well trusted on the net.

With or without formal registration, more and more Netfolks felt lost without their PGP. Father Bill Morton, the Anglican priest mentioned earlier, the one who used PGP to accept confessions over the Net, wrote a parody:

It's one for the money,
Two for the show,

Three to get ready,
Now go, cat, go!
But don't you step on my PGP.
You can do anything, but lay off my PGP

Responding to a query I'd posted in several encryption-related newsgroups, he explained in an e-mail why PGP meant so much to him. Confessions were just part of the story:

> *In the history of Anglican pastoral case, there is a strong tradition of the use of the letter as a means of spiritual guidance. Actually this tradition goes deep into the roots of the Catholic Church. Some of the books regarded as "spiritual classics" are compilations of correspondence between a person and their spiritual director. Until the advent of PGP, e-mail was not a suitable place for such correspondence. It's one thing to have your correspondence published 100 years after the fact; it's quite another to run the risk of having your personal thoughts posted to a Usenet newsgroup or read by the sysop of a BBS. Now they know that even if they hit the wrong button and send their e-mail to the wrong place, it is secure. . . . Legislation that would make encryption illegal or require a mandatory backdoor would totally compromise any trust in e-mail or any other form of electronic text system such as word processors.*

Father Morton's respect for privacy came through when I asked for examples of confidences that people had shared with him by way of PGP: "No matter how I disguise the facts," he told me, "even if I were to create a fictitious person, someone somewhere would believe that they were reading the details of their life story." And so he was vague, other than to say, to give an idea of the gravity of what he heard, "Thoughts, dreams, hopes, as well as lust, anger, and hatred. Sometimes, actually oftentimes, there are things that you wouldn't even tell your spouse. Our lives are based on trust."

Thanks to PGP, Father Morton could maintain that trust not only with people locally in Woodstock, New Brunswick, but with Netfolk from thousands of miles away.

Some people met him in newsgroups. "We'll have an exchange of e-mail on a specific topic," he said, "and at one point it will become evident that I am a priest." He neither hid nor played up his occupation. Upon learning it, he said, the Netter at the other end "may wish to change the topic and enter into a brief correspondence about a particular question. That conversation might last one or two posts and is usually, though not always, in PGP." In addition, he corresponded with a very small group of people regularly about significant events in their lives. These conversations were always in PGP.

"Before PGP," Father Morton said, "e-mail was guarded in its content. A typical e-mail exchange might be to set up a phone conversation or meeting or discuss issues in very general terms. Now, at least in a few cases, the PGP mail is much more open in its content, and as a result the e-mail pastoral relationship can be much more productive."

Father Morton was not alone in his use of PGP to protect personal secrets. For example, the Samaritans, a group devoted to talking people out of suicide, said it would accept PGP-encrypted messages.

"The Samaritans," announced a Usenet post, "have always taken the confidentiality of callers extremely seriously. Indeed the most frequently asked question within the movement about our e-mail service is, 'What about confidentiality?'" Surely, in an era when more and more communications happened to be electronic, it would be folly to deny reliable encryption to the Samaritans and the people they helped. Although the Samaritans felt more confidence about the security of unprotected e-mail than did Father Morton, they understood an important truth: *perceptions* mattered as much as anything. If their correspondents lacked faith in the confidentiality of e-mail, they couldn't write as freely. And, as I saw it, they might not be as open to rescue. If Washington banned PGP, if it replaced it with an inferior, Clipperish arrangement, the Samaritans just might not be as successful as with truly secure encryption.

Privacy wasn't just for confessions and for suicide prevention. It was also for teenagers. Donna—she supplied her real name but I'll protect her with a pseudonym—lived in Florida and was a seventeen-year-old junior in high school who was already using PGP. She e-mailed me:

> *I couldn't speak for other teenagers and their parents, but with my extremely intrusive mother, I use all the privacy devices I can get. I've kept extensive journals since second grade—she's always read them and nosed around, no matter where I've tried to hide them. She's opened letters from friends and pokes her nose into anything that she considers unorthodox; we don't quite see eye to eye on many issues. I'm a good student, responsible, don't drink or do drugs, blah blah blah, but she has continuously invaded my privacy over the years despite her lack of justification.*
>
> *Two years ago I tried a locked drawer where I kept all of my papers, letters, and the like, but she has opened the drawer with my keys. So now I just do everything on the computer and encrypt/password it. I can see how some parents might justify searching their kids' rooms—just as police can under circumstances justify searching homes.*

But, Donna went on, if a child were doing something *illegal,* there "would be physical evidence." That seemed clear: You could encrypt a diary full of unorthodox musings; you could not encode a marijuana stash.

I would have trusted Donna, but I still had mixed feelings about most teenagers using PGP without their parents' sharing the keys. How long until Senator Exon ranted that the young would encrypt dirty bytes? In the end, however, just as with children's use of the Net itself, PGP should be a family decision, not a federal one; Washington mustn't turn into a giant version of Donna's mother. Risks from a ban, even one limited to children, so outweighed the benefits. If Donna's mother wanted to understand her daughter, then maybe she needed to spend less time doing a domestic-level KGB act and more time at a computer—seeing for herself what her daughter was up to. In the process she might understand Donna well enough to tolerate her opinions. She'd better learn to brook them; her daughter was almost eighteen, the age of adulthood in the United States. Soon many parents would be more comfortable with the technology, and then, family by family, parents could decide whether to be Big Mama or Big Daddy and look for PGP-encrypted files. It should be a family, not a government, matter.

If nothing else, parents themselves could use PGP to guard their own privacy. "I use PGP at home solely for keeping confidential information from prying eyes—for instance, from my son and my son's friends, as well as for keeping their information in one central place," said Joe Collins, an employee of an international investment bank based in New York. It guarded his burglar alarm codes, the codes to the family safe, all credit card numbers, and all passwords to software on the family computer. Yes, some popular software came with encryption, and certain people might have argued that home users such as Collins didn't need PGP. But the encryption found in popular software was nowhere near in PGP's league. In fact, Crak

Software, a company in Phoenix, Arizona, even sold "pass-word-recovery software" to crack popular programs such as WordPerfect, Word, Excel, Lotus 1-2-3, and Quattro Pro (for backup purposes).

AIDS activists especially understood the possibilities of good, strong encryption; victims of the disease, after all, were treated about as fairly as lepers had been in biblical times. In New York a group called ACT UP tried to get the public health officials to encourage labs to use PGP to pro-tect the identities of patients. The officials liked the idea. The program died at the hands of a parsimonious gover-nor; but sooner or later, I suspected, PGP would be used in one way or another to protect the privacy of AIDS pa-tients, if it wasn't already.

In the business area, the advantages of keeping PGP legal—and avoiding Clipperish solutions—were just as clear as at the personal level. "PGP is essential," said Robert David Steele, a former CIA agent whose passion for legalized encryption and dislike of Clipper must have endeared him to many hackers.[27] "Security is the founda-tion for openness. In order for a world of open electronic exchanges actually to succeed, electronic persons have to know three things, all of which PGP supports: (a) that the person on the other end of the link is who he says he is, (b) that the information being received is genuine and not altered, and (c) that a digital cash payment will be forth-coming, assuming that this is part of the transaction." Steele was not just talking about the benefits of PGP for business alone, but clearly it was among the major uses that he quite properly had on his mind here.

Many business people on the Net agreed. I was hardly surprised to read in the *New York Times* about the use of PGP "in what was apparently the first retail transactions on the Internet using a readily available version of pow-erful data encryption software designed to guarantee privacy." A Philadelphia man had used PGP to scramble his credit card number and spent $12.48 and shipping

costs on a compact disk with rock music from a New
Hampshire company called Net Market. More benefits
were to come. Already other companies were working on
digital cash, which could let bits and bytes go out over the
Net in ways that prevented them from being easily traced.
They would be, in other words, just like dollar bills.[28] You
could spend them without Big Brother knowing that you'd
bought a *Playboy,* a Rush Limbaugh book, a condom, or
whatever else might somehow cause your neighbors or
your boss to take offense.

PGP also made sense for privacy protection *within*
companies. An accounting firm in Palo Alto, California,
for example, used PGP to guard backup tapes in case of
loss or theft, and a Washington accountant relied on it for
client communications.[29] And when Zimmermann himself asked online for PGP testimonials, a man with a
telecommunications firm on the West Coast told him how
much he loved it as an alternative to Clipper:

> *Once it becomes a standard, the competitive soft-*
> *ware industry will have no incentive to continue*
> *technical development in crypto. And then once*
> *Clipper gets cracked by outsiders or otherwise com-*
> *promised, there will still be a lot of bureaucratic in-*
> *ertia protecting it and keeping the fact that it's been*
> *compromised a secret.*
>
> *We see a serious need for crypto to protect client*
> *records regarding their telephone systems and com-*
> *puter networks, to protect our internal company*
> *memos sent via e-mail, and to protect strategic busi-*
> *ness information sent via e-mail. We figure that a*
> *misrouted piece of client data is a potentially serious*
> *liability issue, and a misrouted sales proposal or*
> *similar business document is like leaving a credit*
> *card on a park bench. Due diligence, fiscal responsi-*
> *bility, and all that. The big plus is simply that we*
> *will be able to confidently move a lot more of our*

*business online, which will make a huge difference
to us. More efficient handling of client requests,
more efficient internal discussions, and more effective communication with investors. In particular I
do a lot of strategic business planning online, and it
always bugs me in the back of my mind—'What
happens if this gets lost on the Internet?' In one sense
good crypto is like a good business dinner. It facilities the flow of ideas in a relaxed atmosphere.*

At the same time, needless to say, PGP could improve
the flow of *political* ideas. In 1993 Boris Yeltsin had been at
odds with foes nostalgic for the old Soviet state. "If a dicta-
torship takes over Russia," a message from Latvia had told
Zimmermann, "your PGP is widespread from the Baltic to
the Far East now and will help democratic people if necessary. Thanks."[30] In Burma rebels used PGP against an oppressive regime. A writer in Thailand said that before PGP
reached them, captured papers had "resulted directly in ar-
rest, including whole families, and their torture and death."
Activists in El Salvador and Guatemala also relied on the
program. "In this business, lots of people have been killed,"
said Daniel Salcedo, a member of the Human Rights Project
of the American Association for the Advancement of
Science.[31] David Banisar of the Electronic Privacy
Information Center told me of PGP being used in Kenya,
Mali, Senegal, Egypt, and Mali, among other countries.

"Wire tapping is conducted in nearly every country in
the world," Banisar wrote in a paper with the marvelous
title of "Bug Off!" "It is frequently abused." A 1992 State
Department report, for example, told of governments and
private organizations snooping away in dozens of countries. And it hadn't happened just in the Third World.
"There have been numerous cases in the United Kingdom
which revealed that the British intelligence services
monitor social activists, labor unions, and civil liberties
groups," Banisar said in a paper written for Privacy

International.[32] What's more, the Canadian Communications Security Establishment had shelled out more than $1.1 million to scan through millions of messages and pick out dangerous words and phrases.[33] Would the CCSE abuse the system and routinely compile dossiers on law-respecting people? And what about the FBI here in the States? Many Netfolks took it for granted that Louis Freeh's people were keeping up with Usenet.

"The FBI has the ability to police the Internet and, indeed, has been doing so," David Nadler and Kendrick Fong, two tech-oriented lawyers, would write later on in *Computer Digest: The Journal of Professional Development for the Washington–Baltimore Technology Community.* "In fact, the FBI has been collecting Usenet postings since the late 1980s."

A formulaic condemnation of all FBI monitoring, however, would be unfair. I could hardly object to the Feds reading the public messages of egotistical nuts with a clear-cut predilection for violence. What better reason *not* to censor Usenet and any audio and video equivalents that might follow? Let the kooks rant away, hour after hour, educating Louis Freeh about their plans. Usenet wasn't anyone's living room. Posting messages there was like publishing a book or speaking in a town square. Via the free Stanford Netnews Filtering Service, I could receive electronic mail messages whenever a specified word showed up in a major area of Usenet. Yes, I could track people by name. I could also choose words associated with a topic. That was the magic of the Net; it gave us small-fry many of the same tools available to the intelligence bureaucracies. The same kind of wizardry that might let Canadian cops snoop on citizens could allow me to track the utterances of Al Gore on the subject, say, of the Internet.

One technology, however, may have bureaucrats more uncomfortable than any other—encryption. A U.S. data-

base expert named Patrick Ball found this out the hard
way when he was in Ethiopia to help the Office of the
Special Prosecutor. Ball efficiently helped build a database
of crimes that had occurred under the regime of Mengistu
Haile Mariam. He was accomplishing plenty. Then a bureaucratic rival started a turf war with him. The man
falsely claimed that Ball had been using PGP for secret
correspondence, probably with the CIA, even though the
truth was a little more mundane. Ball hadn't used PGP for
anything but test messages; the people at the other end
lacked the technical skills. But the rival didn't know. He
confused PGP with unencoding—a way to prepare programs for accurate transmission via e-mail—and unfortunately the chief special prosecutor believed Ball's accuser
and forced the database expert to resign.

So often that was the case with police: They displayed
a mix of fear and ignorance. And they were not totally
wrong to be worried. One computer expert predicted that
in the next few years criminals would routinely use electronic scrambling. "This could signal the end of computer
forensics," said William Spernow, "before it even gets off
the ground." A criminal relied on a double set of books,
employing PGP to conceal the accurate one, and dope-
peddlers in Miami used encryption.[34]

Not only that, just as I was writing part of this chapter,
the newspapers told how terrorists in Japan had killed 10
people and injured about 5,500 by spreading nerve gas in
a Tokyo subway station. Wouldn't restrictions on encryption make such acts harder to commit with impunity?

Strong counterarguments existed, however, against the
jackbooters who would ban strong encryption or impose
the Clipper variety on us. I would rather that nations not
spy on each other. But I fully recall the naiveté of the past,
the fantasy that "gentlemen do not open other gentlemen's
mail"; whether we liked it or not, espionage and coun-
terespionage would always go on. In that spirit, instead of

wasting money on Clipperish schemes, countries could spend money developing more powerful computers to crack encryption, and they could also refine the unscrambling techniques. That would not be cheap. But since bad guys wouldn't let Clipper or successors be the apex of technology, the United States hadn't any other choice. Other countries might feel otherwise. Bureaucrats just couldn't contain technology. Clipperish schemes would be brainless in any country.

As one alternative, governments could rely more heavily on open sources—for example, newspapers and other media outlets, especially those online. The more journalists out there, and the more independent they were, the harder it would be for nations to keep secrets and conspire against each other. The United States and friends had the most selfish of reasons for encouraging the spread of the free press.

The open source idea was hardly original to me. Others had talked about it for years, most notably Robert Steele, the ex-CIA agent, who observed that publicly available material was often far more useful than the clandestinely gathered variety. I didn't agree with much of what Steele said—I wanted more isolation between journalists and government than he might have liked. But his basic point was sound. Information was most reliable when it was in the open and could be dissected, rather than hiding it behind a "secret" stamp. The spread of network technology could only strengthen this premise.

Yet another approach could be the selective use of agents, in new-style roles, taking advantage of high technology. Here again I had mixed feelings. But in an era when countries such as Iraq were trying to develop nuclear weapons, this option should be kept alive.

What about terrorists? As with child-molesting rings and drug cartels, Clipper just would not do any good. Secret groups would be the last in the world to use the

chip. Far better for intelligence agencies to work on more
powerful computers and truly effective software for cracking codes. Breakthroughs might not come immediately,
but would sooner or later, and the civilian sector might ultimately benefit when the technology finally did reach the
world at large. Advanced supercomputers, for example,
could be used for weather forecasting, or for graphics and
design—the same wizardry that had helped make possible
the Visible Human Project described in the last chapter.

Meanwhile an open-source approach could often do
the job. The accused terrorists in Japan hadn't exactly
stayed hidden from the world before the subway inci-
dents. Shoko Asahara, their leader, had delivered sermon
after sermon with allusions to poisonous gas; in the city of
Matsumoto where he had been at odds with authorities
over some land, 7 people had died and 200 had suffered
injuries when a cloud of sarin wafted in the area. Small
wonder that the Japanese government had caught up with
the sect so soon after the Tokyo tragedy. Newspaper databases would have told plenty, beyond any information that
happened to be in the government's own records.

Legally authorized bugs might be yet another solution, and so, at times, might be informers wired to make
the best case. In an era of near-invisible electronics, this
approach would be increasingly practical.

What's more, if Bill Clinton and Al Gore really cared
about protecting citizens in a high-tech age, they would
worry less about snooping on citizens and more about
hardening up points of vulnerability. Steele noted how
easily criminals could "maliciously interfere with the
computers that control the power system. It is relatively
easy to destroy computer capabilities—this takes much
less skill than to 'crack' them and divert computing resources." Also, terrorists could wreak havoc with computers that controlled telephone systems in such areas as
communications for government and banking.

He also warned of interference with the computers of Wall Street and the Federal Reserve. "Trillions in digital data" could vanish into the ether. "A massive global economic panic" would ensue. Preventative measures wouldn't be cheap, but if the American government did care about security, it would prepare realistically for the threats of the information era rather than doing an inept Big Brother act.

To rig up a whole nation for wire taps would be both a waste and a disgrace. I pondered the ironies. Here the NSA and similar agencies were supposed to protect normality—to guard families against dopesters, sex perverts, terrorists, and the rest—and yet Phil Zimmermann the husband and father might go to jail. "I think it's kind of unreal to him," Zimmermann said when I asked how his son felt about this. "I tell him that I have some talented lawyers working for me, and that we're doing the best we can." And Zimmermann's wife? "She thinks that they can't possibly indict me, because that would be wrong— that somehow they'll realize that and just back out. Of course by the time your book is printed, we'll know one way or the other whether she was right."

A Few Words about Library Books, Democracy, and Socks the Cybercat

The White House in the 1990s was extolling computer nets as a way to Bring Government Closer to the People. Americans could dial up "An Interactive Citizens' Handbook" on the Internet, see a photo of a teenaged Clinton with JFK, and listen to Socks the Clinton cat meow. But could Clinton–Gore hear *us?* Just how "interactive" was the White House?

Clinton boosters formed a group called Americans Communicating Electronically to improve electronic con-

tacts between mortals and bureaucrats. Al Gore, meanwhile, had flaunted his typing skills with the famous visit
to CompuServe. But was electronic democracy truly alive
on the Internet and other computer networks? Not quite.
All the techish sizzle notwithstanding, Clinton–Gore might
instead be giving us electronic oligarchy, especially if
Republicans followed the horrible precedents that the
White House was setting. Consider the dubious, somewhat
Orwellian process that was shaping the National Information Infrastructure—the famous data highways and
related endeavors.

So far Washington had not worked nearly as hard as it
should to drive down the cost of knowledge for the average American. At the same time a network-hostile copyright proposal was delighting information monopolists
and imperiling the ability of citizens to share electronic
newspaper clips in even a limited way.

I testified at an official hearing on the NII in 1993, and
what most struck me about Clinton–Gore was the chasm
between words and deeds—the same mind-set that led to
Oceania's propaganda agency being named the Ministry
of Truth. The gospel according to Al Gore was that people
of all income levels would be able to travel the dataways.
His musings later adorned the peach-colored newsprint of
The Mini Page, a newspaper insert for children.

"No longer will geographical location, wealth, gender,
or any other factor limit learning," Gore reassured elementary schoolers. He told how "a child from my home
town of Carthage, Tennessee, will be able to come home
from school, turn on a computer, and plug into the
Library of Congress in Washington, D.C." The NII would
clearly be in the grand democratic tradition, small "d."

The next day, however, the *Washington Post* carried
news of a different stripe from Bruce Lehman, the Clinton–
Gore commissioner of patents and trademarks, who chaired
the NII working group on intellectual property. I learned

that "because of the ease of digital reproduction, Lehman does not foresee that digital libraries will put copyrighted works within easy reach online the way they do books on a library shelf. Copyrighted digital materials are likely to be available only to subscribers—libraries, for example—who pay royalty fees, he said. People who want the material might have to go to their local library and use a computer there that would not allow them to copy or redistribute the work, Lehman said."[35] A few months later Bruce Lehman would graciously tell the *Wall Street Journal* that, yes, he would tolerate children carrying home copyrighted CD-ROMs and floppies of electronic books.[36]

Compared to networked books, however, the CDs and the rest would be pathetic. Distribution over the Internet and other networks could be the cheapest way to get the material spread around, while assuring a wide variety of material for all. When William Buckley likened CD-ROMs to 78-rpm shellac records in the era of the Internet, he couldn't have been more precise. And yet this was the future as envisioned by Bill Clinton's intellectual property czar. So much for the well-informed citizenry needed for a Jeffersonian America. Lehman was beating the bushes for electronic oligarchy.

Once I had felt that the Clinton–Gore people might truly share my own egalitarian dreams. I'd thought that nonlobbyists like me stood a healthy chance. I had been writing about computers for close to a decade; earlier I had covered a poverty beat, and I knew how we could drive down the cost of small computers so that someday even Head Start kids could read electronic books on them. What better way to encourage democracy? The whole country, not just the elite, could grow up understanding abstract thought. Could the Constitution have been drafted by a mob of illiterate TV watchers?

Rather than letting Big Brother choose books for us, we could establish a democratic system with many librarians in many cities empowered to make acquisitions. Never would bureaucrats be able to do the equivalent of tweaking old copies of the *London Times* behind our backs. It would be too damn hard with so many librarians in so many locations, and with the same material reposing on millions and millions of tablet-style computers that individual Americans owned. My vision was one of electronic federalism, not of Big Brother policing our reading tastes. TeleRead wouldn't undermine local schools and public libraries. Quite the contrary. TeleRead would buy affordable, sharp-screened machines for them, sending a signal to Silicon Valley and paving the way for similar computers to go on sale at the Kmart for $99.95 for anyone to buy.

Just as important, unlike the Postal plan mentioned earlier in this chapter, my TeleRead plan would let schools and libraries use the hardware without Big Brotherish restrictions. They could store whatever they wanted on their own computers for local people to dial up. And to make the national library more useful at the local level, they could add special, Web-style links designed for the people they served—not just for whole communities, but perhaps even for individual readers.

What's more, TeleRead would respect diversity and freedom of expression in other ways. Publishers could gamble fees up front to bypass librarians and qualify for royalties, and if censored from the national library, they could post on the Net itself. I took it for granted that Washington would try to censor TeleRead. That was the reason I envisioned a whole network of many librarians, in many places, together with long-range funding. Besides, my plan reflected the old wisdom from hackers: When censorship arises, just route around it. Private companies could make some nice money off officially banned books. Imagine the promotional opportunities; "Nixed by Washington" could be the new "Banned in Boston." What's more, since TeleRead was public and involved many librarians, not just a tiny D.C. elite, any censorship would probably be much more conspicuous than in the world of corporate publishing.

In other ways, too, TeleRead would be anti–Big Brother. Americans would not have to make private companies privy to their reading habits. The national library could track dialups for the purpose of paying writers and publishers—you couldn't retrieve books without reporting past accesses. But TeleRead would include protections. Records associated with individual users could be temporary, just a way to prevent information providers from abusing the system with repeated dialups. People could buy controversial books by way of anonymous digital money. In fact, with sophisticated enough fraud controls, the same techniques might eventually be used to prevent names from being associated with dialup records even for a short time. If nothing else, people could entrust TeleRead records to certified private companies that reported accesses without revealing identities.

TeleRead, then, could provide even more safeguards than public library records in the paper era—significant, since librarians by habit had respected privacy much more than had other government officials. "There was a case back in Nixon's era," Phil Zimmermann would eventually remind me, "where Nixon tried to find out what some of his enemies were reading at the library, and the librarians were, of course, up in arms about being asked to supply a list of books that had been checked out by a particular person or a list of people that had checked out a particular book. They were able to resist the efforts by the government to obtain that information. I think that we need to have the same kind of controls in place for future libraries that are on the Net." I couldn't have agreed more.

Even the hardware could serve to thwart Big Brother by promoting free expression and democracy. TeleRead would let people talk back to bureaucrats and among themselves; the machines would work with keyboards, and someday they might even serve in part as wireless digital telephones, not just computers. TeleRead would let Americans all be more uppity. The information in the national library would enrich public debate; it would at least somewhat blur distinctions between the wealthy and those who otherwise couldn't afford top-quality information.

This needn't be just a dream. The United States had a $6-trillion-plus economy, and if just some of us used electronic forms for government and commercial transactions, we eventually would save tens of billions in time and money. As noted earlier in this book, the same pen interfaces that were ideal for reading would be great for forms. E-forms could help flag errors in tax returns and other documents, "interview" users quickly, and just as quickly narrow down questions to the essentials. And so the saving in time and money could easily justify a well-stocked national library. No magic was involved here, just an old principle of information management. Two applications (smart forms and the electronic books) made more sense than just one (the books). In fact, the American Society for Information Science would later approach me to do a chapter on electronic libraries for an ASIS book from MIT Press, and I would oblige. Clearly TeleRead was a logical link between Gore's plans for reinventing government and his oft-claimed desire to drive down the cost of knowledge.

I was a writer, not an attorney or information scientist, but a number of well-credentialed people understood the logic of TeleRead, even when I showed them a version somewhat less refined than the one just described. At the urging of a distinguished Washington lawyer, I applied to testify at the interagency hearings on intellectual property law in the digital age. But he warned me some bizarreness was afoot. Experts from the Library of Congress would not run the hearings; nowadays electronic books would be more within the domain of the Commerce Department. A Commerce bureaucrat instead would be the main player here—Bruce Lehman. That should have been my tip-off that the proceedings would be big and furry and jump, and come with a pocket for joeys; but I went ahead just the same. The lawyer organizing the hearing seemed friendly, alert, intelligent, receptive. She said each witness would testify just a few minutes, and that after the hearings the Feds would carefully examine our words.

My optimism grew. I expected at least a modicum of electronic democracy, Gore-style, just as promised. So in November 1993 I joined some thirty other witnesses in Crystal City, Virginia, across the Potomac from Washington. Bill Clinton wanted his presidential cabinet to look like America, and, in fact, a black man was secretary of the Commerce. Gazing around the room, however, I saw a sea of white lawyers in dark suits, along with a scattering of women in power clothes. I could have been in California at an elite convocation of the software and entertainment industries.

I ran into one of the members of the intellectual property group, a minor White House advisor named David Lytel, who had promised to read my proposal as sent to him on the Internet. Mr. White House didn't waste a nanosecond. "This is like Hollywood," Lytel said. "Not everyone can be a star. We can't use everyone's idea."

"I'm not here to star," I said, "just to testify. Have you read my proposal?"

He said he had seen the prepared testimony I had left at the entrance to the auditorium.

"But what about the thousands of words I sent you on the Net? I thought you'd have a look and—"

"Excuse me," he said and moved on.

His Hollywood analogy would strike me later as all too apt, for this was shaping up as a TV-centric NII that favored television and movies over books. Al Gore later would not hold his grand information summit at the Library of Congress; no, he would jet off to Hollywood and to a speech punctuated by jokes with a comedienne.

There in the Crystal City auditorium, I saw a tall, gray-haired man surrounded by a cluster of other people. Heads bobbed. Stephen Metalitz was a lawyer and a power in the Information Industries Association, the IIA. "Welcome, Steve," Lehman greeted his first witness in a voice that told me who the true star of the day was. The rest of the hearing unfolded as I now feared. Witnesses from trade associations pounded away at the same theme again and again. Copyright law needed to be friendly to megaconglomerates or they would never bless the dataways with their *Terminator* films. It was as if the Internet, already starting to bristle with small businesses, never existed.

I heard some cogent testimony from some fine people representing librarians and educators, but all in all, I might as well have been at an IIA convention. Lehman's panel of bureaucrats, some of them strangers to copyright law, just about dozed off during my testimony. Chatting with me informally, certain industry witnesses were more curious about my ideas than were the Feds. It wasn't just to size up the opposition. For my plan would divert resources from bureaucracy to knowledge, and could actually *help* many members of the information industry.

A potential obstacle rose ahead, though: the hostility of real, live bureaucrats.

During a break I approached a working-group member from one of the most bureaucratic agencies of them all, the General Services Administration. "What do you think of my ideas for electronic forms?" I asked. "I remember when you guys let a senator benefit illegally from a federal lease on an office building. Imagine what you could have done with better technology to help flag stuff like that."

"Oh," he said coldly, "we can just train our contracting officers better." Better to protect jobs for bureaucrats like him than to offer affordable e-books for schoolchildren.

My foremost opponent, however, as I learned eventually, just may have been Lehman himself—the chairman of the Intellectual Property Working Group, which would help set copyright policy for America's dataways.

Bruce Lehman was Mr. Politically Correct. As his heroes he claimed the career-enhancing names of Bill Clinton and Martin Luther King; never mind the damage that his child-hostile copyright policies might do to ghetto schools, or the fact that the copyright hearing had been about as well integrated as a Klan meeting. The *New York Times* would see in Lehman's office "a handsomely framed photograph taken at last year's White House Christmas party. Bill and Hillary Clinton stand in the middle. Mr. Lehman is to the left, under a portrait of George Washington."

His clothes were as aggressively fashionable as his choice of heroes. The *Times*'s Teresa Riordan would write of "stylish suits detailed with a fresh white handkerchief." He might display "a touch of exotic color, perhaps a mint-colored watchband or the ruby background of a Brooks Brother tie." [37] Lehman needn't haunt any thrift shops. During a twelve- to fourteen-month period before joining the Administration, he had pulled down $430,000 as a lobbyist and lawyer for intellectual property clients. [38]

The patent office's Web site said he had represented "individuals, companies, and trade associations in the area of intellectual property rights as it affects the motion picture, telecommunications, pharmaceutical, computer software, and broadcasting industries." [39] His clients had included Lotus and Microsoft. [40] The latter was buying up electronic rights as if they were soft drinks for the programmers' offices. No, Microsoft would hardly be the world's leading backer of a universally affordable, well-stocked national digital library of the TeleRead variety. I'd lobby anyone, any company, for my idea. But could I ever persuade Microsoft? Oh, come on. This was the company that owned the word "Windows."

Clinton–Gore campaigners had once talked of "People First." Based on Lehman's background and proclivities, however, a better motto in the case of intellectual property might now be "Entertainment, Information, and Software Magnates First." It was as if Clinton–Gore had turned national health policy over to a zealous insurance lobbyist who had spent years crusading for higher premiums.

Even at the local level, Lehman was no stranger to the world of money and politics. In 1991, while a Georgetown lawyer, he had lent $10,000 at 12 percent interest to Washington city council candidate Jim Zais even though local law apparently restricted candidates to borrowing only from the usual lending institutions. Zais at the time had raised less than $13,000 from other sources. Questioned by election officials, the candidate had claimed ignorance of the law and promptly paid the money back to Lehman, along with some $120 in interest.[41]

Like many of his ex-colleagues at Swidler & Berlin, Lehman had kept his checkbook wide open when national politicians needed money. Many months later I learned that between January 1, 1991, and November 28, 1994, the S & B crowd had made at least $191,000 in political donations, including more than $22,000 from Lehman himself during his days there. At least $146,000 of the $191,000 had gone to the firm's political-action committee. Lehman's personal contributions had reached at least eighteen congressional candidates. In fairness, let me emphasize that Lehman didn't just have direct career considerations in mind—he was the first openly gay man whom the U.S. Senate had confirmed as a top federal official,[42] and he had given generously to gay political-action committees.

Gay groups, in turn, showed their loyalty. They had wanted Clinton to appoint Bruce Lehman to *something,* and the White House had made him patent commissioner even though Lehman knew more about copyrights. Ron Brown, however, secretary of Commerce, said: "Bruce Lehman is not here because he's gay. He's the absolutely best person for the job."[43]

I believed Brown. If the Clinton Administration wanted library interests to be kept at bay to placate rich campaign donors, Gore's dreamy rhetoric notwithstanding, no one would beat Lehman the ex-lobbyist.

A few weeks after the intellectual property hearing in Crystal City, a letter arrived from Mr. Reinventing Government himself. I had mailed my TeleRead proposal and a related *Washington Post* clip to Al Gore many months ago in spring 1993, and now he replied: "I am impressed with this detailed and very professional presentation. The information you provided certainly appears to contain ideas that merit careful attention. I will retain this material for future consideration as the President and I work on related policies and programs." I hardly expected a meeting with Clinton and Gore. But was it just possible that one of their GS-14s might deem me worth five minutes of time, and follow up with a few questions?

Months passed. An occasional reporter or academic would read my testimony and call or e-mail, but no one phoned from Commerce. Meanwhile, seeing my TeleRead proposal on the Net, major vendors contacted me. Often they asked the big question: "How are you doing in Washington?"

"Well," I said in effect, "I hope they're keeping an open mind."

"That's nice, bye," the answers would more or less come back—assuming I heard again from people at all. The NII wasn't just TV-centric. It was Gore-centric. If you lacked his blessing, and his bland letter to me didn't count, you were dead or at least comatose unless the right word from the White House revived your idea.

Then a "Green Paper" revealing the Clinton Administration's preliminary views on data highways and copyright came out. It was even more horrid than I could have imagined, an insult to the memory of Andrew Carnegie. The ethos was exactly the opposite of TeleRead's. For example, if the paper became law, one could not transmit a newspaper article to a few friends; the present ambiguities here would be resolved in favor of the copyright holders. Yes, Washington should not allow anyone to bootleg newspaper stories or magazine items for hundreds of people in an electronic discussion group. In fact, I'd once reported a gross offender to a magazine; I believed passionately in property rights. Clearly electronic books, of all media, should enjoy protection, which, in fact, TeleRead would promote by making piracy less lucrative. But we also had to understand the purpose of copyright law—to help spread information in a democracy and further the progress of science and the arts. Lehman either was disingenuous or had let his old $430,000 make him a little amnesic toward Constitutional tradition.

Ironically, if Lehman's side won out, writers and journalists would be among the biggest victims of the very law designed to protect us. After all, we were not just producers of information; we were also consumers. To write a book I would absorb millions of words from the Internet, swapping information with friend after friend along the way, including, yes, some electronic newspaper clips. But the Green Paper bizarrely flouted the natural tendency of most people to *share.* Imagine the effect on teachers and children. Quite rightly, Jim Warren observed that Washington was cheating the public "to avoid controversy among 'important' people."

"The Draft Report comes down firmly on the side of increased rights for copyright owners in all relevant contexts, endorsing the goal of enhanced copyright protection without acknowledging any countervailing concerns," wrote Jessica Litman, a law professor at Detroit's Wayne State University. In a reply to the Administration she said of the report: "It appears to be an advocacy document: It at times misrepresents the state of current law, and gives voice to only one side of complicated policy debates."

Another expert, law professor Pamela Samuelson at the University of Pittsburgh, lambasted the Green Paper in an article for *Communications of the ACM*, published by the Association for Computing Machinery. She said that "not since the King of England in the sixteenth century gave a group of printers exclusive rights to print books in exchange for the printers' agreement not to print heretical or seditious material has a government copyright policy been so skewed in favor of publisher interests and so detrimental to the public interest." Contrary to Washington's claim, the Green Paper was not just a tweaking of existing law but a radical revision in favor of publishers.[44]

Directly Orwellian questions arose. What about enforcement? How to thwart the ease of mailing copies over the Net? The Green Paper's designers thought that laws against circumventing copy protection would provide one of the main answers. But in the case of electronic text, such visions were far too sanguine. People would want the capability to print out material, and if they could print it out, they could scan it and put it online again without the protection feature; what's more, hackers would inevitably develop software to accomplish the same thing electronically.

Yes, the Green Paper would let publishers and others sue makers of devices that could get around copy protection. But just what gear was covered? Scanners? Fax machines? And what kinds of software? What about legitimate programs that also had illicit uses? Were we the new Soviets, living in fear of the digital equivalent of copiers and other subversive gadgets? As William Buckley would write, "fax machines and e-mail outwitted and frustrated even the comprehensive revolutionary orders of Stalin and Mao. This side of what used to be the Iron Curtain, we should have the resources to handle our native bureaucracy." The Green Paper was nothing more than Big Bureaucracy trying to serve Big Business.

The Green Paper had much in common with Clipper. In both cases bureaucrats were reducing respect for Washington by trying to control the uncontrollable. I was hardly a kneejerker crying out for a pigmy-sized government. My liberalism remained. I favored prenatal nutrition programs, Head Start, public broadcasting, and a host of other wonderful anachronisms from the heyday of the Democrats. And yet here was the Clinton Administration blundering along in the most obnoxious way and turning so many of my fellow liberals on the Internet into libertarians.

If nothing else, the White House was complicating my job of trying to sell the Net on TeleRead. It was not just a question of preempting my idea in favor of an inferior solution rigged up for Clinton's powerful friends in entertainment and publishing. Like Clipper, the Green Paper was lessening faith in Washington, period—no small concern for somebody advocating a national program such as TeleRead, even one developed with local sensibilities in mind. Sometimes I wondered if Lehman might be a Manchurian Patent Commissioner.[45] Had the Libertarians brainwashed him to sully Washington's good name?

Again and again I flamed Lehman's Green Paper on alt.activism and at least half a dozen other newsgroups on the Internet. I hadn't any choice. He hated the bytes-want-to-be-free philosophy of TeleRead. Clearly, if Lehman had read TeleRead, it would have driven him nuts, given his apparent belief that copyrighted books must *cost* readers. TeleRead, on the other hand, would mean fair treatment of copyright holders and library users alike. With a

TeleRead-style library, publishers, writers, and private nets could still charge for many categories of information and earn handsome sums from online conferences and other services and products, including customized software to guide people through electronic libraries. Also, they would receive fair royalties for covered material such as books. At the same time, however, thanks to the cost justification provided by the e-forms, we could make electronic books free in this TV-fixated era and thus encourage literacy.

Surely TeleRead could be a logical link between Gore's plans for reinventing government and his oft-claimed desire to drive down the cost of knowledge. With TeleRead, the old scarcities could be obsolete; rich and poor could dial up the same books. It would be a far cry from the present when Beverly Hills spent many times more on library materials than did some poorer jurisdictions. TeleRead was not a cure-all; but in an era of tight budgets, the national library could be phased in carefully, year by year, topic by topic, with minimal pain. The reduction of expensive, onerous paperwork would be like a tax rebate. For once, a program could simultaneously help schoolchildren and small business people.

Perhaps the NII Advisory Council would see merit in TeleRead. The White House didn't necessarily have to follow its recommendations, but wasn't this the age of electronic democracy and citizens' input? A few problems had arisen, however. Bill Clinton's people had tolerated just one librarian among the more than thirty members of the Council. An overworked teacher was there representing education. But no full-time professional writers of books, and just one newspaper publisher, had ended up tainting the Advisory Council.

Nor did any name show up from a distinguished publishing firm such as Knopf or Farrar, Straus and Giroux. Instead the White House blessed the NII with Vance Opperman, a friend of Al Gore's and a money man for the

Democratic Party,[46] who was president of West Publishing. By one estimate West grossed some $600 million a year with pretax margins of almost 30 percent, or twice those of rivals.[47] West-style firms were famous for Cadillac-priced data. Opperman's company had set up collections of court opinions and slapped a proprietary system of citations on them. The meter typically ran at $4 a minute or more, adding up to millions from Feds and taxpayers alike.

Haunted by a group called the Taxpayer Assets Project, the Justice Department had proposed an electronic database with public-domain citations to help users locate material. But West had lobbied away the plans. Nothing must deprive Al Gore's friend, and so many other politicians' friend, of a chance to turn a buck. Opperman seemed about as eager to drive down the cost of knowledge as Bull Connor was to further civil rights in the days of cattle prods and police dogs.

At the same time the Advisory Council teemed with people from such library-like outfits as CBS, Black Entertainment Television, and Walt Disney. Bill Clinton's people also let the movie industry's premier lobbyist sit on the council—Jack Valenti, a former aide to Lyndon Johnson; yes, the same Valenti who had made history years ago by sleeping better at night because, he said, LBJ was in the White House. To the Council, too, went powerful telephone executives, a man from Microsoft, and John Scully, the former Apple executive who had been a Clinton stalwart in '92. A co-chair was a Clinton supporter named Ed McCracken. He came from Silicon Graphics, a billion-dollar company that was hoping to make a fortune off the new video technology.

Clearly entertainment was what counted most here. The term National Information Infrastructure just didn't suffice. A more accurate description, given the paucity of librarians, educators, and journalists on the council, would have been the National *Entertainment* Infrastructure. Yes, people like Vance Opperman were interested in electronic text, but, above all, from a business perspective. Let the masses watch TV. His company would make a fortune selling pricey information to the elite.

Mass literacy just wasn't the main show here, not with all the dutiful suits watching out for the earnings of CBS or Disney or Microsoft or West, and without enough librarians and others to balance them out.

A host of other issues remained. How fascinating that so many of the most influential people in the Clinton galaxy were from outfits such as telephone companies that wanted to profit off both transmission and content. Despite all the rhetoric, I wondered how attentive the Clintonians would be to, say, little companies that were more interested in producing books or folk albums than in financing *Terminator*s or laying fiber optic cables.

Could money and politics have mattered just a little in the selection of people for the NII Advisory Council? If nothing else, a few questions arose in the case of West Publishing, the giant publisher of legal information. Vance Opperman was friends with Mack McLarty, Clinton's first chief of staff.[48] What's more, Opperman cochaired the finance committee during the 1994 reelection campaign of Dianne Feinstein, a Democratic U.S. senator from California who sat on a copyright subcommittee within the Judiciary Committee.[49] A study by the Taxpayer Assets Project, one of Ralph Nader's groups, revealed how civic-minded West was. By way of a political-action committee and gifts from lawyers, lobbyists, and family members, the West crowd in five years had given more than $738,000 to Congress members and the Democratic National Committee.

Judges, too, must have loved the company. A West-run foundation had dispensed $15,000 awards to federal judges for "distinguished service to justice." Over a dozen years, the selection committee had included seven past or present members of the U.S. Supreme Court, the ultimate in-

terpreter of copyright law. West had paid for trips to places
as far off as Hawaii and the Virgin Islands. Benefiting, ac-
cording to the *Minneapolis Star Tribune*, were Justices
Anthony Kennedy, Sandra Day O'Connor, John Paul
Stevens, Antonin Scalia, and now-retired Justices Lewis
Powell, Byron White, and William Brennan.[50]

West impressed me. Via campaign gifts, friends, and
favors such as the trips, Opperman's crew had cozied up
to all three branches of government—the executive, the
legislative, and the judiciary.

Eager to see how representative West was with its
people's political gifts, I phoned the Center for Responsive
Politics, the Washington-based group from which I simultaneously got information about Lehman. Would the
Center please send me a printout of congressional and
presidential donations from some other members of the
NII Advisory Council and from people and political-action
committees associated with their companies?

A list arrived for the period between January 1, 1991,
and November 28, 1994, and I scanned down the names on
the laser-printed sheets. The Walt Disney people hadn't disappointed me. Advisory Council member John F. Cooke,
president of the Disney Channel, had given at least $48,000
to politicians from coast to coast and to Democratic organizations. Non-Council member Jeffrey Katzenberg, then
with the Disney conglomerate, had donated at least $63,000
in one way or another.

I saw *at least* $400,000 in Disney-related gifts—dona-
tions from top executives were just the start. Cook and
Katzenberg on their own couldn't sway the White House
and Congress, nor even could all of Disney; but imagine
what Hollywood and other rich industries could do en
masse to influence copyright and telecommunications policies. What counted most wasn't the person but the industry.
At one recent gathering at Steven Spielberg's mansion—in
spring 1995, a time not covered by the laser-printed sheet—
Bill Clinton had raised $50,000 per couple.

Whatever the case, the stray change added up. Over at MCA, Advisory Council member Alvin Teller gave at least $28,250 between early 1991 and late 1994, while Lew Wasserman, a nonmember, gave at least $87,000. Advisory Council member Jack Valenti, Hollywood's big lobbyist in D.C., donated at least $56,250.

Advisory Council member Stanley Hubbard, chairman and chief executive of Hubbard Broadcasting in Minnesota, also made a good showing. He and relatives gave at least $74,000 to people on the Hill, political-action committees, and the Democratic Party. Confronted with $1,000-per-election limits on political gifts to members of Congress, Hubbard just spread his money around, as if using greenbacks like calling cards. His donations reached powers such as Representative Ed Markey of Massachusetts, who, until the Republican victory in 1994, chaired the House Subcommittee on Telecommunications and Finance. Many saw Markey as one of the more progressive NII players. Just think, however, what such politicians could have done without the distractions of special-interest money—donations not only to them but also to colleagues who would be more susceptible to pressure.

Telephone executives made the NII sugar-daddies list, of course. Advisory Council member Bert Roberts Jr., MCI's chairman and CEO, gave at least $28,000 to an MCI political-action committee and to politicians, ranging from Senator Bob Packwood to, yes, Edward Markey. A supporting cast came from the ranks of the MCI employees, including one of my techie heroes, Vint Cerf, "Mr. Internet," who contributed at least $1,000 to the same PAC as Roberts.

Advisory Council member James Houghton of Corning Glass donated more than $50,000 to members of Congress across the country, and to party, presidential, and PAC funds. Corning, of course, was rooting for fiberglass cable—a rival in some ways to wireless technology, which some on the Internet considered the future.

No, the millionaires on the Advisory Council had not committed crimes or bribed anyone. Under the law, they had a right to give massive amounts to campaigns as long as each gift did not exceed the legal limits. To my knowledge no money had come from anyone's corporate tills, just from individuals and the political-action committees to which they had lawfully contributed. Besides, just like Lehman, many other rich donors must have had the most heartfelt of reasons for personal donations, going far beyond copyright and telecommunications issues. Even though copyright holders had donated to many well-positioned politicians such as Senator Dianne Feinstein, who was active on intellectual property matters, that was hardly the only reason why Hollywood millionaires gave. The woman was a California Democrat. Many people at companies such as MCA were the same. If a Californian, I myself might have voted for her.

Likewise, the people of West Publishing must have had varied motives in contributing.[51] Vance Opperman was a former antiwar protester and probably still saw himself as a force for social good. I suspected, too, that he loved seeing his old friend Al Gore grow in power. At the 1992 Democratic Convention Opperman had described himself as a "political junkie" who enjoyed hosting political receptions for fun. "I don't expect to get any political benefits out of them."[52]

Replying on February 22, 1995, to questions from the *Minneapolis Star Tribune*, Opperman's company noted that all donations were legal and on record at the Federal Election Commission. "It appears that you believe the laws regarding these matters should be changed," West said. "If so, the proper thing for you to do is to seek to change these laws rather than criticize those who carefully comply with existing law." The company denied any efforts to influence officials improperly. West said that its employees, its political-action committee, and its counsel all had "long histories of being active in the political process. It is inaccurate to tie their donations over the past 20 years to any specific issue of legislation pending before a government body. Your inference that such donations have been made as one collective effort is also totally untrue."[53]

West pointed out to the *Star Tribune* that people from rival information companies were also making contributions. But of course! Money always counted in politics. Vance Opperman had put it well several years ago as head of Opperman Heins & Paquin, a leading law firm notable for PAC gifts to Minneapolis politicians. "If we have those who oppose the interests of our clients," he said, "we do not support them." He said the law firm's PAC ran under this philosophy: "Support your friends. Punish your enemies."[54]

Presumably Bill Clinton and Al Gore would rather avoid punishment from the Oppermans of this nation. While almost ignoring librarians and educators, the Administration had appointed to its Advisory Council some members of the elite who were already over-represented in the political process. Did Vance Opperman, as a friend of Gore's, really have to worry about the Vice President reading *his* letters? I wouldn't have been surprised if he had Gore's private e-mail address. Just how many electronic entreaties to the Hill, or to the Clinton–Gore area on the Web, would it take to neutralize the little fortune donated by friends of West Publishing? I couldn't have agreed more with Cliff Stoll when he wrote that Washington often ignored citizens' e-mail. It all figured. The Power People were too busy raising donations from millionaires and political-action committees—hardly the biggest champions of low-cost knowledge.

Granted, some optimists hoped that the Internet itself could help turn around Washington. Aided by the Net, a group in Washington State had gathered $26,000 to help defeat Tom Foley, then the Democratic Speaker of the House.

And NewtWatch, an anti-Gingrich effort on the World Wide Web, had registered as a political-action committee. Some members of both major parties were hoping to use the Net to raise money efficiently from small donors.[55]

That was far from a full answer, though. Even before I learned of all the campaign cash from some members of the Advisory Council, I had wondered about the group's odd composition. Not everyone on the council was rich, of course, far from it. But why had business prevailed so brazenly over the general public and Al Gore's little neighbor back in Tennessee, the one who was supposed to dial up books from the Library of Congress regardless of family income? Just one teacher and one librarian? In politer language I'd sent the question on to a White House staffer, and he had patiently explained to me that Washington had to serve the needs of the "stakeholders."

I loved the word. It sounded so innocent, so natural, so philosophical. What if this were eighteenth-century France, the revolution were on, and Marie Antoinette looked like guillotine fodder? Armed with such a marvelous locution, she could forego all references to bread and cake and simply say, "Stop! I'm one of the stakeholders."

Now having documented a nice flow of money from "stakeholders" to politicians, especially Democrats, I remembered how many Watergate-era ambassadorships had gone to the highest bidders. Wasn't the same ethos at work here as Richard Nixon's? I knew of no broken laws—but perhaps that was the trouble.

"I remember when I got on Energy and Commerce, everybody jumped for the Telecommunications Subcommittee first," Peter Kostmayer, a former Democratic representative from Pennsylvania, said as quoted by veteran political journalist Martin Schram. "There was a member sitting next to me, and every time another member bid for that committee, he went 'Ding!'—as if a cash register was going off."[56] When politicians talked about the need for election reform and clean, ethical government, many were themselves superb examples of the need for action.

Maybe, I'd thought earlier, I could at least enjoy an open-minded hearing from a nonmillionaire on the Advisory Council. Bonnie Bracey was the only elementary school teacher. She should have loved TeleRead.

But during an official virtual conference organized on the Net by the Commerce Department, she went after not Opperman but *me*. "I am not the least interested in the TeleReader," she said in a public message, "and I don't have any money after trying to do this job to invest anyway." I was and am a writer. Last I knew, I had not been selling computers. Bracey needed to scrutinize my proposal. Maybe she could then dismiss it as a nefarious writer's plot. TeleRead did, after all, propose a massive shifting of resources from bureaucracy to various forms of knowledge, including—*gasp!*— electronic *books*.

At times, Bracey would e-mail me that my proposal intrigued her, but somehow she would never get around to *study* it, or at least to telling me that she had gone beyond summaries. She would repeat the usual clichés that citizens didn't want to spend money on schools. Toward TeleRead's cost-justification mechanisms, toward the support that it could win among frugal, business-oriented conservatives such as William Buckley, she was unresponsive. Granted, she wasn't callous about the children TeleRead could help. At the personal level she had been exemplary, spending hundreds and perhaps thousands of dollars on hardware and software that she could use in her classes. But TeleRead for her could have been a bother. Offensively, perhaps, it meant a national library online for all, regardless of whether they happened to be students anywhere.

TeleRead, however, was hardly antischool, given all the new possibilities it could open up online for teachers and students. Looking back, I just wished that Bracey had seen a note I received from a teacher in Illinois who had

asked more than sixty magazines for permission to
reprint articles for her small class at no profit. Only
twenty-five publications had gone along. "We were ignored sometimes," the woman had e-mailed me, "and
once I was told, by phone, never to use any articles from
that publication. That was *Windows Magazine*, and I
didn't renew my subscription." Of her anthology, she had
said: "It's a better textbook because it's more up to date."
Clearly we could never separate "educational" uses of the
NII from the rest; an article from a commercial magazine
could actually prove so much more valuable than an instantly obsolete textbook. TeleRead would make back issues of magazines available for free, make current ones
easier to obtain, and, above all, allow free textbooks to be
updated instantly, complete with hypertext links to the
rest of the national library.

But predictably the NII Advisory Council ignored
TeleRead and more or less green-lighted the Green
Paper. The council for the most part came out in favor of
publishers enjoying control over transmission rights. In
effect these people were kissing off the idea of a comprehensive, cost-justified library that all Americans could afford to use online, whether for school or for self-
improvement. As I was concluding this book, it wasn't
certain that the Green Paper would slither its way into
law in more or less the original form. But the news from
Capitol Hill didn't cheer me. The Republican Congress
appeared to be at least as skewed in favor of copyright
holders as were the Democrats.

Even diluted (and renamed the White Paper in the
final version), the Green Paper might well be a disgrace.
I worried about the rest of the world. Imagine the
Australians or Europeans looking to the United States for
leadership in Net-related copyright matters. To me, the
Green Paper bore the stains of greenbacks. People around
D.C. had a polite little word, "access." It didn't mean legal
violations, but rather purchases of policymakers' ears.

Information magnates had access. I wondered if the little child in Al Gore's hometown gave so faithfully to major politicians, flew Supreme Court justices to Hawaii, and doled out $15,000 "justice" awards.

The Green Paper, alas, was just one indication of many big shots' willingness to work against the citizenry. Again and again the denizens of Capitol Hill bragged about Americans being able to dial up the text of proposed legislation through a service called Thomas. And yet some Congress members still hoped to work out deals before the public saw the results on the Net. Friends of West Publishing used exactly such tactics on the Hill to try to reduce the amount of information that the government re-leased for free. West and similar companies wanted to be able to profit off public data. So their congressional allies were hoping to cancel out the Freedom of Information Act in cases where federal contractors had created records.

Any weakening of the act would make me *very* grouchy; it had opened up many kind of government in-formation for free or at affordable costs. I had benefited. Two decades ago the General Services Administration had tried unsuccessfully to charge me $20,000 to learn details about the government's office-leasing program. Using this first-class muck, I had shown that then-Senator Abraham Ribicoff secretly owned a stake in a building that the GSA leased for the Central Intelligence Agency. I had learned, too, of a friend of Spiro Agnew who had been able to avoid building a half-million-dollar cafeteria required by the lease for the headquarters building of the Environmental Protection Agency. Because of the Information Act, I had been able to report both stories and get them out in the press and on network television. I had spent months camped out at the GSA, perusing documents; imagine what I could have done with a computer to ferret out digi-tized muck. And so I was dismayed to learn that some in Congress wanted to weaken the Information Act—this in an era when the Internet supposedly would open up

Washington. If not fully Orwellian, such hypocrisy didn't promote democratic alternatives to Big Brother.

Uppity activists used the Net to thwart West at least for the moment. A bill introduced by Representative William Clinger, a Republican from Pennsylvania, was to be heard in a subcommittee and rushed through a committee edit in just a few days with West-friendly provisions. But James Love of the Taxpayer Assets Project caught wind of the shenanigans; Jim Warren pitched in with his own jeremiads in *Government Access*, his online newsletter; and furious Netfolks called and faxed the Hill. West may have really lost when the Republicans found out through the Internet about the firm's generosity toward the *Democratic Party*, to which its executives gave far more than to the competition. "Why are we doing this?" the Republicans, in effect, may have wondered.

Only because of some extraordinary diligence by Love and allies did the public win here. Newt Gingrich could talk all he wanted about the Net putting citizens and lobbyists on an equal footing, but without a constant watch on the Hill, scene of so many crimes, the same power cliques would keep winning again and again, banana-republic fashion. West might yet succeed.

Around this same time, Sally Katzen, a top bureaucrat with Clinton's Office of Management and Budget had asked Congress to make certain that the Feds could charge more for information in some cases than the cost of spreading it. They would be able to do this after posting notices in the *Federal Register*. And then, if insufficient protests ensued, the info-gouges could begin. Katzen's proposal didn't fly, but its very existence was bothersome enough. The idea hardly jibed with all the nice rhetoric from the White House about using the Net to promote open government. So much for freedom of information, Clinton style.

Meanwhile I forged ahead with my TeleRead efforts, perhaps not for this Congress and this White House, but maybe for those in the future—once enough voters understood that we mustn't replicate online the "savage inequalities" of our schools and libraries. TeleRead if nothing else was a handy litmus test to find out which policymakers were sincere when they talked about the need for true public libraries in cyberspace, as opposed to just digital storefronts with links to publishers. Good people could disagree with me. But when politicians and their flunkies did not bother to hear me out despite my idea's credentials, I was reminded of how democratic Washington was toward Power People and how oligarchic it was toward the rest of the cosmos. Sometimes I felt that my location, in Alexandria, Virginia, was metaphorical. My apartment was just inside the Washington Beltway.

The question of the moment wasn't just one of copyright. It was also one of democracy itself, both the decision process and the aftermath. What about the Copyright Gestapo? In the future might the Feds monitor the activities of Republicans more closely than they would those of Democrats? Would Republicans be more susceptible to charges of intellectual piracy when they did the inevitable and tried to share old newspaper clips over the Net? Or vice versa? Would the Democrats suffer discrimination? What about Italy, where the machine-gun-toting cops had invoked software piracy laws against leftist bulletin boards but not against conservative ones? But the Clintonians, so eager to serve their political friends, were just as cavalier toward these possibilities as toward the civil liberties risk of Clipper.

Ultimately the copyright-holders' victory just might be Pyrrhic. Someday the political terrain could shift and millions of children might grow up on free, government-commissioned books. Or, perhaps instead, videos in too many cases would replace text. So we were better off if, as soon as possible, we used networks to spread *privately* originated books through a free, well-stocked library system. TeleRead could indeed help many in the information industry. From Lexis-Nexis to Random House, companies could turn profits off dial-up fees, either from works they commissioned directly or from rights they bought from authors. TeleRead wasn't a threat to information companies if they truly added value such as editing or marketing. Even West could benefit. TeleRead would let Opperman's company reap many millions off dial-up rights—not only to legal writings but also to other kinds—if the market favored it.

No, the real losers would be the bureaucrats, whose work, after all, would be less in demand in an era of electronic forms in mass use. And even they could have a soft landing. TeleRead would hardly take place instantly, and it would remove much of the scut work from the remaining jobs in government. TeleRead was anti-bureaucracy, not anti-bureaucrat. For the moment, however, as shown by the obtuseness of the GSA man at the hearing, the resistance was there.

Some lessons were emerging. Hundreds of people had e-mailed me for copies of TeleRead. "Even anti-taxers like me would be willing to foot the bill for something so practical and knowledge infectious," a home schooler in Illinois had said. The head of the Digital Publishing Association, an organization consisting mostly of small publishers and writers, had loved TeleRead. "Instead of flooding the young mind with yet another sitcom or soap," he had said, "TeleRead would allow video to present them with quality reading materials." And yet our wishes had not meant squat.

David Lytel, the White House staffer, may have pressed his delete key almost as soon as the TeleRead proposal reached him over the Net. He and his colleagues at the Lehman hearings hadn't followed up my official testimony with a single question in person or by phone or e-mail. The hearings had been a big farce, a caricature of a public relations exercise. I might as well have been Winston Smith deviating from the plot and making a few friendly suggestions to one of Big Brother's TV cameras. No one would shoot or torture me for saying the wrong things, but on the major NII issues the Clinton people were about as open as Big Brother to ideas from below, Net or no Net.

I wasn't the only writer with a few feelings on the subject of Executive listening skills in this networked era. A *New York Times* columnist later told how cavalier the White House crowd had been toward the e-mail from her. I'd actually gotten farther than she had. At least Gore had sent me a higher class of boilerplate. Perhaps that was because I had actually used conventional rather than electronic mail, and had enclosed a photocopy of a TeleRead article from the *Washington Post.* Article or not, however, the White House had thumbed its nose at me. While Clinton and Gore couldn't reply to every citizen, the composition of the citizens' advisory council had made clear what the NII priorities were, even in the age of Cyber Socks: Big Government serving Big Business.

Clinton–Gore had better change if they wanted my vote in '96. Rather than just sharing Sock's meows and feeling ever so smug about high-tech democracy, they needed to spend time more listening to us nonlobbyists and a little less time keeping Vance Opperman happy. Democracy should not mean just a dialogue between the White House and the usual "stakeholders."

• • •

As is obvious by now, intrusive government officials love to fixate on net.sex. But something else is happening as shown in the next chapter: net.*love.* Let's hope that Exon and company can tell the difference.

SEVEN

The Electronic Matchmaker

Gregory Smith* had yet to kiss Susan Olson* good night or run his fingers through her hair. But he could do something else with his fingers: type to her. Greg was a library and information-management student in Adelaide in South Australia, she worked for a real estate firm in Kansas City, Missouri, and they were carrying on a romance by way of the Internet. "We write letters constantly," he said, "and exchange our thoughts on newspaper clippings, music, all manner of things. About the only thing we haven't exchanged are marriage vows."

The outcome, as I began this chapter, wasn't clear. If the Smith–Olson affair was like many on the Net, they would pull the plug long before all the typing destroyed their wrists. "For every good story," Greg said of love on the Internet, "there are at least 100 bad stories—people meeting and realizing there's a major difference between virtuality and reality." A few months later, I decided, I

would check back in with Greg and Sue and report the results at the end of "The Electronic Matchmaker."

For the moment I was optimistic. Greg and Sue had
been at this for a good two years; they spent several hours
a day pouring out their thoughts to each other, Greg at his
UNIX workstation, Sue at her lowly Packard Bell computer. He had bought her a diamond ring on a layaway
plan; she was giving him a ring. She would fly Down
Under at some point, and then the next summer, Greg
would to go to Kansas City and meet Sue's family, including her father, a retired auto worker who, ah, had a few
surprises ahead.

I think of good people like Greg and Sue when I read
the tacky, hacky stories about unhappy affairs online and
Net sex. While many politicians and reporters delve into
the sleazier areas of the Internet—and, yes, regions can
look like Silicon-era Sodoms—something wonderful is
also happening on the Net. It's connecting lovers with uncannily matched interests and values. Remember, the
Internet teems with more than 12,000 newsgroups. If
you're quirky and picky, if you insist on a lover whose
hobby is Esperanto, the international language, try
soc.culture.esperanto. If you want to find a fellow Peace
Corps alumnus, you can choose from among several
newsgroups and lists. If you're a Libertarian stalwart and
insist that your girlfriend be nothing but—well, the search
may take longer.

Some philosophies just don't hold out as much appeal
to women as do others. But that has not daunted a smart
young Libertarian in California, Eric Klien, who started
what may have been the Internet's first matchmaking
service, an operation later taken over by Electric Clas-
sifieds. Match.Com offers a long questionnaire that
should appeal to many of the detail-oriented habitués of
the Internet.

Whatever your taste, the Net probably has a dating service if that's what you want. Operating with a French ad-

dress on the World Wide Web, Babb's Personals shows up with a photo of a green-eyed, dark-complected woman, and a number of free, anonymous ads in French and English. Christie's Internet MatchMaker claims to reach more than 14,000 users in seventeen cities. On the Net, too, you'll find HIV Positive Dating Services ("Meet other positives, negatives, and neutrals locally, regionally, nationally, and even globally"), Web Personals ("Now over 4,200 different visitors each day!"), and Virtual MeetMarket ("I believe that the people who browse through here, and more importantly the people who bother to publish personals here, are somewhat intelligent and Internet-savvy enough to know the difference between FTP and FTD—you know, the flower delivery guys?").

I found some of the catchiest ads on Virtual. One showed a beautiful twenty-five-year-old brunette in Los Angeles touching an empty set of casual clothes labeled "Your picture here?" "I'm looking for somebody who's [*sic*] personality has a shelf life longer than a month," she said, and California spelling notwithstanding, she clearly deserved just that sort of person. A graduate student, hungering for a "sweet SWM of my dreams," inserted a picture of a knight in armor. Seeking "a Scandinavian beauty," a graphics designer from South Carolina posted an almost magazine-quality layout with photos of himself and his cats and even an aerial shot of Charleston. The prose wasn't the most imaginative, and his Scandinavian requirement was rather limiting, but in a flash the ad showed women what kind of life he could offer them. Other possibilities exist on the Web. Instead of just saying you like certain musicians or artists, for example, you might write Web links to take people to an area with sound or graphics files.

The best matchmaker is the Internet itself, with all its ways of bringing well-meaning people together. If Greg married Sue, this would hardly be the first Australian–American marriage born on the Net. Australia is the e-mail capital of the universe, or at least the romantic regions thereof. Until surpassed by the United Kingdom and Canada, Australia had more Net connections than any country except for the United States. Recently the Aussies' telcom people started charging institutions for net connections according to the amount of use, and that just might crimp future Gregs and Sues. But at least in mid-1995, Australia's e-mail laurels remain unthreatened.

American women love Australian men because they speak the same language—more wittily than we Yanks do, of course—and because they all carry huge knives with which they can defend their girlfriends against crocodiles and muggers. Isn't that so, just as in the movies? American men worship Australian women because we know they are unappreciated down on the sheep ranch, they're literate, and have brilliant careers ahead of them. Don't knock stereotypes if they help bring the right people together.

The film *Crocodile Dundee* may or may not have been on the mind of Laura Goodin when she was wandering through soc.culture.australian. She saw "a message from an Australian composer studying in the U.S.," who told of "an alternative tune to 'Waltzing Matilda.'" Laura asked for the music. Within months the Aussie proposed, right over the Net in the same newsgroup. "Congratulatory messages came from all over the United States, Australia, and New Zealand." Today Laura Goodin and Houston Dunleavy are married and living together in the Washington, D.C., area, with a baby on the way. They exchanged more than 1,500 messages during their courtship, not to mention countless sessions of typing together in Teletype fashion, just as Greg and Sue have done. It is not the same as talking the old-fashioned way but can save enough in phone bills to pay for an engagement ring or maybe a more powerful computer. "A long-distance relationship is hellish," Laura says, "but the pain is eased somewhat by the Internet."[1]

This isn't just happening on the Internet itself. When a New York City woman was testing a service that became America Online, marriage was the last thing on her mind. Nevertheless she ended up married in Virginia to a lover she met via e-mail. Rush Limbaugh, the conservative radio host, met his wife on CompuServe, where, supposedly, she had sought his advice on coping with a liberal professor. A chef and a substitute teacher met on Prodigy and flew off to Las Vegas together, thinking they would enjoy the video poker if nothing else; they won $4,000 and each other.[2]

A psychiatrist has even written a novel about online relationships, *Virtual Love.* "E-mail has been called the singles bar of the 90's," Dr. Avodah Offit told the *New York Times.* "And that concept intrigues me a lot. The traditional ways that people meet now do not allow much access to each other's minds, and that has not led to enduring relationships." What's the best place to find out about your potential spouse? By sitting silently through movies or boozing it up in noisy, smoky nightspots, or by sharing intimacies over the modem? "I find people are more open on e-mail," she says. And I agree.

The Internet, to be sure, is hardly a romantic nirvana, and although this chapter will be positive about net romance for the most part, I'll mix the praise with some lengthy warnings. Some sections of the Net will please fundamentalist preachers no more than will the red-light areas of New York or Calcutta. From alt.sex.bondage I called up a digitized photo fit for the Marquis de Sade. The caption accurately read, "Japanese girl tied to rack while master pours hot wax on her breast. Looks very painful and her face shows it." Just about all of those posting to the forum are male despite the heterosexual orientation of the typical messages. This area of the Net is about as woman friendly as *Hustler.* Offensively, too, the Internet also comes with sections devoted to bestiality, and, yes, discussion of adult–child sex. In every case, of course, society must distinguish between shared fantasies and real acts. (As indicated in chapter 6, Exonian laws aren't the solution—parental vigilance and access-control software are.)

A more serious worry, from the viewpoint of women hoping for romance on the Internet, is the locker-room attitudes that can show up even in some respectable areas. Consider the cause of this: the numbers.

If you go by one network veteran, fewer than one in twenty of the early Netfolks were female. By popular belief, maybe a tenth of the people on the Net are female, a far smaller percentage than on other services such as Prodigy and America Online. The truth, however, is a bit more complicated. John Quarterman and Smoot Carl-Mitchell of Texas Internet Consulting, which regularly tracks the demographics of the Net, reported in the May 1995 issue of their publication *Matrix News* that according to a survey in October 1994, 64 percent of Netfolks were male and 36 percent female. And among educational institutions the percentage of females was as high as 41 percent. Borders between the Internet and commercial services are breaking down Berlin Wall fashion, so you can expect the Internet to show an increasing amount of female influence.

The old stereotype, however, that the Net is male dominated, would seem to hold up for the moment. Even the virtual dating services tend to have far, far more men than women despite, in some cases, better terms for female customers.

The reasons for the ratios are world famous. Computers in the past were to girls what trucks and catchers' mitts were also: the province of boys. Thousands of men in the computer industry are still oblivious to the existence of another sex. When I write popular-level computer books, male editors often demand that I stick to the technology rather than show how *people* use it. Most women, however, recoil from the Internet and other high tech unless they see practical reasons for bothering with UNIX commands and similar horrors; they have been raised to favor humans over gadgetry. Let's hope that the old fears vanish as more women befriend computers and programs grow easier for both genders.

Meanwhile, however, on some areas of the Internet, women can be treated like females in Asian countries that pamper baby boys but all too often let sickly girls die or even kill the fetuses. A few men ignore female Netfolks except for purposes of humiliation, sex, or combinations of the two. Although messages from women tend to draw more replies on the Net than those from males, the end results can dismay; one man reportedly welcomed a woman to a discussion group, launched a political dialogue, then shifted in a nanosecond to a request for a swap of nude pictures. Women tell of weirdoes stalking them via e-mail, flooding their Net accounts with unwanted messages. One victim, as reported in *Mother Jones* magazine, suffered "an untraceable e-mail 'bomb' containing hundreds of sexual and violent messages, the mildest of which was 'Shut up bitch.'"

At the same time women on the Internet can enjoy less of the sort of attention they desire. Some Netfolks don't pay as much attention to the public messages of women, and besides, female Internauts may not want to post anyway in some areas, given the outright insults and sarcasm that may await them. Women seek harmony and compromise; much of the Net thrives on controversy.

My wife, who, like most of her gender on the Internet, hates flame wars, has even run across a newsgroup whose people venture forth to start arguments in other groups. What is a hobby to some men can be an antisocial practice to women. Many women hesitate to speak up on the Net, whatever the topic under discussion. Disturbing statistics come from Gladys We, a graduate student at Simon Fraser University in Vancouver, Canada. Writing in the magazine *Virtual Culture*, she says at least four-fifths of several hundred postings to alt.feminism were by men. She tallied figures almost as lopsided in soc.women. "Only in soc.feminism," We writes, "amid accusations of censorship, were there comparable numbers of postings from women and men."

Given the obstacles that women often face on the Internet, then, it is amazing at times that *any* romances happen there. When they do, yet another danger arises—the risk of missed cues. A friendship online may cause either sex to ignore mismatched words and gestures that might put them on guard. One Los Angeles women met her boyfriend on a BBS and suffered a disaster that could just as well have happened by way of the Net. He got her pregnant, begged her not to abort, married her, and made life a real hell, not just a virtual one, until they divorced.

Worrisome, too, are the eternal tensions that go on in cyberspace between sincere Befrienders and not-so-sincere Gamesplayers, who the former have trouble detecting. The Befrienders seek friends and lovers; the Gamesplayers would just as soon toy with a human as hack a program. An argument might even be made that high tech attracts more than its share of people who thrive on impermanence. You do not last long in computers if you believe that Pentium-level chips are forever, or that 28.8K-bps modems are more than throwaway technology in the general scheme of things. Faster chips, higher speed modems, and new girlfriends or boyfriends are sure to come along. That's the mind-set. Let's just hope that the girlfriends and boyfriends will last.

"I am burning with a need to talk with you, to share with you my fears, my joys," one Australian women cooed via modem to a man in the Canadian province of Alberta. Within two weeks her ardor did not just cool, it inexplicably froze. "This is the very last time I will write to you," she said. Very possibly—we can't say for sure without ESP—the Australian woman was a Gamesplayer.

Gamesplayers enjoy at least one big advantage on the Internet. They can post their electronic want ads through computers, known as anonymous servers, that strip their names and other compromising identifiers.[3] And replies can come through anonymous servers. The same technology used to protect privacy can let Gamesplayers fool victim after victim, and even mask genders. Particularly in fantasy games on the Net you can never be sure if you're typing to a woman or a man who just wants more attention—abusive or not. What's more, for the skillful there are ways to forge messages to unsuspecting neophytes.

Another negative is that the Net can be as helpful to adulterers as to the moral and sincere. A techie has just poured out to me a story of the kind that Carson McCullers would have written if she had fixated on the Internet rather than on the American South. His wife, the mother of two children, has been using the Net to cheat on him in a massive way. She befriended two alcoholics by way of her modem, the marriage counselor says he has done all he could, and now comes word that she just might have the AIDS virus; I hear it's too early for a conclusive HIV test.

If sexual excitement is the only goal of *certain* Netfolks, and if the crowd in alt.sex.wanted is too creepy, some professional women just might meet their needs. As noted earlier in this book, a little outfit called Brandy's Babes advertised on the World Wide Web—complete with hints of more than just visual stimuli. The babes are apparently off the Net now, but some would say that successors are inevitable. In *limited* ways the Net and the world of professional sex are much alike: both have their jargon and, for those who seek it, their anonymity.

Both worlds are rich in eccentrics. For example, I recently ran across a woman in her late forties who was about to bear a baby with a computer scientist she met on the Net "an hour before April Fool's Day." She says the child was accidentally "conceived about two weeks after meeting 'in the flesh.' We are having the baby first. *Then* we will talk about marriage on a serious basis. I'm delighted at the prospect of being a mum at last, and I am not your average clunky woman at all. I generally feel much better about myself. I introduced Tom to sex, and he says he had no idea how cuddle-deprived he was. He's now quite addicted to me." Tom and his computer are now part of her household; like many Netfolks he can use his modem to work virtually anywhere, which in some cases is yet another advantage of online romance.

Like most denizens of the Internet, the e-mail lovers just mentioned are well educated. And, although the woman was between jobs, Netfolks are normally at least affluent. If they are students, their parents are middle class or better. While the price of Internet service is coming down, and while access is free in some cities and at many American colleges, the Net doesn't exactly teem with welfare mothers.

So what other patterns emerge among lovers who meet through the Net? "I haven't done a study of the personality curve, the introvert–extrovert ratio," Avodah Offit, the psychiatrist who wrote *Virtual Love,* told me, "but my experience is just the opposite of what one might expect. My 'high user' contacts are all very sociable types who hate being out of contact with others at any time of day or night. Of course my correspondents are not generally engaged in romance with me, but they do write to others online in a variety of relationships." My own observations suggest that while many net.lovers may be introverts, her thoughts would hold true.

Judging from lovers whose photos I've seen, the plugged-in couples are neither more nor less attractive than the world at large. But the plainer ones can use prose to compensate for looks; this is a medium where words are everything.

I hope that the people's love letters don't just vanish, because the output of *some* Netfolks can be charmingly Victorian in style, feeling, or sheer volume. "My family took it pretty hard at first and were a bit skeptical, especially my Mum," says an Australian college student who fell in love with an American more than a decade older than she is, "but then I gave them some of the early letters to read, a pile of 100, the only ones I had time to print out, and the next day my mother came up to me and said, 'I am very happy for you. I am glad you have Frank.' I was waiting for the 'But,' but it never came." A New England woman, who married a fellow clarinet player she met on the Internet, says he once showed her a $1,000-plus telephone bill. That's Love, capital L. Maybe the nineteenth century is alive in some quarters, whatever the medium, voice or e-mail.

Below I'll tell stories of Greg and Sue; a bachelor who was looking for a woman who wouldn't treat him like "a peripheral"; and a man who, to his distress, found himself cuckolded more easily because his wife was on the Net.

Greg and Sue

Adelaide was where Greg Smith majored in library studies at the University of South Australia. It was a graceful port and state capital with a Mediterranean climate, a population of a million, the Torrens River in the center, and swarms of college students from three schools. Named for Queen Adelaide, the wife of England's King William IV, the city dated back to the 1830s. Kangaroos still hopped around in the countryside, but Adelaide itself was both urban and urbane. It was full of churches and bars alike, along with trendy shops in Rundle Mall and elsewhere. The State Theater put on Shakespearean plays at an internationally known festival center.

Not surprisingly, Adelaide has been described as the Boston of South Australia. While some young locals may shrug off the place as too churchy and sleepy, others might disagree. Adelaide in many ways is a young person's town—a good place to meet the opposite sex. Greg Smith, in fact, did find women in the corporeal world around him, but the relationships never took root, and in the early 1990s he was still on the lookout in the bars ("universities are great for this"), the parks, the buses, the mall—you name it. He had his attractions. Greg, in fact, was on the handsome side, if you went by the digitized photo and other information conveyed over the Net. He stood six-foot four, weighed around 190, kept in shape by walking, and had thick, dark brown hair, and a winsome smile.

"I'm a physical person," Greg told me. "I like to be with people. I like 'reading' people for body language and all that." From the very start he was aware of the perils and limitations of the Internet in such areas as love. You had to trust the words of strangers, not sharing their own reality. "Relationships are established where one party is totally sincere and all that, and the other one is just getting a laugh out of it." Just the same, he could not resist touring the Internet and the bulletin board to which his international connections led.

Young people like Greg Smith, who sought out new places on the Net, whether bulletin boards or electronic libraries, were vaguely like the Jack Kerouacs of '50s who liked bumming around the United States for its own sake. Some would describe the high-tech Kerouacs as "net surfers." But the phrase "net surfing" has become so trivialized in the media that perhaps we should return to the Kerouac analogy.[4] *Kerouing*, not surfing. Stark differences, of course, existed between the international Internet and the American towns of *On the Road*, the famous Kerouac novel. Greg had spent some time in the United States when he was ten years old and loved to keep up with

American sports, but he was very much a creature of Australia, with a distinctly Aussie flavor in his accent and values. Nor was he a rebel in the true Kerouac tradition. You could be a library science major and still soak up the culture of the Net; you didn't have to hop on and off freight trains and risk poverty or a severed leg.

In fact, while hooked into an established institution such as a corporation or a university, you just might do better than if you had to buy all the gadgetry yourself— just so you didn't flunk out while you were partaking. A *teacher* might even encourage your wanderings. And that was how Greg ended up on the Net for the first time in 1992. He found himself logging onto electronic bulletin boards all over the planet, with bizarre names such as "Badboy's Better BBS System" or "Chatsubo." He was at least partly drawn to such places because they were so much like neighborhoods or small towns. Each came with its own set of friendships, love affairs, and feuds that could reach an intensity even greater than those on the discussion areas of the main Net.

The woman who married Rush Limbaugh is said to have exchanged tart words with Limbaugh on Compu-Serve at the start of their relationship, and the same happened with Greg and Sue. They did not attempt an alt.personals-style romance. Via Chatsubo he and she were just patterns of dots on each other's cathode ray tubes. In fact, the two even butted heads over the question of whether certain people were abusing computer resources.

Sue, it should be noted, was not a true technophile; she could fire up a modem and use easy UNIX commands and that was about it. Even so, the two shared much else. Greg was around twenty at the time, just a year or so older than she was. Sue was a college student, at Northwestern Missouri State University. "I like her intensity, her sarcastic wit, her humor, and her, I dunno, just her way of seeing things," Greg would say of the Sue he came to know.

"Politically we're very similar, as regards political policy and all that. Our tastes in music are close. Our pleasures are drawn from simple, similar things. For example, we are both mad about long walks, NFL football, curling up in front of fires, walking in the mall, playing in the rain, and on and on it goes." Sue had been thinking about teaching, among other possible careers (political work and diplomacy happened to be others), and she enjoyed museums. Greg's father had taught Shakespeare once, and his mother had also been a teacher. So while nothing Oedipal was at work here, Greg might well be more comfortable with a woman who shared familiar priorities.

Just as important, both Greg and Sue could breeze along on a keyboard and say *plenty* online. In the near future, people might be able to speak into a microphone with those at the other end seeing words pop up on the screen, but for the moment the Net was friendliest to good typists, especially those who could write well, as Greg and Sue could. They could almost be playwrights, the way they loved stage directions such as "Hugs" and "Wave good-byes." If a feeling occurred to either, they could transfer it from their brain cells to the keyboard and make the recipient *see* their thoughts. When Sue sent a letter to Greg and me, it was obvious she wanted to get back to her private correspondence with him. She ended her note: "*hugs greg* hold your horses sweetie, I'm typing as fast as I can :-)." I could see that techie or not, Sue felt at home at the computer keyboard.

Without trying to woo each other across fourteen time zones, the two friends grew closer as they made the rounds of the BBSs on the Net. One of the boards carried a gallery of digitized photos, and Greg enjoyed Sue's face. The look was American-Midwestern. Her light blonde hair flowed in a way that must have pleased him.[5] She had green eyes broken up with what she has described as a "strange shade of yellow." The skin was pale, the Scandinavian in her. In one of the shots she posed with a knee resting on a well-padded armchair. She wore a crocheted sweater, pants, and flats, and looked sexy but in a fresh, friendly way that would not have threatened a schoolteacher's son. Greg, in turn, pleased Sue; in fact, even more so later on when she learned of his height; she herself stood five-feet ten and favored tall men.

Sue especially relished his sense of humor. "I could log in after a totally crappy day in classes and I'd have some corny e-mail from Greg that would send a smile to my face no matter what I felt like. He was, still is, and probably will be, the only person who can really cheer me up no matter what the circumstances are." Love, however, just wasn't on the minds of Greg and Sue in those early days. She had family and friends in Kansas City and counted on braving the frigid Missouri winters while she went to college. Meanwhile she had experienced her share of romances off the Net, including one with a shy friend who helped introduce her to the online world by suggesting that they *type* to each other. Sue may or may not have been ready for yet another relationship.

Even if she and Greg were just friends, they were paving the way for something more by slowly trading secrets about themselves. Lois Shawver, a California psychologist often online, warned me of the lack of trust that can afflict many long-distance relationships via computer. And yet paradoxically, the Net could bring people closer to each other. "It's so easy to end a relationship," Shawver told me, "you simply stop corresponding." So "people seem to be more willing to take a chance and disclose intimately. That helps to create trust. I do think that also explains the medium's ability to help people bridge cultural gaps." It was all certainly true in the case of Sue and Greg.

Helpful, too, was the emphasis that they placed on the platonic at the start, without even meaning to do so. Is it just possible that horny young men and women on the Internet and elsewhere could declare a one-year moratorium on the raunchier forms of "cybersex" where men and women exchanged lewd remarks with each other, Teletype fashion, in group settings? Ditto for the online world's many homosexuals and bisexuals. Ironically the aftermath might be *more* sex and better sex after some true friendships developed by way of electronic mail and one-to-one chats. One test of friendship, of course, might be this: Would a couple still write to each other if their Net connection ended? And Sue and Greg had passed so far: Her Internet account had vanished after she left Northwestern Missouri State University to work and go to school part-time. She ended up at an insurance company. Letters written on pulped trees, comic strips, editorial cartoons, music cassettes, material of all kinds, had traveled between Australia and Missouri. "We got closer and closer with each postage stamp," Sue told me, "and believe me, there were a bunch. The post office likes me a *lot.*" Finally, however, Sue had returned to the Net, this time with a private account.

On August 7, 1994, she had to break off an online chat to leave for work. "And I had one more question for her," Greg recalled. "She asked what it was. And I asked her plain and simple, 'Will you marry me?' There was a pause of about thirty seconds, and she asked me if I was serious. I said, 'Yes, never more so,' and she said 'Yes.' " Sue let her mother and a sister in on what was happening. She told certain friends, too, but not her brother and father. "It's just going to be incomprehensible to them," Greg told me, "that this could happen over a chunk of cable. Add to that I'm stealing away their last child, not just out of the home, or the state, but out of the country, and I can understand why her father is not going to understand."

The same shocks would presumably await Greg's mum and dad. "I think it's more the medium than anything else. It's way new to them, but for me it's just part of the way we do things now. *Grin*. Mum's department just got Lotus' cc:Mail,[6] and she was telling me about it and I was like 'Yeah, so?' but she was really excited about it."

Although Greg did talk to Sue from home, not just his university, he could do so without his parents knowing, because of the late hours he keeps, and because he lived in a converted shed out back of his house. I pondered the ironies here. Suddenly the Internet held out a new peril for parents. Having fretted about electronic pornography, Mom and Dad could now worry about children with more noble but equally secret activities. Parents might erase porno from a hard drive; it was not so easy to wipe out love as sincere and intense as Greg and Sue's.

But had the two actually *talked*, telephone style, over a real phone? "We've had a grand total of one phone call," Greg told me. Sue dialed him up. He said she'd kept putting it off because she was scared. "I know, I know," he wrote, "we should talk more but I'm just a poor student." Greg inserted the computer symbol for a smile to show he was kidding. "The one thing that surprised me about that call was how naturally the conversation flowed. I think it came from the fact that we are friends first and a couple second—that the pressure of the relationship was negated by the fact that we are such good friends. I seem to recall impressions more than anything else, like the lilt of her laugh, the timbre of her voice, the accent. We just talked about stuff—us, love, Clinton's screwups in Congress, sports, everything. Very tough to put the phone down."

"Still," I asked Sue by telephone, "won't it be quite a transition from the American Midwest to Australia?"

In a friendly, steady voice she told how she had overcome her hesitations. When Sue toured the local museums now, she saw graffiti on statues, and she said the neighborhoods were slipping. I thought of my grandmother's old place in Kansas City years ago, how it had been block-busted by sleazes who frightened the whites away and resold the houses at handsome profits to Afro-Americans. Hotrods had roared up and down Chestnut Street; Grandma had been the last white holdout. The memory still enraged me. Although I hadn't been to Kansas City in years, I believed Sue.

"My brother and sister are quite a bit older than I am," she went on, "and they both have children of their own, and I'm not crazy about the idea of leaving them to know their aunt through phone calls and video tapes. But I have no intention of staying in the Midwest just for my family's sake.

"It's my life and what I want to do requires more than the Midwest has to offer. I can fit in well wherever I go. And I've gotten a few books on Oz. From what I've read, I'll like Australia just as long as I don't have to wear one of those damn hats and worship Paul Hogan. I have Greg to worship. They may drive on the wrong side of the road and drink beer with lunch, but it's not like I'll have to learn a whole new language." Besides, she loved the idea of the children growing up with an accent as delightful as the one she heard from Greg.

I asked Greg if his virtual romance with Sue had changed him. "It's relieved a lot of the pressure that exists between myself and women, because it's no longer that I'm looking for something more than friendship—I have a relationship which satisfies those needs and so don't need anything from those friendships. What is most interesting is that change that I haven't picked up but that other women must have. In the two-and-a-half years I've been at the university, I've been 'hit on' a grand total of zero times that I can remember. In the twenty days or so that I've been engaged, I've been hit on three times. And for the life of me, I can't figure out exactly what is making women see me as attractive. And they weren't friends or acquaintances either—completely unknown to me. Weird."

So how much had Greg changed Sue? "A lot," she e-mailed back. Sue said: "Being with Greg has taught me, if anything else, that my life doesn't have any boundaries, be they physical or emotional or geographic." This was more than lover's mush; I noticed her use of "With Greg," as if they were in the same room.

Asked for love letters—no pressure, let me emphasize—the two obliged with thousands of words just from their August 1994 writings alone. Mostly the letters were from Sue whose feelings were more conveniently preserved in digital form than were the letters from Greg. He wasn't holding back: He was the one who had contacted me about their romance. What followed from Sue was more affecting than anything I'd read in a novel, for it was real, and I learned about it in the same way that Greg did, through a series of pixels on a computer screen. Reading this one message would help explain why she was willing to leave Kansas City; why she felt that, regardless of a father with heart trouble, she had felt free to move on; perhaps even why she was willing to share her life so openly with me through this book, for a chronicle was an affirmation of sorts.

New to me but old to Greg, the revelation did not come immediately. Sue's August letters started out mainly with the routine, the glue of long-range relationships, the confirmation that she wanted Greg to know her life and likes. There was talk of food ("I love you more than I love munching on peanut butter and crackers"), diets ("I splurged on Chinese and probably regained the three pounds I lost"), art (at the Nelson museum she favored the impressionists), friends' babies ("Barbara went to the doctor this morning to check and see how the baby was doing—she was about ten weeks along, and she had a miscarriage"), school (Sue was attending community college and could not resist sharing a few unabashedly corny jokes about her anatomy course), places to go on vacation ("Hey," she said, in a discussion of Mount Rushmore, "do you Aussies get weird and chisel the faces of dead leaders onto mountainsides, or is that a distinctly American thing to do?"), and jobs ("this working full time and college at night is starting to wear me down a bit, but for the time being it's what I want to do").

Like almost any woman she *planned.* The word was that Greg should wrap some paper around his fingers and snip it off at the right place and send the results on to her so she'd know the size of his ring. And should it be silver or gold? They discussed pajamas. "I always thought it would be cool to share a pair of PJs with someone," Sue wrote. "I'd wear the tops, you'd get the bottom. Okay, so I'm cheesy, but I guess it's the American upbringing :). Shrug." In her mind Sue saw the "really cool chapel in Rapid City, South Dakota, where my grandparents on dad's side renewed their vows for their fiftieth wedding anniversary. "I wanna get married in it," she wrote Greg. "There's a place where you can light a candle for a loved one and say a prayer to keep them safe. Well, I lit a candle for Barbara, and then I lit one for us. It felt weird to be in a church for a good reason. Seems that all the last ones have been for funerals."

Another close friend had died some time back, and she reflected on the connection between that and a period of heavy activity on the bulletin board circuit. "When I logged on, I could just be some faceless person—no one had to know that my best friend was in the hospital room semicomatose because he had developed full-blown AIDS. There were so many people in my life that just up and left because Ralph* got sick; it was almost as if I had AIDS just by association. So I got online and became everyone's favorite sweetheart."

Then a signal fact emerged in the correspondence, something that explained who Sue was, and why Sue felt like Sue, although I believed that she and Greg would have wanted to be together even if her circumstances had been different. "I had just found out," she told him, "that I had won a fight against a terminal illness while Ralph was losing his. I don't talk about the fact that I am a cancer survivor very much, because I haven't been in remission that long. It will be two years in September.

"All I want to do is make it to the five-year mark and forget the pain and the tears and the chemo and the treatments," the letter said. "I want to look forward and be able to see a future without constant trips to the hospital, to days and nights when I can just be healthy and happy. I have a tendency to block out when I was sick because if I don't think about it, I don't remember it, and if I don't remember it, I don't worry about it coming back. If you ask, I will tell you everything." Very early on in their friendship, Greg had known that the cancer was cervical; any children would have to be adopted. Sue ended the message by assuring him that she no longer wanted "the foreign policy degree from Georgetown anymore, or the chance to have the President asking my opinion on things." Her goal now was Greg, an affordable flat, and a roomful of kids to teach.

The rest of her letters went on to discuss such cosmic questions as Sue's love of long showers in the mornings, her tendency to roll around a little in her sleep, and Greg's hatred of his cataloguing duties.[7] "I love love love love love you," he wrote, and heated up the wires some more while he and Sue dreamed of hugs at the airport, unstoppable passion, and a wedding.

"Know," he told her, "that there's a goofy, tall, dark, Australian, madly-in-love man here dreaming of you, and us, and the future." I was betting right now that they'd make it to that South Dakota church.

Lee Chen: The Lover as a Peripheral

He was a hacker, a true denizen of the Internet, and a poet at times. A word in one poem told all: "peripheral." It means a printer, a modem, a scanner, or any other gadget that plugs into the main computer, yet is not one of the *very* most important parts. And that's how some women on the Net saw him, the human equivalent of a printer, someone on the peripheries of their minds. He was among their friends but not their lovers. His own love went unreturned. So he called his poem "Song of a Peripheral"; he posted it to alt.romance, soc.couples, alt.support.loneliness, and alt.support.shyness. It read, in part:

> *You feel you're nothing special in her life.*
> *You never get a sense that she wants you to be close*
> *   to her.*
> *You're just a pleasant, polite friend around the*
> *   periphery of her world.*
> *But you still care for her, because she is that special*
> *   woman—*
>
> *A sweetest heart who cares for the well-being of*
> *   others.*
> *A most sensuous soul who is full of life and passion.*
> *And a beautiful intellect who brings realist precepts*
> *   to balance out those disillusions in the world.*
>
> *. . . It's painful to feel you're just a Peripheral, isn't it?*

"How could I *not* print part of 'Song' in this chapter," I thought, and wrote Lee Chen for permission. Back came a letter from the Department of Computer Science at the University of Calgary in Canada. People on the Internet love to end messages with "signatures" telling how they see the cosmos, and Lee had picked a quote that looked as gentle and logical as his poem. The speaker was the President of the United States in the movie *Dr. Strangelove or How I Learned to Start Worrying and Love the Bomb*. And the words went, "You can't fight in here, this is the War Room."

Sometimes I thought that in the battle of the sexes, certain areas of the Internet could be that war room. No man could claim to be a superhunk or millionaire without risk-

ing a female retort in the vein of, "Yeah, sure." The Net was
rich with put-downs worthy of an old Tracy–Hepburn
movie. Clearly the men had started this war, however.
"When a female shows up," said the author of an explana-
tory file on alt.sex.wanted, "clueless folks tend to e-mail
'wanna fuck' messages no matter *what* she has said. This
means many of them don't post, only listen." Fights had
also broken out between the gays and certain heterosexu-
als, who came up with the witless fag jokes, and who, in
turn, had drawn equally stupid remarks about "breeders."
In this sexual war, the biggest losers were SMHGs. That
was Netspeak for Straight Male Horny Geeks, who, as
noted earlier, suffered from the laws of supply and (lack
of) demand.

Lee Chen was an SMHG in a nice way. His style had
been to try in alt.personals rather than one of the tackier
areas. When Lee had placed a recent ad, he had described
himself as "a romantic dreamer," and he wanted "a single
woman between the ages of nineteen and thirty-three
who is sincere, intelligent, attractive," and "passionate" as
well. Lee was twenty-six and entitled to feel his age.
Moreover, based on his self-description, women would
have no more reason to run away from him than they did
from Greg Smith in *his* lonely days.

"I'm five feet eleven inches, 185 pounds, have dark
brown eyes and short black hair," Lee said. "And I'm a
healthy, disease-free nonsmoker and considered attractive
looking." He told me he held a master's in computer science, was continuing his studies, and obviously was des-
tined to earn a comfortable living at the very least. Lee
enjoyed "going out to movies and romantic dinners, discussing current events and politics, visiting museums and
natural parks, walking along the rivers, listening to various kinds of music, giving and receiving pleasures with a
sensuous partner." So far, however, Lee lacked a woman—
he was new in town. Maybe a minor part of his problem, at
least among females off campus, was the kind of place that

Calgary was. He saw it as "a cowboy city, big in the oil business, very similar to Dallas culturally, except for the cold winter climate." This particular SMHG might have felt more comfortable in a more intellectually minded city such as Boston or San Francisco. But he was no snob and still held out hope of meeting one of the locals rather than confining the search to university people ("I'm sure there are many wonderful women in this town"). Simultaneously he decided to try the Net.

The first time out with a personal ad, Lee heard from a woman in, yes, Australia—E-Mail Central. Dozens of love letters threatened to melt down any fiber-optics on the Net; in fact, she sent Lee her erotic poetry and encouraged him to reply with the same. Through it all, he was high minded. "I believe in the mutual respect between women and men," he said, "but am also saddened by the gradual decline of romantic chivalry in our society. I feel they don't need to be mutually exclusive." His poet in Australia seemed to feel the same. Within a month she promised to fly to Canada.

"My darkest knight, my love," she called him. She was "burning with a need to talk with you, to share with you my fears, my joys. I ache to be able to brush a falling raindrop from your cheek and hold your handsome face close to my heart. I miss you already though we have not met."

This woman could have been crafting bodice-rippers for Harlequin Books. "I thrive on every word that falls from your sensuous lips," she wrote Lee. "I feel I am being too bold for a lady of my breeding, but what I feel has gone from my control before I was aware of my feelings." More letters followed, more fire, more steam. And then, out of nowhere: "This is the very last time I will write to you. You have to leave me alone. Any future mail you send me will remain unanswered. We do not know each other. Words across a net aren't a firm basis of a relationship and it takes time to form a friendship. We have neither and I cannot currently give either to you. I have strong personal commitments at the moment that leave me unable to commit to anyone, especially a man in a romantic way. Please understand. It may have been special and beautiful, but it has to be over. One day I may be in a position to explain further, but currently I cannot. I apologise once more and wish you well in your life."

"Maybe," Lee looked back, "it was just a game for her." And, no dummy, he had learned from such experiences. Nowadays Lee was wary of anonymous addresses with low numbers that suggested their owners had been cruising alt.personal for a long time.

He had also learned of the usefulness of friendship as a prelude to love. "Of all those ladies who answered my original personal," he said, "only one is still corresponding as a friend." Another female friend was also in his life online, somebody he met in an unrelated newsgroup. She typed out an popular opinion and he wrote in to agree, and they found they shared interests. But neither saw romance immediately ahead. Nor was that true of the other friendships he had online. Although vague about them, he suggested that he was still on the periphery.

Reached some months later, Lee told me he had gone on to befriend "quite a few nice women around this campus." In person and on the Net, however, he had yet to meet just the right one for those river walks, museum tours, and "giving and receiving pleasure."

"Well, sorry, David," Lee said, "but I didn't have a happy ending. "I'm sure there are some people who actually find their true loves this way. Although I didn't find true love, I've found many sincere friendships via the Net. So I'm glad that the Net has worked for me." I was, too, and I wished him all kinds of wonderful surprises ahead. Chivalrous SMHGs like Lee Chen should be more than peripherals.

Net Adultery

Places like New York or Tokyo abound with museums, art galleries, movie houses, universities, and large pools of single people who hope to meet the same. Something else, however, awaits those looking for it—more opportunities for adultery than in small towns. And it is the same with the Internet. It isn't just that straying wives and husbands can use those identity-stripping computers in Finland to make swap shopping easier. More importantly, the Internet teems with bright, funny, people who hate convention, including, in some cases, marriage.

For a stretch, a support-style mailing list came across as a Peyton Place in cyberspace. A man and a woman met there. He told her he would be leaving his wife and children. She spent that weekend with a *third* member of the list; after the original man publicly confessed, she popped up out of the blue to give her side. If anyone doubted that computers could bring people together in person, this was proof positive in the worst way. Most members of the list were horrified. They pleaded for Peyton Placers to go off-line. Clearly the Internet does not turn people into saints—it just makes it easier to do what comes naturally, good or bad.

But some context, please. The same Net could bring together old-fashioned romantics. As shown by the Smith—Olson pairing, the Net could actually *strengthen* traditional values among those who so inclined.

Besides, much of the illicit action on the Net was by the mutual consent of husbands and wives. When I ventured into a seamy area called alt.personals.poly, I saw an ad posted by a swinging couple from Florida. "I am 6'3" brown haired, considered attractive," said Hank*, the husband. "She is 5'0" busty, blonde, blue eyes, very pretty. We're not weird or disturbed or wanting to beat people, hahaha. We are very sensual, passionate, and are good at ya know the fun stuff." Was this the 'Bahn that Bill and Al had in mind for us? Not quite. But it wasn't as if some pervert was cheating on his wife and hiding behind an anonymous server while lusting for a nineteen-year-old coed who was new to both life and the Net. Although I did not condone Hank's swinging, I actually felt a little sorry for him after he wrote me a short but touching letter: He told how a woman had stood him up and the Missus. Better luck next time, Hank.

Suppose, however, that a man and woman had been married for fifteen years and had two children, he was a straight-arrow programmer type, she was funny and sexy, he introduced her to the Internet, and she got crushes on men whom she befriended over the wire—a marriage just might fall apart because a stranger might actually fly in from out of town wanting to get to know her in a biblical way. Such was the case of Phil* and Jayne*. While I have scrambled the details of the story, it is entirely true in spirit. They lived in Cincinnati, and Bill worked as a programmer and an Internet administrator for his employer. He had arranged for his wife to be able to dial up the office computer from home and send and receive e-mail. That, as we'll learn in a moment, was a key fact.

In many ways Phil and Jayne were a contrast. He could "readily repair my hurt emotions when it comes to betrayal, be it from friends, or from my wife." Phil held himself to the highest of standards no matter how low-minded the rest of the cosmos was. Jayne, on the other hand, was wild and loved to party and speak up. "She can drink anyone under the table," Phil said. "She has a loud voice and a happy disposition. She can talk to anyone and make them feel at ease. She is a joy to be with. A blonde with striking blue eyes. She has the attitude of a redhead but we never fight. She rarely sports a smile, but when she does, it is radiant. She has an excellent body, but she keeps on thinking it is not quite desirable. She has gone in for plastic surgery because of her low self-esteem."

For some years in her life, Jayne suffered from another problem—stodginess, of all things. Taxiing children
around, nagging them to do their schoolwork, playing the
good mother, had made her too conservative. Phil wanted
the old sparks back. So he introduced her to "an e-mail
friend of mine who had been a catalyst for many parties
as well. I hoped this would spur her into action." It did.
She began a love affair over the Net. "I often ran to the
computer room after getting home from work to find
Jayne engrossed in some letter writing. She would immediately cover the screen and ask me to leave. I could see
the discomfort in her face. This was one of my clues to ask
around and to check up on what might be happening. I
caught them in the act in a swank hotel." For the sake of
the children, however, Phil forgave her and did not divorce. He even revived his friendship with his e-mail
friend.

A second man, however, cuckolded Phil a few years
later, and like the first, he was an alcoholic. "He would
hound her," Phil said, "and send copious amounts of e-
mail, call her from wherever he was regardless of how
distant. He had an attitude that 'no one can tell him what
to do, even if it is an affair.' " So Phil, despite his forgiving
nature, did what many red-blooded men would have done
in his place as a local Internet administrator. He deleted
their electronic mail from the office system. "The second
affair rekindled after the lover's wife left him," Phil says.
Lawyers successfully pried Jayne and the man apart.

"She has 'fallen' into love with other people on the
Net," Phil said, however, "and some have even taken the
trouble to fly in to meet her." Fortunately the moon and the
stars and the hormones weren't right. So where on the Net
did Jayne hook up with these winners? Alt.sex.wanted? No,
Phil said—rec.humor. And he actually feared rec.humor
more than he did the plain, sex-oriented areas of the Net,
because it might pave the way for a relationship based on
more than carnal impulses.

I asked, "As a local Net administrator, do you think that people on the Net play around more or less than does the general population?"

"About the same," Phil said. "But there are a lot more insecure personalities acting out an alternate personality on the net. This will often lead, I think, to more misunderstandings. Someone can appear to love you a lot, over e-mail, but cannot carry through in person." And then Phil came up with another fascinating insight, which could also apply to some relationships on the Internet between single people. He observed that certain Netfolks really didn't care that much about the men or women at the other end. Rather they used electronic mail as a diary. "Jayne cherished the e-mail she got from one of her lovers," Phil said, "but in person he is a lying, cheating, and abusive drunk with a far more shallow agenda."

Phil and Jayne were doing what they could to repair the damage. The two had undergone marriage counseling. "Stop trying to think so much," Phil was told. "This makes you appear to be walking on eggshells, making it harder for Jayne to be honest with you." I hoped the counseling would work. As if her infidelity weren't enough, she now cried because she might have contracted the virus that causes AIDS. "One of her lovers has slept around a lot and shot up drugs," Phil said. "He hasn't seen a doctor in ages because of his alcoholic tendencies, and on one occasion he has said he could have the HIV virus. I assured Jayne . . . we will handle any result from the test one day at a time." The same thought might apply to his life with Jayne. One day at a time. In the future, I hoped, she won't be so secretive about the dots on her computer screen.

Greg and Sue, an Update

I promised to update you on Greg and Sue. In late May 1995 Greg told me they were still moving ahead, except

that they'd decided it would be much easier for her if they
lived in the States. He would arrive at the Kansas City airport on Wednesday, July 12, at 11:11 P.M. on American
Airlines. "My parents know," he said. "On the surface
they're bitchy about it—well, Mum is—but underneath
they're cool with it. Especially my dad. He wants to come
too." The older Smith had taken his family to Colorado
years earlier during a teacher-exchange program.

"Work?" Greg went on. "Heck, I can do a lot of things.
My preference would be systems administrator or network maintenance or even Internet guru–trainer."

Jokes about Adelaide's sleepiness notwithstanding,
Greg would miss life down under. He cherished "the laid-
back nature of Australia. I spend a lot of time talking to
people, and in 99 of 100 cases, the shopkeeper will take
time out to have a chat about something going on in the
world. People are so open and friendly, gosh darnit. I
mean friendly, not lazy." He would hate to give up, too, the
summer days at the sea, the music festivals of Adelaide,
and the programs of the Australian Broadcasting Commission ("it's government funded and turns up some really cool and alternative stuff"). He would also miss
Australian Rules Football. "Mostly that's an art form,"
Greg said. "Unlike NFL, every player has to be able to do
every other player's job. There's no offense or defense, and
it's such a quick game that offense can turn into defense in
the blink of an eye."

E-mailing me on a rainy, thundery day—from
"America's Heartland soon to be changed to America's
Flood Plain"—Sue wrote: "Thoughts and hopes? Well, I
think the one thing I've had to struggle with lately is facing up to the fear that we won't get along. I know there's a
chance. I've pretty much come to grips with it, so I think
that's a good sign. I think we'll work it out. I *hope* we will,
but that's yet to be foretold—I'm just looking forward to finally meeting my best friend.

"Where we'll live is a little uncertain. I'm still making the rounds of apartment complexes, trying to pick one that I like, that I think he'll like, and that is central to work and school.

"Telling people about Greg and me is a little tricky. Most of the people I work with understand the basic concept of the Internet, but don't really understand the idea of love at first talk session. I've pretty much just told people I met Greg through friends. It just makes things a lot easier, seeing as how I don't have to explain things over and over again. Maybe it's a cop-out, but everyone knows how committed I am to Greg regardless of how we met, and that's the important thing.

"My father remains in the dark," she said. "My mom and I had a big discussion about things and she felt that was the best way to handle things with him. I'm just taking things one step at a time and dealing with them as they come. I don't want to throw it all in his face. He's still my daddy and has the best interest of his baby girl at heart." Earlier I'd told Sue that the hassles would vanish when she met Greg, and she had agreed. "'Cept maybe the fact Greg will be the tallest one at family reunions *grin*. We'll all be arguing over whose side of the volleyball net he's on. Mine of course. :-) *grin*."

Sue brought me up to date on work and school. Recently she'd switched jobs and was now a file clerk for an appliance company where the pay was higher and the boss friendlier. "I can pretty much study during the slow periods, which helps a great deal. *brandishes her grade card*. Got it in the mail today—all A's. I'm framing this sucker—I actually pulled an A in algebra!"

Her net.lover was getting a cc of the note to me. "Oh, Greg," she couldn't resist adding, "I did some rearranging for you today. I think you might be able to have a drawer or two in the dresser *grin* just kidding. I cleaned my room today and vacated one-half of my drawer space, a major accomplishment almost tantamount to the A in algebra. Just don't look in the closet."

Redirecting the note back to me, Sue said: "I've always been up front with Greg about who I am and how I look and how I act and all that stuff. There's going to be a lot of rough edges we'll need to smooth out, but I'd say we've got a strong foundation to build on." Concluding, Sue said she had undergone a round of antibiotic-hormonal treatments for an ulcer and gained weight. "The bad news is the weight gain that went along with it. Least now I have the bust to fill out my bathing suit."

A few days later I heard from Greg. Uh-oh. "To put it bluntly," he wrote, "I am not a happy camper." I hoped I hadn't offended him. He and Sue had given so much of themselves by sharing their letters with me. As I read on, I found out the true reason for his dismay. It wasn't an ever-curious writer, or parents, or friends, or professional colleagues: Greg had graduated from school and was doing fine with temporary consulting work. "Visa—problem, big problem. My visitor's visa has been denied on the grounds that I have insufficient reason to return to Australia. The upshot of this is that our wedding and my travel plans have been severely disrupted, delaying us by anything upwards of about two months—gawd, I hate the sound of that. I talked to Sue on the phone last night-her morning, and we're confident we can make it through this."

In character Greg was using the Net, and specifically the newsgroup alt.visa.us, to help him cope with the visa'crats.

"It makes no sense to me that the U.S. government won't let in someone with a college degree that's in demand in this country," Sue wrote, "and who speaks English with such a sexy accent."

She had one last update later in June: "There's one thing you *have* to change in your chapter, and it's just one line. I went to the oncologist and he said I'd had enough tissue regeneration that was healthy to give me some hope of being able to have kids. So I guess I just might get to explore the world of labor pains and stretch marks after all. *Ugh.*

"And I know this sounds cheezy, but would you mind altering names?"

I was happy to oblige.

"The press here in Kansas City," Sue said, "has an absolute field day with stuff like this. A guy got a mail-order bride from Russia a year or so ago, and they had a five-part segment on his life story in the paper and on the news. I'd just rather not be looked at as someone who had to go to a whole other country to find a date. Which is how my father puts it *sigh*."

Oh, she had finally told. I wished I could see her father's face when Greg actually materialized in K.C. In the most direct way Fred Olson* might understand how fortuitously the Net had enlarged his daughter's range of choices. What counted wasn't her finding a man, but the best man for her—whether he was next-door or an ocean away.

• • •

So that was how matters stood with Sue and Greg as the presses were about to turn. I pondered the visa problem. Damn the feds. Already the ayatollahs of the Senate had been trying to turn the Internet into *Mr. Roger's Neighborhood,* while the crew in the White House was crusading to make the Net more snoop-friendly. Now Washington was getting in the way of both a romance and a more definitive ending to my love chapter.

As I typed those words I was listening to a RealAudio replay of Senator James Exon pushing his censorship bill on the Senate floor—an outrage that could harm not only net.sex but net.love, given the major danger of abusive enforcement. I loathed the man's voice. The bullying self-righteousness struck me most of all. Exon's tone was too close to that of the late Senator Joseph McCarthy, the anti-Communist zealot from Wisconsin. In a very narrow way I regretted that the Cold War was over. Now the bigots and bullies could focus on *domestic* troublemakers. Listening to the digitized Exon, I heard him say that a Nebraskan football coach had cheered him on. I reflected. Perhaps the senator and the coach could do a RealAudio broadcast from the locker rooms and show that in their territory even the after-game talk was G-rated.

My thoughts drifted. RealAudio reminded me of another recent wrinkle, The Internet Phone, which let Netfolks talk all over the world for free if they paid flat rates for Net service. What a joy this might be for people like Greg and Sue in the days before they rushed into each other's arms at the airport.

There were a few catches. You needed a deluxe Net connection, alas, which Sue lacked.

So she and Greg would still have to reach out and touch type to each other.

That wasn't so bad, actually. They were saving their e-mail, and someday the files would remind them of all the promise, all the anticipation, that the Net had held out for them in the form of each other.

Although I tinkered with The Internet Phone, I preferred electronic mail, just as I'd normally favored international Morse code over voice during my amateur radio days. Now that art might be lost. Code didn't matter as much on the airwaves as before. The U.S. Coast Guard was phasing it out. Any future SOS would apparently be in bits and bytes rather than in dots and dashes, assuming the initials remained at all. What would also perish—writing on screens, eventually? Just what would happen to typed words on the Net?

Whether seriously or just as a discussion provoker, a Seattle columnist had imagined the following: "It's the year 2020; your daughter Emily is nine years old and she can't read or write. Is this your worst nightmare about our schools come true? Nope, Emily just doesn't need to read or write anymore." That, of course, was exactly the kind of nightmare I'd had on my mind in proposing TeleRead. We needed graphics, not just words; but surely we could do better than the Emily scenario.

I'd asked Avodah Offit for comments on net.love rather than on the effects of the technology in general, but she couldn't help warning about the almost inevitable transition of the Net to sounds and images for all.

Delighted by the renaissance of writing on networks, she'd e-mailed me: "I think two-way TV will bring us down to earth. It will be a loss rather than a gain to those of us who enjoy using our imaginations and our writing skills. Right now we all have an opportunity to use the literacy that humans have spent thousands of years developing."

That was how I felt, too, whether the topic on the Net was romance or gerbil care. An old pop lyric came to mind: "These are the good old days." I wondered about the Snubbites and how they would have felt about Greg and Sue and the many others the Net had brought together; about the leather-jacketed kids up in Nova Scotia who, for the first time in their lives, were looking forward to *writing*, however rudimentary the elite Snubbites might have considered the children's prose; about all the love letters that might go unwritten if TV-centric politicians let Emily and friends live out their lives as illiterates without electronic books or keyboards or equivalents.

Some things were forever worth our being reactionaries in an enlightened way. Literacy was one of them. We mustn't ever let the romance and civility of the written word die on the Internet.

Once again I recalled some e-mail Sue had sent, in which she had not meant to be profound but was. Sue the cancer survivor had reminded us of the need to enjoy both Life and Net, and I wanted similar thoughts to grace the screens of many lovers, in many countries, and for many years. "*hugs greg* hold your horses sweetie," she had written, "I'm typing as fast as I can. . . ."

Notes

Chapter 1—The Terrain

1. The three Net-hostile quotes are from Joshua Quittner's "Back to the real world: New books from the front lines of the information revolution urge cyberspace cadets to get a life," *Time*, April 17, 1995, page 56.

2. Luddites, of course, were the loom smashers of the nineteenth century who protested automation.

3. Goldberg is author of the book *Questions and Answers about Depression* (Charles Press, 1993), but the book is clearly *not* his main reason for being on Walkers—mentions of *Questions* have been well within limits. Sheer altruism is clearly his true motive.

4. Reid Kanaley, "Computers to the rescue: Internet becoming a worldwide safety net," *Philadelphia Inquirer*, January 17, 1995, page 1.

5. Kanaley.

6. John Schwartz, "On the information net, creativity is its own reward," *Washington Post*, April 10, 1995, page 23 of the "Washington Business" section. Schwartz is a *Post* reporter and columnist.

7. Quittner.

8. Stoll himself noted the Maine–Texas allusion.

9. Irwin Lebow, *Information Highway & Byways: From the Telegraph to the 21st Century* (Piscataway, New York: IEEE Press: 1995), page 17. A good book. Highly recommended. It even comes with the *Walden* allusion, although from a rather different perspective from that of Stoll.

10. Thanks to my friend Andy Oram for the buffalo analogy.

11. With hypertext links, readers could click on mentions of the *Star Tribune* and immediately go from my area of the World Wide Web to the one where the newspaper had posted the West article. I didn't reproduce the material; I just pointed my readers in its direction.

Chapter 2—Business on the Net: From White Rabbit Toys to "Intel Inside"

1. The physical description is based on photographs in local newspapers.

2. *Advertising Age*, January 9, 1995, page 22 of the "Interactive Media & Marketing" section.

3. Peter Lewis, "Prodigy is leading its peers onto the World Wide Web," *New York Times*, January 18, 1995, page D1.

4. *Interactive Publishing Alert* is available for $195 for 12 monthly issues via e-mail, and $245 by regular mail. Contact 71333.1473@compuserve.com or rosalind@ harrison.win.net for more information, or write Rosalind Resnick at 1124 Harrison St., Hollywood, FL 33019.

5. *The Cook Report*, written for the Net savvy and dealing heavily with local and state Net issues, costs $85 for individuals and $350–$650 for corporations. Cook's e-mail address is cook@cookreport.com; his physical address, 431 Greenway Avenue, Ewing, NJ 08618.

6. Rates for new customers increased after the *Times* article on Larry Grant appeared in mid-1994.

7. Mark Lyon, "Firm gives air freight a lift on Internet," *Air Commerce Special* supplement, page 8, distributed with the *Journal of Commerce*, December 19, 1994.

8. Of course, on occasion, electronic mail can be delayed for several hours and maybe even longer. So Telnet or the World Wide Web would probably be better in situations where couriers are on tight schedules.

Chapter 3—EntertaiNet: A Few Musings on Net.Rock, Leonardo da Vinci and Bill Gates, Bianca's Smut Shack, and David Letterman in Cyberspace

1. ISDN means Integrated Services Digital Network, which allows transmissions faster than the 14.4 Kbps and 28.8 Kbps rates so common today.

2. Barry Walters, "The Internet is a punk rocker now," *San Francisco Examiner*, February 27, 1974, page D3 (Style section).

3. Laurel Taylor, "The speed of sound," *Good Times*, August 18, 1994.

Chapter 4—Pulped Wood versus Electrons:
Can the Print World Learn to Love the Net?

1. A.C.'s work is on the Net, but in the strictest sense he himself isn't. His daughter at a paper in Florida can enjoy his columns online but can't even swap e-mail with him. Perhaps she'll eventually conquer his technophobia. A.C., I'm rooting for you.

2. Frank Daniels III, "One newspaper's journey on the Internet," *T Leaves: A Newsletter for NAA Members,* October 1994. NAA is the Newspaper Association of America.

3. David Streitfeld, "Book report," *Washington Post,* September 25, 1994, page 19 of Book World section.

4. Lewis and many other journalists here do not necessarily serve as official spokespeople for their publications.

5. Teresea Martin, "Like a newspaper, but better: Tablets will succeed where others have failed," *Digitial Media: A Seybold Report,* September 13, 1994.

6. Jonathan Seybold, "How the rise of electronic media is affecting paper prices," *Digital Media Perspective,* March 27, 1995.

7. To Baker's credit, he seems to have learned about the new media since writing the article. Commendably he came out for an online royalty-collection approach that would be less onerous to readers than the approach favored by the Clinton Administration.

8. As usual, for aesthetic reasons, I'm using italics to show emphasis in place of the original capitalization.

9. Not to be confused with the former speech writer for Ronald Reagan.

10. I'm not beating up on the late professor, one of the best teachers I ever had. In his place, I'd have given the same advice. The limitations of 1960s technology made it difficult to think otherwise.

11. E-mail from Bruce Siceloff.

12. Katherine Fulton, "Heirs to newspaper make unlikely pioneers. So why is Frank Daniels III out on the frontier?", *Poynter Special Report: Converging Technologies,* 1994, pages 5–7.

13. Ibid.

14. Daniels, in *T Leaves.*

15. The speculation about *Time*'s role in the cable trade is my own. Jim Kinsella, one of the organizers of Pathfinder, told me that he liked this approach but was not necessarily speaking for the company.

16. In Raleigh, a locally oriented arm of Time Warner might enjoy a big advantage over the *N & O* someday if the newspaper lacked access to cable for Internet purposes. Cable will probably be much better than phone connections, the kind the *N & O* uses. The best cure, of course, would be laws that (1) assured the *N & O* a place on local

cable and (2) also let the phone companies there go into the cable business. Then the *N & O* could choose between Time Warner and its phone company allies of the present. Perhaps such laws will be on the books by the time you're reading this. Meanwhile, I'll hardly blame the people at Time Warner for unofficially talking up cable for the Internet; as noted before, I'd do the same, given the technical benefits.

17. Conspiracy theorists may take note that another arm of the Newhouse interests, Ballantine Books, is distributing *NetWorld!* for Prima Publishing.

18. Laurie Flynn, "Getting on-line—the Microsoft way," *New York Times,* November 20, 1994, page F10.

19. The Stahlman and Smith quotes are from "Time Inc. raises its multimedia profile with an Internet test," by Deirdre Carmody, *New York Times,* October 24, 1994, page D10.

20. Laura Fillmore, "Online publishing: Threat or menace," speech to the Online Publishing Conference, Graphic Communications Association, March 1993.

21. Ibid.

22. Ibid.

23. Fillmore, "Slaves of a new machine: Exploring the for-free/for-pay conundrum," Fifth Conference on Organizational Computing, Coordination, and Collaboration: "Making Money on the Internet," Austin, Texas, May 10, 1994.

24. Ibid.

25. Vannevar Bush, "As we may think," *The Atlantic Monthly,* July 1945.

26. Interview with Fillmore.

27. Fillmore, "Slaves."

28. Ibid.

29. Ibid.

30. Ibid.

31. Rory J. O'Connor, "News firms plan on-line network," *San Jose Mercury News,* April 20, 1995, page 1F.

32. Reuter Information Service, "Newspaper executives see online services as prime competitor," carried by *The NandO Times,* June 9, 1995.

33. David Streitfeld, "Cyberstrokes: For authors, e-mail offers some novel reader feedback," *Washington Post,* June 9, 1995, page B1.

Chapter 5—Wired Knowledge:
When They Let a Murderer Loose on the Internet

1. Ronnie Crocker, "Executed killer lives as computer image," *Houston Chronicle,* December 18, 1994, page A1.

2. To be technical, these weren't true physical slices, just images taken of the remaining surface as researchers ground down Jernigan.

3. From an essay that Chris Gazunis wrote in a 1994 contest sponsored by the National Center for Education Statistics, the NASA K-12 Internet Project, and the National Science Foundation.

4. Randy Hammer was another contestant in the competition that Chris Gazunis entered.

5. Peter West, "Wired for the future," *Education Week*, January 11, 1995. The senior analyst quoted was Kathleen Fulton.

6. The University of Colorado got a great package deal. While I couldn't rate Helen according to her medical knowledge, she appeared to know her computer imaging cold.

7. Not to confuse detachment with callousness. In Pelster's place—working with the cadaver day after day, not just writing about him—I'd have coped the same way.

8. The Associated Press quoted Oxford and Nelson.

Chapter 6—Governments and the Net: Making Sure Orwell Was Wrong

1. Encryption is the scrambling of messages into codes.

2. Simson Garfinkel, *Wired*, March 1995, page 44.

3. To simplify a bit, cryptography is the study, or the technique, of making secret messages.

4. Peter Huber, *Orwell's Revenge: The 1984 Palimpsest* (New York: The Free Press, 1994).

5. Sandy Sandford, "The intelligent island?" *Wired*, September/October 1993.

6. Rosalind Resnick, "Cyberbiz" column of July 3, 1995, published in the *Miami Herald*, on the Knight-Ridder wire and her Web site, http://www.netcreations.com. One of the best sites on the whole Net. Drop by!

7. Exon has announced plans not to run again—his term ends in 1997. But who knows what can happen in the meantime?

8. My favorite observation on the passion for censorship comes from Phil Kirby, a former editorial writer for the *Los Angeles Times*, by way of Nat Hentoff, in the book *Free Speech for Me, But Not for Thee*. "Censorship," Kirby said, "is the strongest drive in human nature; sex is a weak second." Thanks to Bob Chatelle of the National Writers Union for bringing this gem to my attention.

9. The example of messages violating local standards comes from a syndicated column by Lawrence Magid that appeared in the *Washington Post* on March 13, 1995.

10. Buckley and George Will are the most famous conservative journalists in the United States. Among other accomplishments, Buckley is founder of the *National Review*. His comments appeared in an "On the Right" column released through the United Press Syndicate on February 24, 1995.

11. Perhaps the idea will have been changed by now to allow more freedom to librarians and the public.

12. David Buerger, "Our lives are quickly becoming an open book," *Communications Week*, May 9, 1994, page 52.

13. Simson Garfinkel, *PGP: Pretty Good Privacy* (Sebastopol, California: O'Reilly & Associates, 1995), page 88.

14. Ibid.

15. Ibid.

16. William M. Bulkeley, "Cipher probe: Popularity overseas of encryption code has the U.S. worried; Grand jury ponders if creator 'exported the program through the Internet'; 'Genie is out of the bottle,'" The *Wall Street Journal*, April 28, 1994, page A1.

17. "Tidbits on the PGP/Zimmermann case—Protecting Americans' privacy," an item that Jim Warren released in the March 6, 1995, issue of his online newsletter, *Government Access*.

18. Steven Levy, "Crypto rebel," *Wired*, February 1993.

19. Ibid.

20. Garfinkel, *PGP*, page 112.

21. Ibid.

22. Ibid.

23. As of this writing, it looked as if Warren wouldn't testify—perhaps because his remarks would have been so helpful to Zimmermann's side.

24. To its credit, the White House at least called attention to the First Amendment nightmares of the Exon "decency" bill. Given how bad the bill was, however, that was a little like denouncing slavery.

25. If the case is still on, contact Hugh Miller at hmiller@luc.edu for information on making donations.

26. "Another chop at the Clipper chip," *Business Week*, February 13, 1995.

27. "I oppose the Clipper Chip and all forms of key escrow because it's impossible to use bad legislation as a substitute for bad engineering," Bob Steele told me. Yes, he's the same CIA alum as in chapter 4, the one with whom I agreed in a friendly way to disagree. Hi, Bob—you're right on about Clipper!

28. Peter Lewis, "Attention shoppers: Internet is open," the *New York Times*, August 12, 1994, page D1.

29. Bulkeley.

30. Ibid.

31. Ibid.

32. Privacy International is an international human rights organization founded in 1987 to oppose privacy invasions worldwide. It led the campaign to fight a national card proposal in Australia that ended up causing Parliament to dissolve in 1987.

33. *Ottawa Citizen,* January 31, 1994, as reproduced by David Banisar in his "Bug Off!" paper for Privacy International.

34. Bulkeley.

35. Elizabeth Corcoran, "Bit by bit, an online collection of the Library of Congress to digitize artifacts," the *Washington Post,* October 10, 1994, page A1.

36. Junda Woo, "Big copyright curbs sought by industry," the *Wall Street Journal,* December 27, 1994, page B5.

37. Teresa Riordan, "Profile: Even in a 'Big Tent,' Little Insults, Little Compromises," the *New York Times,* May 29, 1994. The *Times* is the source of information on Lehman's heroes. To answer the obvious question—yes, I asked Lehman for comment on a number of topics ranging from campaign donations to his use (or possibly nonuse) of the Internet. No reply came. I also asked him about his controversial $10,000 gift to a local politician, the one described in this chapter and in chapter note 41.

38. Saundra Torry, "Many of Clinton's chosen earned big bucks in private practice," the *Washington Post,* October 18, 1993, page F7.

39. Found at http://www.uspto.gov/combio.html.

40. Riordan.

41. Pamela McClintock, "D.C. council candidate returns questioned $10,000 loan," the *Washington Times,* February 19, 1991, page B4. In a "Notebook on Politics" column on February 21, Rene Sanchez of the *Washington Post* described the loan as "apparently in violation of D.C. campaign finance law, which sets a $400 ceiling on individual campaign donations."

42. Riordan is the source of the "first" information.

43. Riordan.

44. Pamela Samuelson, "Legally speaking: The NII intellectual property report," *Communications of the ACM,* December 1994. On the Web at http://gnn.interpath.net/gnn/meta/imedia/features/copyright/samuelson.html.

45. *The Manchurian Candidate* was the film in which the Communists captured a GI, brainwashed him, and groomed their man to be president of the United States.

46. Marcia Berss, "West will always be three," *Forbes,* November 21, 1994, page 47.

47. Ibid.

48. Ibid.

49. Ibid.

50. Sharon Schmickle and Tom Hamburger, "West Publishing and the courts: U.S. justices took trips from West Publishing," *Minneapolis*

Star Tribune, March 5, 1995. In of July 1995, at least, the lead article showed up on the Web at http://www.startribune. com/westpub/west.htm. The home page for the *Star Tribune* is http://www.startribune.com/.

51. I can only speculate since, like Lehman, Opperman refused to answer my written queries about donations and other matters.

52. Bill Salisbury, "Minnesota 'bit players' enjoy the show; Democratic colleagues happy with their role at convention," the *St. Paul Pioneer Press,* July 14, 1994, Page 1A.

53. West's 6,000-word letter of February 22, 1995, was available on the World Wide Web at the following address in July 1995: http://www.startribune.com/westpub/perspectives/response. htm

54. Jack B. Coffman and Thomas J. Collins, "Bankrolling the legislature part 6: Who has the clout," the *St. Paul Pioneer Press,* April 17, 1992, Page 1A.

55. Margaret Engle, "Virtual money trail: The Center for Responsive Politics on the Internet," *Capital Eye,* June 15, 1995, Page 2.

55. Martin Schram, *Speaking Freely: Former Members of Congress Talk about Money and Politics* (Washington, D.C.: Center for Responsive Politics, 1995), page 85.

Chapter 7– The Electronic Matchmaker

1. The Goodin quotes appear in the paper "The Net and Netizens: The impact the Net has on people's lives," by Michael Hauben (hauben@columbia.edu).

2. The America Online example is from a personal interview, the CompuServe one from online messages, and the Prodigy example from *People* magazine.

3. Although anonymous servers protect privacy in most cases, this could be happening only up to a certain point. Many on the Net take it for granted that national security agencies in the United States can monitor traffic to and from the servers and determine the identities of the senders.

4. I won't even bother here with the term "Cyberpunk," which nowadays can mean anyone from a rebellious hacker to a technophobic teenager who is trying to make a fashion statement.

5. Sue tells me her hair is shorter these days, "a little past my chin now." I doubt the change will imperil Greg's ardor.

6. A program for sending and receiving electronic mail over a network.

7. I look forward to an era of electronic books where librarians can function more as book reviewers and information hunters, and less as clerks.

Index